FROM GLOBAL TO LOCAL

FROM GLOBAL TO LOCAL

THE MAKING OF THINGS
AND THE END OF GLOBALIZATION

FINBARR LIVESEY

PANTHEON BOOKS

NEW YORK

All rights reserved. Published in the United States by Pantheon Books,
a division of Penguin Random House LLC, New York, and distributed
in Canada by Random House of Canada, a division of Penguin
Random House Canada Limited, Toronto. Originally published in
paperback in Great Britain by Profile Books Ltd., London, in 2017.

Pantheon Books and colophon are registered
trademarks of Penguin Random House LLC.

Library of Congress Cataloging-in-Publication Data
Name: Livesey, Finbarr, author.
Title: From global to local : the making of things and
the end of globalization / Finbarr Livesey.
Description: New York : Pantheon, 2017.
Identifiers: LCCN 2017008955. ISBN 9781101871218
(hardback). ISBN 9781101871225 (ebook).
Subjects: LCSH: International economic relations. Economic development.
Climatic changes—Economic aspects. Corporations. International cooperation.
BISAC: BUSINESS & ECONOMICS / International / Economics. POLITICAL
SCIENCE / Globalization. BUSINESS & ECONOMICS / Exports & Imports.
Classification: LCC HF1365 .L58 2017. DDC 337—dc23.
LC record available at lccn.loc.gov/2017008955

www.pantheonbooks.com

Jacket design by Janet Hansen

Printed in the United States of America
First American Edition
2 4 6 8 9 7 5 3 1

For Tom and Renee, with love

Contents

Acknowledgments

A BOOK LIKE THIS is an effort of many years and is based on discussions and arguments with many people from many countries and backgrounds. My thanks to everyone who took the time to listen and debate what is happening in the global economy with me, challenging me to sharpen my arguments and in many cases to reflect on what I was really trying to say. Over the years Tim, Eoin and James have been patient, supportive and encouraging in equal measure.

My U.K. agent, Sally Holloway, has been a calm and very wise guide as we've journeyed from the initial idea in her office in Oxford, through proposal and on to the final version of the book. Similarly, Andrew Franklin and his team at Profile Books in London have been great to work with, my thanks to them for taking on the project. On the other side of the Atlantic Zoe Pagnamenta has provided patient counsel and Erroll McDonald at Pantheon has been a wonderful supporter of the book from start to finish.

None of this would be possible without the support of my extended family (Jim, Mary, Rick, Joanna, Tim, Emily, Johanna, Rob, Sheila and Andrew). Most of all, though, this is possible because of Charlotte and our children, who have to put up with long mental if not physical absences when the writing takes over. My love and thanks to her and the littles.

FROM GLOBAL TO LOCAL

1

Go East, Young Man?

FOR THE PAST THIRTY YEARS or more, the global economy has been run based on three big assumptions: that globalization will continue to increase, that trade is the route to growth and development, and that economic power is moving from the West to the East. More recently, it has been taken as a given that our levels of interconnectedness—both physical and digital—will rise without limit. But what if some or all of these assumptions are wrong? What if everything is about to change? Indeed, what if the global economy has already started to change its rules, but we just haven't noticed?

This is a story that is hard to tell. When there have been thousands if not millions of books, articles and academic papers claiming that globalization is the only game in town, saying that it isn't so may lead to me being put to the back of the class. If you are to believe much that is written on the evolution of the global economy, we have arrived at the equivalent of Fukuyama's (in)famous *End of History,* but this time for companies.[1] The caricature version of Fukuyama's thesis was that liberal democracy had won out over all other forms of political organization. Communism had fallen, socialism was nowhere to be seen, there were no more challengers left on the field. Twenty-five years later what was an irresistible thesis had fallen from grace. "Today, it's hard to imagine Fukuyama being more wrong."[2]

Globalization has become something analogous, portrayed as the end of economic history in many articles. In the common currently accepted version of the story of our world economy, offshoring of production to

Asia by the developed economies came, made and won. The specter of China in particular looms large, with millions of cheap workers, huge industrial cities created instantly where there was nothing and a scale of ambition that seems to dwarf that of the West. For many commentators, politicians and economists this is a game that is already over. In their eyes we've seen a permanent deindustrialization of the West and economic power has shifted significantly and permanently eastward.

But sometimes the stories that seem the most secure are actually fading away from the inside out. Our faith in the shining city on a hill, the project of American democracy, appears to have been significantly tarnished through the presidential election campaign of 2016. The long running Syrian conflict and the refugee crisis that it has spawned have challenged our ideas of progress and the march of peace through democratization. And there are new voices questioning whether we've really settled on this new global economic order, questioning whether we are telling the right story about the world economy as we move further into the new century. These are the voices that will be heard in this telling of the global economy.

THE CORE ARGUMENT of this book is that the accepted interpretation of the future of globalization is misleading and flawed. We are running the global economy on a model that went out of date without anyone noticing at some point in the past decade. But working as if continuing globalization (or hyper-globalization for some) is the only show in town opens us all up to huge risk, potentially as dangerous as the financial crash of 2008 that brought the world economy to its knees.

The *Titanic* provides an unexpected metaphor for this phenomenon. Apparently, the most senior officer to survive its sinking, Second Officer Charles Lightoller, said on his deathbed that there had been an order to steer away from the iceberg but that it had been misinterpreted. If true, how could such a thing have happened? Left is left or in this case, port is port—surely? Maybe not. At the time of the *Titanic*'s maiden voyage the shipping industry was going through major changes as sail was giving way to steam. With that came a change in how ships were steered, from tiller to wheel. Why is that important? Well, with a tiller you steer *away* from the direction in which you want to go, whereas with a wheel you steer toward it. So the order the captain would have given to turn to port on

a steamship such as the *Titanic* was the exact opposite of that used on a sailing ship. And the helmsman may have misunderstood his command. The order and the execution were carried out in two different languages.

This may be just another great tall story to add to the *Titanic* archive but, whether it is true or not, it highlights the importance of having a narrative that reflects how the world works today, rather than how it worked yesterday. For if the story or shorthand we carry in our heads is out of date and wrong it can lead to catastrophic consequences, whether it is the loss of a ship, the greatest recession in a hundred years, or, as this book will suggest, many countries entering an economic wilderness in the coming decades.

Out-of-date stories and understandings are everywhere once you start to look, from our private lives up to narratives about the world itself. On a personal level, for how long after a relationship has effectively ended does one of the soon-to-be ex-partners cling to the belief that all is well? And how long do we hold on to a mental picture of ourselves in our twenties when we've long ago passed into our forties or fifties? On a macro level, the world has a long history of out-of-date stories causing more than a little trouble—the long and bloody history of proving that the earth revolves around the sun, the Cuban missile crisis and, of course, every financial crash from the South Sea Bubble to that of 2008, in which many individuals, investors and governments believed wrongly that risk had been designed out of the financial system when the exact opposite was true. It is hard to shake a story once it has become established. But without challenging our world view on a regular basis we run the risk of steering the global economy into another iceberg.

"GLOBALIZATION IS AN IRREVERSIBLE PROCESS, not an option."[3] Writing in 1999, the secretary general of the United Nations Kofi Annan didn't leave much room for doubt. Here at the cusp of the new millennium there were large questions being asked about the role of the United Nations and other multilateral organizations in promoting development in the context of globalization. The 1990s had seen the consequences of the fall of the Berlin Wall, the opening up or the fall of communist countries and the emerging powers of China and India beginning to take a greater role in international trade. It is not hard to put yourself in Annan's shoes,

looking at what appears to be an inevitable and unstoppable process playing out in front of you. Following decades of international negotiation on trade agreements the path forward was clear. Globalization was the engine of the global economy and there was no need, no reason to turn it off.

Similar statements on globalization were made by the leaders of various states and international organizations throughout this period. The then prime minister of the U.K., Tony Blair, speaking to the 1998 World Trade Organization (WTO) Ministerial Conference, argued that "the global economy is a fact" and that the question was "not so much whether there should be free trade, but how best to manage what I believe is an irreversible and irresistible trend."[4]

Statement after statement, newspaper article after newspaper article pointed in the same direction. The world had globalized and would continue to globalize, resulting in greater prosperity for all. For the liberal elite the question of the day became how this new prosperity could be shared to raise the standard of living for the millions living on less than a dollar a day. Globalization was never in question.

In some ways this statement of intent to raise all boats on the tides of globalization was a response from those in power in the multilateral organizations and Western governments to the many critics of globalization. Joe Stiglitz, Nobel Prize winner and former chief economist at the World Bank, wrote a scathing critique of how multilateral organizations, in particular the International Monetary Fund (IMF), were working. Commenting on the decision-making process at the IMF he said, "Decisions were made on the basis of what seemed a curious blend of ideology and bad economics, dogma that sometimes seemed to be thinly veiling special interests."[5] The street protests at the Seattle meeting of the WTO in 1999 were a clear signal of the level of public discontent with the process of globalization. But again these were not a denial of the process. Even those opposed to the negatives of globalization were not denying its existence. They thought it should stop because of the damage it was causing.

As the financial crisis of 2008 was bringing the global economy to a very sudden and painful halt, the IMF was no less certain of the long-term outcomes for the world economy. "Globalization is irreversible. In the long run, globalization is likely to be an unrelenting phenomenon."[6] It did, however, caveat this with a warning that for periods of time the

momentum could be lost, as occurred following the outbreak of the First World War. This, in the IMF's eyes, would be a pause in the long-run trajectory of development, with greater and greater economic integration expected as the world turned. The more things change, the more they stay the same.

Eight years after the start of the financial crisis, there are many voices again speaking out against globalization, in particular arguing that it has not delivered on its promises. There are fears of a rise in protectionism in many countries, most clearly seen in the political rhetoric of the race for the White House that has played out in tabloid form through 2016. Throughout the campaign Donald Trump returned again and again to plans to increase tariffs on foreign goods, pledging to remove the United States from all its large-scale trade deals, including the North American Free Trade Agreement (NAFTA), and to kill off the multilateral deals being negotiated such as the Trans-Pacific Partnership (TPP).[7] Now in office, President Trump has signed an executive order pulling the U.S. out of the TPP, has talked up but not yet carried out plans to renegotiate NAFTA and has danced around the idea of a border adjustment tax.

The United Kingdom's vote to leave the European Union is another flashpoint, highlighting that the economic and social ties some take for granted are not as durable as they may believe. Attempts to unravel why the vote went in favor of exit are many, with commentators unable to agree on a clear story of what led to the result.[8] For some it is the long-term neglect of those negatively affected by globalization in the poorer regions of the U.K. that led to the Leave campaign's success. For others it is simply about perceived levels of migration, having seen David Cameron pledge to reduce net migration to the tens of thousands only to see the flow of people into the U.K. increase significantly. Whatever the reason, the U.K. entered a period of great uncertainty in 2016, clinging to the reflexive statement that "Brexit means Brexit" from the new prime minister Theresa May to try to stay afloat and see where it was going.[9]

According to Global Trade Alert, an independent initiative coordinated by the Center for Economic Policy Research in London, there have been close to 6,000 protectionist measures introduced worldwide since 2008, leading to what it calls "global trade disorder."[10] These interventions can be anything from an increase in local content control (more of what is

in a product has to be made in the home country) to the introduction of tariffs on products as they come across the border. It seems that as global economic conditions deteriorate countries cannot resist trying to protect their domestic industries at the expense of trade.

In a curt response to those hinting at protectionism and the end of globalization the current director general of the WTO, Roberto Azevêdo, wrote in a comment piece for the *Financial Times*: "Complementing the antitrade rhetoric is the notion that we have reached 'peak trade' or that globalization has ground to a halt. One argument is populist, one is intellectual—both are wrong."[11] While his language was forceful and backed up by the status of his office, his argument or lack of one was shored up by faith alone.

What if those who run our multilateral organizations and many political leaders are wrong about the inevitable continuation of globalization? Whether the process of globalization has been managed well, whether it has fulfilled its promise to lift the poorest out of their precarious situations, is not the main argument of this book. What I want to explore is whether the process of globalization is as inevitable as is being asserted, and, if not, the effect that will have on trade and international relations. We need to be clear both about whether countries are actually coming closer together or not and about the limits to globalization.

THE STORIES WE TELL help us to make sense of the world. Each of us has a set of stories, some generated from personal or professional experience, some from our time as students, some handed down as tradition or history.[12] Thinking of what economists, historians, scientists and other thinkers do as a form of storytelling is uncomfortable for some, but the hope is that as the stories get better over time, we all gain a clearer sense of the world as it is rather than as it might be.

It is difficult to change a story that has existed for a long time, in particular one that has support from many people. This phenomenon, well recognized in science, was most clearly captured by Thomas Kuhn in his classic 1962 book *The Structure of Scientific Revolutions,* in which he speaks of paradigms, that is a shared understanding in a discipline of the methods that can be used and the problems that are worth studying. Once established, paradigms remain until there is a crisis that forces a move away

from "normal science." But these "paradigm shifts" are hard, for "Novelty emerges only with difficulty, manifested by resistance, against a background provided by expectation."[13] There usually has to be a significant build-up of contrary evidence, specifically a large number of anomalies which challenge the dominant view, to force a change of paradigm. So is there evidence which contradicts the continued expansion of globalization? Can we see the anomalies in the globalization story?

When Allied forces invaded Iraq in 2003 there was a large question hanging over the operation: would any weapons of mass destruction (WMD) be found? In the run-up to the invasion two dossiers were produced by the U.K. government which detailed claims about Saddam Hussein's possession of weapons of mass destruction and whether he could launch those weapons within forty-five minutes. The first, referred to as the "September Dossier," had a foreword by Tony Blair in which he claimed that Hussein's "military planning allows for some of the WMD to be ready within forty-five minutes of an order to use them."[14] The U.S. Secretary of State at the time, Colin Powell, made a presentation to the United Nations Security Council in February 2003 to convince them and other skeptics not only that Hussein had weapons of mass destruction but also that he was working hard to conceal them from inspectors in violation of UN resolutions. In that presentation he depended on the second British dossier, the "February Dossier," calling it a "fine paper [that] describes in exquisite detail Iraqi deception activities."[15]

The problem was that the dossier was not all it claimed to be. As *The Economist* politely put it, "This [dossier] mixed genuine intelligence with bits of an old academic thesis, lifted without attribution."[16] There has been much written on the motivations of those producing the documents that supported the invasion of Iraq, but one probably generous view is that the signals they were receiving were simply misinterpreted. The intelligence they were trying to interpret didn't stand up to the weight that was placed on it. As we try to make sense of the global economy we are in an analogous situation as our data, our intelligence, is also weak, even if we don't realize it.

The second reason we do not see what is in front of us is subtler and harder to correct. This is when something accurately describes a situation but over time the context changes and what was initially a correct

interpretation becomes misaligned. This is the slow-boiling frog problem applied to our understanding of the world. As the temperature changes slowly the frog doesn't realize it is being cooked. For us, no individual change is large enough to grab our attention and so it isn't until very late in the process that we suddenly see that there has been a very significant if gradual shift in the world.

The way in which a population changes over time, absent a large shock such as a war or a great pandemic, is an example of this kind of change. Successive generations will have varying numbers of people in every category (class, race, religious affiliation) and as the changes are driven by births and deaths in the main, they happen at a pace which is too slow to observe on a day-to-day basis. In May 2015 Ireland voted to amend the constitution of the country to allow same-sex marriage. This in a country that had been referred to by Pope Paul VI as the most Catholic country in the world and which in 2011 still had 84 percent of the population indicating their religion as Catholic.[17] But the cultural make-up of the country had changed over generations, becoming more socially liberal, and so Ireland became the first country in the world to use a popular vote to legalize gay marriage.

The changes in the structure of the global economy are happening one company at a time. There is no one seismic moment that leads to every company siting all their production facilities in their home markets. Instead, older companies adapt or die and new ones with different ideas come into the market, again a rate of change too slow to see on a day-to-day basis.

Sometimes we try to mistakenly apply a story from one part of life to another that doesn't connect to what we are trying to understand. For instance among tech commentators and writers a common mistake is to apply digital models to the physical domain. The breathless way in which we talk about digitization, disintermediation and the weightless economy distracts us from the actual rules of the physical world rather than those of the digital.

The perception of the past thirty years is that the world has become more and more connected, that it costs less and less to get anywhere or to contact anyone. And that there is a direct correlation in the decline of the costs between the movement of people, the shipping of things and

the sending of bits of data around the world leading to one story—globalization. Most of us have spent all our lives in this period of correlated change and so it is very hard for us to imagine an existence in which things are otherwise.

However, there are many popular examples of correlation not being causation, a field so rich it has led to a book and a popular website by Tyler Vigen, who was a law student at Harvard when he started the whole thing.[18] He created a blog, collecting data and looking for spurious correlations pretty much from anywhere. So you get Nic Cage and drowning put together, or the divorce rate in Maine with the per capita consumption of margarine, things which clearly have nothing to do with one another but which have an incredibly high level of correlation.

We have done the same thing with our understanding of the global economy. We've tangled up many things which are different—like falls in transportation costs, the deployment of dense communication networks and changes in production technologies—and put them all in a box labeled "globalization" without putting a health warning on the outside.

Over the past thirty years or so the signals on globalization have all been moving in the same direction. The costs of communicating have been falling quickly, as have global transportation costs. But just because these two things happened at the same time does not mean that they are linked.

We'll talk more about the actual costs of these two phenomena in Chapter 5 and about their differing dynamics. For now, the most important thing to realize is that globalization is not a single entity, a simple concept that is becoming either more or less prevalent. There are many things that can be moved between countries and they all have different dynamics. There are separate elements of globalization and they can all move in different directions, complicating still further our picture of how the global economy is developing.

So what is globalization? And what is the evidence for globalization happening over the past ten, twenty or thirty years?

Most of us are aware that there has been increasing economic integration around the world since the end of the Second World War. A key measure of how integrated the world economy has become is the ratio of world trade to world gross domestic product (GDP). Looking at what is referred to as "merchandise trade" (essentially physical products as opposed

to services or financial flows), there have been significant changes since the 1960s. As flower power was taking over, global merchandise trade was about 20 percent of world GDP. Then, following the energy crisis in the 1970s, the ratio varied but was roughly 30 percent until the early 1990s. From that point on the ratio takes off, climbing to 40 percent by 2000 and on to a high of just under 52 percent in 2008. The story here is one of increasing economic integration through trade as more countries are becoming connected through the goods that move between them. Global trade grew at 3 percent per year from 2000 to 2006, and for the year before the financial crash climbed 6.5 percent.[19]

On any measure of trade the world has reached out more and more beyond national borders over the past half century. And this is another reason the concept of deglobalization is so foreign to many economists and commentators—increasing integration has been with us over a generational cycle. It is hard to imagine the global economy working in any other way.

Following the financial crash of 2008 there was a severe contraction of growth and trade, with a ten percentage-point drop in the ratio of global merchandise trade to GDP. After such a spectacular crash, trade has recovered some of its intensity, but the ratio of trade to growth has flatlined. Having had trade growing at about twice the growth rate of global GDP, to have them now increasing at the same pace has got some people worrying whether we've reached "peak trade."[20] In relative terms we probably have, even if with an increasing global population we may have an absolute rise.

These are special circumstances and we have only four or five years of post-crash data to work with, but there could be a new trade dynamic emerging. It appears that, at a gross level, for the first time since 2008 growth in world trade no longer outpaces global economic growth. This may become the new normal. The question is whether this relative decline in trade in goods should be a concern, or whether it signals a new mode for the global economy. Does it signal a slowing or a shift of the pattern of growth? If so, is it going to last and what are the causes of the change?

HOWEVER, WE HAVE TO BE CLEAR—the making and trading of physical goods is only one part of globalization. There is also the money side of

the world. The old phrase should probably be flipped on its head—it is the world which makes money go around. As well as the movement of things across the globe, we have a long history in moving money or capital from country to country. The pace of financial globalization was relatively slow up to the 1990s, and most companies were funding their developments using domestic sources of finance. Now, though, a company director can "choose between issuing stocks and bonds in domestic or foreign financial markets. He or she can reduce his or her cost of capital if foreign currency loans are available at more attractive terms than the domestic loans. These loans can be hedged by using a variety of financial products. He or she can also consider selling equity at foreign bourses."[21] There are many ways to find the money to build the factories that are needed to keep pace with global demand for new products.

Investors will always look at risk and return, and if that means investing across borders, so be it. One measure of the globalization of finance (of which there are many) is the ratio of foreign assets (financial claims held by companies in another country) to world GDP. This ratio was 17 percent in 1914 but by the end of 1945 it was only 4.9 percent following the disintegration of the international system in the inter-war period. The peak of the ratio of foreign assets to GDP in 1914 was not reached again until 1980, and it then continued on to much higher levels, reaching 56 percent in 1995.[22]

The financial crisis saw many of the indicators of international finance collapse, leaving many commentators concerned that there would be a lackluster recovery in international capital. A 2011 issue of the magazine *The International Economy* had a special section which asked the question "Is financial globalization beginning a process of reversal?"[23] The fourteen experts consulted included a former president of the Federal Reserve Bank of New York, a member of the executive board of the European Central Bank and the chairman emeritus of the Chicago Mercantile Exchange. Even in this relatively conservative group, three responded that there was a process of reversal, five said definitely not, while the other six hedged their bets, indicating that there would be a change or pause in financial globalization. This is the one aspect of globalization where there is a widespread conversation on whether things will continue to integrate or whether there will be a retrenchment.

The two main modes for foreign direct investment (FDI) are mergers and acquisitions (M&A) and greenfield investments (setting up a new facility, for example). Using the United Nations Conference on Trade and Development (UNCTAD) figures for FDI we can see clearly the peak of $1.9 trillion just before the financial crash in 2008, and, while there was an initial recovery, since 2011 the level of inward FDI has fallen again back to $1.2 trillion in 2014.

Is global finance the canary in the coal mine for how strong the forces of globalization will be into the future? It is unclear which way the numbers on FDI will go, given the uncertainties in the global economy. However, if international companies are having to invest in new facilities in the countries they want to sell into, we should see a spike of FDI especially for greenfield investment. We will discuss this more in Chapter 8 when we are hunting for the weak signals of deglobalization.

Cambridge is a very international city, with students and professionals coming from all over the world to study and work here. It makes for a transient environment in some ways, but there is a shared sense of having come from somewhere else that is good to have. I'm originally from Cork in Ireland and our extended family stretches over nineteen time zones, from New Zealand to the west coast of Florida, so it can be very hard to keep up with what is going on. Without digital globalization it would be impossible to maintain family connections across that span of geography.

Skype has been a godsend, allowing my partner and me to pretend that grandparents and friends are literally at the end of the table, catching up over a coffee while the kids bounce in and out of conversations. This is a shared experience of digital globalization, where the most far-flung parts of the planet are connected through data and video rather than roads and aeroplanes.

While trade and finance have struggled to recover from the 2008 economic crash, levels of data interconnectivity seem not to have slowed in the slightest. Between 2005 and 2015 cross-border flows of data (measured according to used bandwidth) have apparently increased by a factor of 45.[24] Imagine if that was a property increasing in price—your house that was worth £200,000 in 2005 would be worth £9 million by 2015. Or think of this as flows of people: if there were 1,000 people arriving in a city per year in 2005, by 2015 this would be 45,000. The scale of the increase is hard to comprehend.

The internet is another country in many ways. The number of

subscribers for the major platforms—Twitter, Facebook and the like—now number into the many millions. Early in 2016 the "about" page for Twitter claimed that it had 320 million active users every month (which may mean the total number of accounts is much higher).[25] The numbers for Facebook are even more astounding or terrifying, depending on your perspective. Their latest update claims that they had 1.59 billion monthly active users at the end of December 2015.[26]

Powered by increasing processing power in our phones and tablets and the building of thick digital pipes across the globe, this is one aspect of globalization that doesn't appear to be flagging. Barring strong negative interventions on the part of governments, our increasing rate of digital connectivity doesn't appear to have a "natural" brake either.

MOST GLOBALIZATION INDICATORS were increasing through the nineteenth century up to the shock of the Great War. There was a significant retrenchment in the inter-war period, with trade tariffs and other restrictions being imposed. Then there was a general reopening, with globalization tending to increase as the world recovered from the devastation of the Second World War.

How to sum up the changes that have occurred under the banner of globalization over the long run? There are six times more people on the planet than in the mid-nineteenth century, producing sixty times more stuff and trading more than 140 times what was traded then.[27] So it is beyond doubt that there have been significant shifts in trade and an increase in this form of globalization. The question is whether these changes are well understood and are likely to continue in line with the patterns we have seen in the past.

Our lived experience doesn't encompass these major rises and falls, we have only experienced the continual increase in globalization. Now the challenge is to see clearly what is happening in each of the elements of globalization, to see the digital and the physical processes for what they are rather than assuming that they are one and the same, heading forever in the same direction.

SO FAR WE'VE BEEN DISCUSSING the process of globalization and in the rest of the book we'll discuss whether there is going to be a

retrenchment of some kind. But does this matter to you and to me? Does it matter where things are made? Does where your washing machine, car or bookcases are made have any impact on you? Should we care about the geography of companies at all?

Depending on where and when you grew up you will have a very different view on whether where things get made matters. If you're a son or daughter of the rust belt of America, raised on Bruce Springsteen and bathed in the glow from factory doors, the decline of manufacturing is personal. For many it has struck at the heart of their identity and that of their town, their state and their country. If we are not making we are losing. Companies which were the lifeblood of a town have become unable or unwilling to carry on that role as competition has increased and the economics of making and trading has moved against producing in the U.S. Generations of families have been severely impacted by plant closures and the inability of both individuals and their towns to adapt and find employment in other sectors.

The identity of the U.K. has similarly been challenged. While the Industrial Revolution provided the power and muscle for empire, the relative decline of industry through the 1900s across the country has been a large social shock to absorb. In 1841 a full third of the country worked in manufacturing, compared to just 9 percent by 2011.[28] That shift means that manufacturing touches many fewer families than it used to and is a weaker part of the national identity than before. But beyond an attachment based on family history and continuity, does it matter if a country doesn't make things in significant quantities?

Well, the answer to that question for companies or countries isn't a simple case of do whatever makes us money, whether that involves a physical product or not. Nor is there an automatic value to be put on products over services (or vice versa). We shouldn't fetishize manufacturing just because we can see the products and be awed by the industrial design skills of companies like Apple. Nor should we dismiss steel making because of the smoke and the heat of the furnace. However, there are some aspects of manufacturing that impact far beyond the making of things.

Key to the model of growth for countries such as the U.K. and the U.S.A. is innovation. The ability of companies to develop new products, new means of production and new business models is built on the

innovative capacity not just of a given company, but of the industrial system surrounding it. Without the impetus of innovation, the introduction of new ways of making and delivering products and services, as well as the development of new products and services themselves, growth would weaken significantly.

Looking country to country, a key measure (though not the only one[29]) of the strength of their innovation systems is how much companies and the countries in which they reside are spending on research and development (R&D) in total.[30] This is usually expressed as a percentage of GDP and is seen as one of the major investments that leads to improvements in productivity and consequently to economic growth.

Those sectors making physical products have for a long time accounted for the lion's share of R&D spending. Currently manufacturers make up two-thirds of the business R&D spending in the United States.[31] While you might expect companies with physical products to spend more on R&D, due to the cost of the machines involved in investigating new materials or trying to find new ways to make the product itself, this contribution to innovation is well beyond the scale of manufacturing in the economy. Manufacturing as a share of GDP is only around 12 percent for the United States, so the contribution of manufacturing to R&D spending is five times what you'd expect if all sectors carried out R&D equally. That pattern is repeated around the world in roughly the same proportions. The manufacturing base can have a disproportionate effect on the level of investment in R&D and through this possibly the long-run innovation potential of a country.

Another aspect of the future growth potential is whether there are path dependencies, that is, how difficult it is to change course once you've decided to go down a certain path. If you decide to let manufacturing go and it turns out that was a mistake, how easy would it be to reindustrialize?

In 2009 two Harvard business professors took apart an Amazon Kindle 2 and analyzed whether it could be made in the United States. Their verdict was no.[32] The injection-molded case was made in China and the ability to make that had left the U.S. when toy manufacturing migrated there. Similarly the electrophoretic display was made in Taiwan, and required expertise in flat-panel LCDs which was no longer available in the United States. They showed that element after element of the

Kindle 2, made in various countries and assembled in China, could not now be easily made or sourced in the U.S.

They refer to this as "the hollowing out of the industrial commons." As more and more manufacturing leaves a region or a country, so do the skills and infrastructure that go along with that manufacturing. And this not only impacts on what can be made now but also stops the evolution of the processes of making, as neither the people nor the machinery are around to keep them going. We'll discuss this later, when talking further about the industrial commons, but it would appear that there are effects that are hard to reverse.

The impacts on companies of moving manufacturing around the world are significant, but to many commentators they are invisible. Innovation is an abstract concept that isn't easy to measure and long-run trajectories are just that, long run. However, one aspect of this story that is well discussed is the balance of trade and what this means for countries like Germany or China that have export-led economies, as compared to the U.K. and the U.S., which run persistent trade deficits. We'll come back to this in Chapters 8 and 9 when we discuss the pattern of trade now and into the future and the implications it will have for international relations and the operation of the existing multilateral system. But where do our perspectives on international trade come from? And do they affect our interpretation of what is about to happen?

Perspective really matters. Where you stand will determine what you see and how you interpret the world around you. Our common perspective on international trade and our attempts to understand and model the patterns of trade have their roots in the 1700s, with Adam Smith and David Ricardo. Their writings form the ground where most commentators stand when thinking about international trade and they unintentionally block us from seeing clearly what is happening at the moment in the global economy.

Smith kicked international trade theory into a new place when he discussed "absolute advantage." "If a foreign country can supply us with a commodity cheaper than we ourselves can make it, better buy it of them with some part of the produce of our own industry, employed in a way in which we have some advantage."[33] The logic is fairly intuitive: each country looks for opportunities to trade one good they are efficient at making,

either because they have easier access to raw materials or their workers are more skilled, for a different good that the partner country has an absolute advantage in. It appears that everyone has something to gain and we're off to the races.

The next move was with Ricardo, who instead of focusing on absolute advantage thought about comparative advantage, where rather than just looking at the between-country differences for producing a product, you look at the in-country differences to produce goods and then compare across countries. This means that even if you are a country with absolute advantage in making every product that could be traded there are still gains to be made in trade.

So far, so historical. These are the theories of trade that were developed before the high formalism of economics kicked in and which now provide us with guides on how to think about the benefits that might come from trading between countries, so what's the problem? The problem is the "unit of analysis," or, to put it another way, whom we cast as the characters in our trading drama. These wonderful minds of Ricardo and Smith saw the world more through the perspective of countries rather than from the point of view of the companies doing the actual trading (in many cases the companies were of the state, instigated and supported by the government of the day). This way of looking at trade has stayed with us in almost all commentaries about the global economy, where the United States, South Korea, China, Germany and others are treated as competitors in a "global race," with each country looking for opportunities and advantages.

Although this country-based perspective is still the prevailing one in macroeconomics, there has been some recent progress in the last three decades. New trade theory (and its daughter, imaginatively referred to as new new trade theory) does include some aspects of company differentiation, for example taking into account that not all producers have access to or use the same levels of technology. Paul Krugman, the MIT professor as famous for his *New York Times* articles and blog as for his Nobel Prize in Economic Sciences, is a key figure in these developments. In 1991 he published an article with the simple title "Increasing returns and economic geography."[34] He opens up with an admission of omission on the part of mainstream economics. "The study of economic geography—of the

location of factors of production in space—occupies a relatively small part of standard economic analysis." This is even though where factories are and how goods move about the world "are surely among the most striking features of real-world economies, at least to laymen."

Krugman goes on to build a model for why within a country manufacturers of a given type would agglomerate in a few locations instead of spreading across the nation. While acknowledging the oversimplification contained within the model, Krugman finishes with a hope that it would spark a "revival" into research in economic geography. Remember that he was writing at the start of the 1990s, not the 1890s, and so many commentators and policymakers on the political field of play at the time, even if they had a background in economics, would not have been exposed to this thinking, and would potentially be stuck in an economic world without geography.

IN OUR RAPID, 24-hour-news-cycle lives, we often elide companies and countries, assuming that their goals are aligned. But countries are not the actors carrying out the trades, they do not steer the ships or stock the shelves. Companies, not countries, make the decisions on what to send to market, but they appear very rarely in the literature, especially in early theories of trade. Put simply, countries are not companies, and companies are not countries.

This has implications both in theories of trade and in our wider debates on how the global economy works. But still the public and the 24/7 news channels that keep us informed on the global economy want to talk in terms of countries competing. While the overall situation of some countries is better than others, this is not because the countries themselves competed for trade. The trade position of any country is determined by the decisions hundreds of company managers made on what to make, where to make it and how to structure their financial operations. If we want to understand how the global economy is performing and how it will evolve into the future, it is a mistake to think only in the overarching terms of countries trading, which may not align with the perspective of the company and its managers. Or, to put it another way, from the perspective of the firm it is no longer the case that what is good for the country is automatically good for the company, or indeed vice versa.[35]

This muddling together of companies and countries has been going on for a long time in both directions, companies represented as larger and stronger than countries, and countries interpreted in the framework of a company. Neither viewpoint is particularly useful. Frustrated with how the discussion on economic policy was being misrepresented in the media and in American politics, Paul Krugman wrote a classic piece for the *Harvard Business Review* in which he made a plea for politicians to heed economists above businesspeople when it came to questions of national policy: "[E]conomics and business are not the same subject, and mastery of one does not ensure comprehension, let alone mastery of the other. A successful business leader is no more likely to be an expert on economics than on military strategy."[36]

As we have seen, companies do not appear very often in international trade theories, with one or two exceptions.[37] However, if anyone is to gain a clear perspective on what is happening in the real world, that has got to change. Some economists are investigating the limits of trade theories to describe what is going on in the world. In their 2013 book on offshoring (when a company moves or starts an activity outside of their home country) and outsourcing (when a company contracts an activity out to another company),[38] William Milberg and Deborah Winkler comment that "there are considerable limits to the economists' own models. In particular, the economists' views on offshoring are closely tied to an outmoded theory of comparative advantage."[39] The main problem is that the economic models don't capture the broader institutional context, including company strategy or the actions of governments to regulate products and trade. We have to look at what companies are doing—they are the main actors in our drama—rather than being led by either the claims of countries or the outputs of models.

HOW DO COMPANIES come to a decision on where to place a piece of production or which supplier to work with? Most companies work with the concept of total landed cost, which is essentially the total cost of raw materials, labor, logistics and any other cost incurred as you make and ship a product to a customer. Simple to define and very hard to measure.

The trade-off in terms of offshored production has usually been interpreted as the search for cost savings. Many of the early moves into China

by American or British companies were made in order to access very cheap labor. While statistics on China can sometimes be misleading, the best numbers available on the hourly compensation for manufacturing workers show an average ratio between the United States and China of about fifteen to one. On labor costs, offshoring is the only game in town—right?

Well, those averages cover many sins, as the costs of labor in China's coastal cities can be three times higher than those inland. So where in China you are working can make a very significant difference to your cost calculations. Next, that multiplier of fifteen only really makes a difference if labor costs are a large share of the total landed cost. Say you have a product that you're making domestically that all in costs $15 to make. If the labor cost is $1 of that, then replacing costly U.S. workers with cheap Chinese workers saves you ninety-three cents on first look.

A recent series of reports by the Boston Consulting Group (BCG) looked into the cost comparisons for U.S. versus Chinese production and they came to a very interesting conclusion. They concluded in 2011 that:

> within five years, the total cost of production for many products will only be about 10 to 15 percent less in Chinese coastal cities than in some parts of the U.S. where factories are likely to be built. Factor in shipping, inventory costs, and other considerations, and—for many goods destined for the North American market—the cost gap between sourcing in China and manufacturing in the U.S. will be minimal.[40]

This is not just a U.S./China story; it is a global story, with all the elements of landed cost under pressure for every company in the world. Some of the costs are being removed by automation and others are being driven high by regulation or market forces. But it is the complex interplay between them all that we have to try to understand if we are going to make headway in understanding where globalization is heading.

In this book I will primarily take the perspective of the company and its managers as the decisions that they make aggregate to give us the pattern of trade and investment flows in the main. The person who decides where a new factory will be placed or which supplier will be used is a senior company executive, not a macroeconomist or a politician. The context in

which these decisions are taken can be highly political—you only have to look at the incentives countries offer companies in attempting to influence their location decisions—but ultimately it is companies, not countries, that are making those decisions.

THIS BOOK DOCUMENTS the story of the changing context for decision making in the global economy, a story that takes us from humble cottages across the north of England to the sprawling Special Economic Zones and manufacturing cities like Shenzhen or Guangzhou in China, via the political capitals of the West and the rising innovation powerhouses of Asia.

It is important, though, to stress that this book is not making a judgment on globalization. It is neither pro- nor anti-globalization. That may be a surprising statement to make in a book about the changing nature of the global economy, but to understand whether globalization is good or not for various countries, people or the environment requires a series of different books, a number of which have already been written. Our task is to be clear on the decisions managers of companies face and how those decisions are changing, given the changing context for manufacturing.

This story challenges the conventional discussion on the global economy. You may feel that the numbers are too strong even to contemplate the idea of a reversal for globalization.

And yes, the numbers are brutal. Across the developed economies manufacturing employment has cratered. In the second half of the twentieth century there were 18 million or so people working in manufacturing in the United States. Then from the turn of the century to the financial crash, manufacturing employment dropped by a fifth.[41] This is one of the reasons manufacturing has become of secondary importance to the majority of people in the West—they no longer have any direct connection to manufacturing except as consumers.

The narrative of the move to the East can also be summed up in terms of the share of things that are now made in China. According to one article, "China accounted for just 3 percent of global manufacturing output in 1990. Today it produces almost a quarter, including 80 percent of all air conditioners, 71 percent of all mobile phones, and 63 percent of the world's shoes."[42]

Given that context, even typing the word "deglobalization" feels

slightly revolutionary, countercultural. With container ships continuing to grow and grow and countries like the U.K. running record trade deficits (the deficit at the end of 2015 for the U.K. was a new high, reaching 7 percent of GDP) the immediate signals don't point to a great redrawing of the economic map of the world.[43]

However, the early signs of a shift are there. Companies in many countries are deciding to have their production either in their home country or nearby, reshoring and nearshoring their supply chain. Automation is attacking the costs of labor and shifting the calculus for managers. Political forces are constraining the space for manufacturing, for example restricting emissions from transport. All these issues will be discussed in more detail in the chapters that follow as we unpack the forces moving us toward deglobalization.

THE PROCESSES OF GLOBALIZATION are a complex mix of trends that play out beyond our control and clear choices we are making as individuals, companies and countries. I have written this book in order to clarify our understanding of what globalization is and what it can become. Whether we think that globalization is good, or that free trade is a negative force, we all need to have these discussions based on what is actually happening on the ground and what is most likely to happen next, rather than on a caricature of what the global economy used to be like in an era that no longer exists. For this reason choices about trade deals and membership of regional trading blocs made now will have impacts far into the future. The popular vote in the U.K. to leave the European Union was made in the current context and did not have any real sense of the changing nature of making, trade and what it will take to be a successful company or national economy.

My argument is not that trade will cease, that countries will fly apart and that integration will be no more. This will be a relatively subtle shift. The key is that the geography of production is changing and ownership will matter more as companies will have to be producing in their final market. If we understand this we can have productive growth. However, if we keep trying to re-create the economy as it worked in the 1990s, many companies and possibly economies will struggle.

There is no simple one-time choice, either for companies or for

countries, between importing and exporting, or between producing an item within the company and outsourcing production to another company. The sum of the costs of moving things, data and people are core, and these are changing all the time due to new technologies and new models of co-ordination for companies. The question this book raises is whether we've become too wedded to one answer to this problem of location and organization, based on an outmoded, out-of-date understanding of technology and organization.

Exploring how the diversity of manufacturing will be impacted by changes in manufacturing processes will be a key part of this book, showing how different products are more or less adapted to the new context and how this aggregates to a restructuring of the global economy. To understand this properly, though, first we have to understand how "making" has changed over time—that is, how we used to make and how we structure the making of things now.

2

From Putting Out to Getting Out

IT IS EASY TO FORGET how dependent we all are on manufactured products in our everyday lives, from shoes to cars to smartphones. Most of us give even less thought to how these products are designed, made or delivered to us. We are living in a densely manufactured world but with a lack of public interest or understanding of how things are made. There is an important social history to be written on our relationship to products and whether we ever were concerned with their provenance, to use the food industry's word of the moment. But our understanding of making is important as it changes the quality of debate we have on manufacturing, globalization and the future. Without any sense of how we make things it is very hard to have a sensible conversation about what is likely to happen to industrial organization over time. Into the future, what kind of industrial system do we want? What types of jobs will we want to do? Will we want to be environmentally neutral and how do we think the profits of the system should be shared? These are questions that should be made more explicit and asked on a regular basis.

To tell any story of the future of making it is important to discuss the nature of "making," from early industrial systems of "putting out" (see below), through the Industrial Revolution, right up to the relatively recent emergence of global value chains, or "getting out"—that is, paying others to make for you. We've seen changes spanning over two hundred years of industrialization and deindustrialization, with different countries at

different moments having a falling share of output based on manufacturing and at others a rising share. These variations over time in different parts of the world highlight how complex the changes are in manufacturing and how they contribute to the rise and fall of globalization.

Which country had the greatest share of world manufacturing output in 1750? Was it (a) Germany (b) the United Kingdom (c) China or (d) India? It is not a question that comes up very often in either a pub quiz or on any of the many television game shows but it is a question that most people get wrong. Time's up—what is your answer?

Well, if you chose (c) China you can give yourself a pat on the back.[1] The relative shares of manufacturing output around the world at the midpoint of the eighteenth century looked very different than most people would assume. China accounted for a third of all manufacturing output for the world. The United Kingdom, at this moment in time just before the Industrial Revolution kicked off, had only a 2 percent share and the nascent power that would become the United States had just 0.1 percent at this very early stage of its development.

As the 1700s started out the global industrial landscape was about to be ripped apart, with the global north industrializing and a relative deindustrialization about to happen in the global south. The Industrial Revolution emerged across England, changing the nature of making and powering the country into empire. But nothing stays still for long and after the initial dominance for the British, power moved around the world, landing next in the United States. As these shifts have occurred, how have the relative shares of manufacturing output for each country changed?

For the United Kingdom there was rapid industrialization through the late eighteenth century and into the nineteenth. In 1880 Gladstone and the Liberal Party took over from Disraeli and the Conservatives, gaining 110 seats in an election dominated by foreign policy. Gladstone inherited a manufacturing base that produced nearly a quarter of all goods in the world, the peak of production for the United Kingdom. From there, in a relative sense it was downhill, with the once great empire on the eve of the Great War having only 13 percent of world production. This decline continued through the twentieth century so that currently the U.K. has around 3 percent of world production, only slightly higher in a relative sense to where it was in 1750, although of a very different quality.[2]

There is a different path for the United States, coming from nowhere and gaining and retaining a very significant share of world production. Remember, it had just 0.1 percent of output in 1750, and it did not achieve a very significant share until the latter half of the nineteenth century, with 7.2 percent in 1860, 14.7 percent in 1880 and fully one-third of world output in 1913, just before the outbreak of the First World War. The United States' relative share of production peaks in the 1950s, topping out at just under 45 percent, almost half of world output within the shores of America as the global economy recovered from the Second World War. Employment in manufacturing as a share of total employment in the U.S. peaked at the end of 1945 at just under 40 percent (although the absolute number of manufacturing workers peaked at the end of the seventies).[3] No wonder that manufacturing and industry form such a strong thread in the identity of many people and families in America.

While there has also been a decline for the United States in the relative share of manufacturing in its economy and a fall in terms of its share of global manufacturing output since the 1950s, that decline is not as extreme as for other developed economies. Currently the United States, at just under 20 percent of global industrial production, is in a very different position from that of the U.K. The U.K. went from being the self-declared workshop of the world, leading in manufactured output in the late nineteenth century, to now being the eighth largest producer. From that lead in terms of production, the U.K. now produces about 11 percent of what the leading manufacturing nations of China and the United States each make.

And what of China? Having been the heavyweight in 1750, it consistently lost ground up to the start of the First World War. At that point it had just under 4 percent of world production and wasn't going to see that relative level surpassed until the 1970s. What some have referred to as the reindustrialization of Asia is underpinned by China as a leading world producer, now vying with the United States for first place.

There are many messages to take from this whistle-stop tour of how dominance of industrial output has shifted among countries: from Asia in the eighteenth century to Europe through the nineteenth century and then America became the unchallenged hegemon until the reindustrialization of China toward the end of the twentieth century. Today, no one country has more than roughly a fifth of world production within its

borders, and it is questionable whether any nation will ever again reach the level of concentration that the United States achieved during the postwar period.

The first message we should heed is simple—the landscape of manufacturing changes continually; there is no "end of history" in the sense of the relative powers of each country locking in a position and staying there for decades and centuries to come. Any forecast that manufacturing in any given country is dead and buried should be treated with suspicion, as each change in technology, costs and demographics alters the landscape that manufacturers face as they make their decisions. It may be very difficult to restart making in a country, but it is not impossible.

The second message is that, yet again, our narratives and our expectations can be at odds with the facts. Not knowing who was top of the pile in the eighteenth century might not matter much now, but would most people get the current top five manufacturing countries right?[4] Before making any claims on what is and is not right for our economies, we all need to make sure we're actually talking about the reality that the economy faces.

If this is the story at the level of countries, how are companies who operate in those countries organizing themselves to make? How has the organization of individual companies evolved over the past two hundred years to get us to where we are today?

One of the earliest recognized systems of production has the unfortunate, in a modern sense, title of "putting out." Owners of raw materials or an agent of an enterprise would go from house to house parceling out supplies that each household would turn into individual products like shoes or clothes, or an element of the final product which could later be assembled by another household. Echoes of the practice remain in the term "cottage industry." The men and women involved were paid piece rates, that is a fixed amount for each item they produced, rather than for their time, as there was no way for the amount of time or effort expended to be measured accurately.

Such cottage industry was not a small aspect of enterprise in the United Kingdom during the Industrial Revolution. There were thousands of people working in this way, either to provide their main source of income or to supplement income from agriculture. The cotton manufacturer

Dixons of Carlisle had over 3,500 handloom weavers working for them in the early 1800s spread over the counties straddling the border between England and Scotland (as well as some in Northern Ireland).[5] Production organized in this way was necessarily relatively local, confined within one country and usually within one region, but this way of organizing making didn't always imply a lack of scale.

Cottage industries were a form of proto-industrialization and served as a necessary step in the evolution of what we would now consider to be more traditional factories. This approach to making, which has been used since antiquity, survived up to and through the Industrial Revolution in Great Britain, Europe and the United States and is still seen in many developing countries, such as in Ghana, where home handicrafts are exported and there is a cottage industry focused on recycling scrap aluminum into new products such as spoons and cooking pots.[6] Las Mujeres Solares de Totogalpa (The Solar Women of Totogalpa) build and sell solar ovens in Nicaragua as part of the Grupo Fenix. These twenty women have also discovered that the cheap green coffee beans left after the best have been exported could be transformed into high-quality coffee if they were roasted in one of their solar ovens.[7] This is a modern-day cottage industry that is both contributing to local development and innovating using their key technology and the local environment.

Curiously, the cottage pattern of organization has been revived in many developed economies with the rise of the teleworker or telecommuter. Most of these modern distributed workers are not producing physical goods. They are enabled to work from home by superfast broadband replicating office work in a domestic environment. But they have become a significant element of the labor market. In the United States those who are employed full-time and who spend at least half of their working hours at home make up around 2.5 percent of the workforce or over 3 million employees.[8] The feasibility of a digital and distributed version of manufacturing, making use of distributed makers working out of their garages, is another question altogether that we'll discuss in later chapters.

JUMPING FORWARD, the next significant version of industrial organization was the factory system, with large numbers of men, women and children producing, for example, textiles or metal products under one roof.

There was no rapid transition from putting out to this new and more centralized making. Rather, gradually over time, there arose a mixed system of production whereby some work was contained within a factory and some was still undertaken at home by piece workers. The early factories brought together different groups of workers to take advantage of tools or sources of power, but bore little resemblance to the integrated production lines we have become accustomed to in a modern context. These intermediate institutions were referred to as manufactories, distinguishing them from what were to become factories in the full sense.

Why did factories arise when they did? The answer is complex and plays out over time for different types of products. According to one study, "On the whole, the transition from domestic manufacture to factory was the most dramatic in textiles, but even there it took over a century to complete."[9] Generally, as the costs involved changed (shifting in emphasis between labor, materials and machinery) and the complexity of the production equipment increased, it was more likely that production would move to a factory rather than stay organized as put-out piecework. As new machines like the power loom became available the scale that they were efficient at became larger than could or would be accommodated within a domestic dwelling.

The method of making also changed, moving from individuals working at their own tempo to something called "continuous flow." Here the speed of production was set by the production manager and the workers had at keep up. Piece-rate pay was becoming less common and workers were beginning to be paid a daily wage now that they were together, in view and able to be controlled.

The regimentation and control that appeared at this point in the history of making have been integral to our interpretations of manufacturing ever since, written into the fabric of our understanding at this point. What had been a relatively fluid system of production became more rigid, less flexible. This has carried on to the present day, with each operation within a factory controlled to the second and optimization being the goal. That thinking, so embedded that it is out of sight, could hold many companies back in the current environment, in which the methods of production are changing so that they might need to become more fluid again.

Our usual interpretation of the Industrial Revolution, the emergence

of factories and the increase in wealth for countries such as the U.K., can obscure some of the realities that changed at this time. A key impact felt across families and economies was that there was now a separation between where people worked and where they lived—or, to be slightly more formal, between the locations of production and consumption.[10] Instead of using their houses as workshops more and more people—men, women and children—were now leaving their homes, to work in a factory. Max Weber highlighted this change, commenting that the place of work was separate from both the worker's house and that of the consumer of his or her labor.[11]

We feel that this is the norm, heading off to work each morning, leaving behind an unused space that will not see activity again until past knocking-off time. But it changed the nature of family life, possibly alienated this new workforce and removed manufacturing from the view of the broader community. This is important for later in our story as this alienation of production happened again at the national level, as the West deindustrialized and started to place manufacturing over the horizon. Out of sight, out of mind.

AS NEW WAYS OF ORGANIZING MAKING were being tried out, changing where things are made and who was making them, a number of key ideas emerged that allowed these experiments to happen. Many of these concepts are part of our common vocabulary now, so we don't need to spend much time lingering on them, but it is important to see the conceptual roots of our current organization of manufacturing.

Two ideas—division of labor and interchangeability—and a category— general purpose technologies—are at the core of what was happening in industrial organization through this period. Without these we could not have made the journey to global value chains with production spread around the world. Ideas and modes of organization are as important as technology in constructing new patterns of making.

At the beginning of the Industrial Revolution in the late eighteenth century, one of the most important ideas on the organization of manufacturing was formulated by Adam Smith, a man who rarely entered a factory. Yet the story of pin making is central to the argument of Smith's *Wealth of Nations*. The making of pins, which the uncompromisingly intellectual

Smith referred to as a "very trifling manufacture," showed how production could be broken into a number of steps or activities, and that by having each worker concentrate on just one step the amount produced could be significantly increased. Smith claimed that one person making pins could produce one a day, but that he had seen a "small manufactory" in which ten men produced 48,000 pins a day.

Smith, thought of by many as the father of modern economics, knew enough to realize that, in order to give substance to his theories, he had to see the world in action. His travels (primarily in Britain and France) convinced him that an increase in the division of labor would automatically lead to an increase in productivity, for him the "greatest improvement in the productive powers of labor."

The division of labor was adopted as a core concept across economics in the late 1700s and has dominated our thinking on how to organize manufacturing ever since, from the level of the individual through assemblies and on to whole products. There have been amendments and improvements made, for example the introduction of a moving production line, but at its heart division of labor still dominates how we think about organizing the manufacturing world.

IN ORDER TO BE ABLE to increase production volume, reduce the time to make and utilize less skilled labor, companies needed a simplification strategy. Even with the introduction of machines to help with cutting, pressing or spinning materials, making had a very high element of craft through the period covering the rise of factories and early industrialization. The skill of those using the machines had to be relatively high to deal with their inherent variability, the diversity of the products they were making and the difficulties in fitting everything together into a finished product.

The idea that allowed many manufacturers to move forward appeared in the late 1700s in the form of standardization or interchangeable parts. The idea is simple—that the worker should be able to make the parts of a product and swap these parts between products without having any doubts whether they will fit or whether they will work. The idea of interchangeable parts works hand in glove with the division of labor, as each subcomponent or assembly that is part of a product can be specified and

made without further reference to the rest of the product once the design is agreed.

War has been a depressing but effective driver of innovation for many products. The desire or need for weapons of greater destructive power has fueled spending on research and development throughout our recent history. The making of new weapons was the test bed for the use of interchangeability in manufacturing. What is referred to as the "American system of manufactures" arose after the American War of Independence, following the embargo imposed by the United Kingdom on the export of machinery and skilled mechanics to the United States.[12] The foundations for this system are based on the two armories founded after a 1794 Act of the Third Congress of the United States titled An Act to Provide for the Erecting and Repairing of Arsenals and Magazines, and for Other Purposes.[13] These were developed under the guidance of the first president of the United States, George Washington, the first a continuation of works that had started in Springfield, Massachusetts, and the second located at Harper's Ferry, Virginia.

In the midst of all these changes was Eli Whitney, credited by many as being the father of the American system of manufacturing. He was the first private citizen to be awarded a government contract which had a cash advance attached. This contract was worth $5,000 immediately and another $5,000 on proof of progress toward the production of guns for the government.

Whitney claimed in 1798 he would produce 10,000 muskets by 1801. This was a ridiculously ambitious goal as the existing armories and their gunsmiths had never produced anything like that number in the time he gave himself. When, by the middle of 1800, he realized he could not meet the deadline, instead of admitting that he had not produced a single weapon, Whitney arranged for a demonstration in January of 1801. This demonstration is the root of the claim that Whitney invented interchangeability.

"Whitney had made sure the right people were invited . . . President John Adams and President Elect Jefferson witnessed Whitney, using only a screwdriver, assemble ten different locks to the same musket."[14] But Whitney hadn't cracked interchangeability—he didn't take apart the gun locks and had specially prepared the ten muskets to make sure

that everything would fit. Convinced by his sleight of hand, the government gave him more time and more money to continue toward his goal. The muskets were finally delivered by 1808, seven years after the original deadline. Yet again we see the difference between the reality of the world and how perception can be manipulated.

So, if Whitney didn't introduce interchangeable parts, who did? The first successful attempt to demonstrate interchangeability in weapons happened many years before in a completely different country. At the Hôtel des Invalides in Paris on a cold November day in 1790, a gunsmith named Honoré Blanc took parts which he had made in a Vincennes dungeon from different bins and assembled working gun locks. He was watched by French politicians, military leaders and academics, who were stunned with the precision of the work. What is even more interesting is that five years before that, the then U.S. ambassador to France, one Thomas Jefferson, had written a letter home recounting a demonstration in the workshop of Blanc showing the interchangeability of parts. Jefferson knew about and had seen interchangeability working by 1785 but was still willing to be taken in by the performance of Whitney in 1801. Seems there might have been some hometown advantage.

But these events were for many years forgotten. "When, in the 1850s, English investigators brought word back to Europe of the 'American system of manufacturing,' they found that the French military had never heard of the method—let alone of Honoré Blanc."[15]

This retelling of the history is an important example of how again our worldviews can be at odds with what has happened and what may happen. It also highlights that there is no inevitability to technological progress, as the French system was discarded as much for social reasons (artisan makers rejecting the ideas of "rational production") as for technical or economic reasons. We should remember this when we are discussing what versions of the future industrial system we think are likely to emerge.

Interchangeability is a key moment in the development of mass production. It allows for separate pieces, subassemblies, to be made in volume and then finished products to be assembled from any mix of those parts. This depends on precision engineering, each part made to within a set tolerance. However, it also points to the importance of standards in manufacturing which as we move into the future of digitization of manufacturing will be

even more important. As we will see later, the control of the standards in the digital version of making will be key.

FOR MANUFACTURING in the eighteenth and nineteenth centuries the importance of the steam engine, the new power behind the factories that were spreading across the United Kingdom, cannot be overestimated. This is an example of what is referred to as a general purpose technology (GPT)—one that has applicability in many areas of the economy, has scope for improvement and increases the opportunities for innovation in a diverse set of sectors or products.[16] For some macroeconomists technology rather than the long accumulation of labor and capital is key to growth. Some changes in technology are such a leap forward that they create a discontinuity, a "drastic innovation."[17] Such technologies are rare and until recently have not received significant attention. That might be why we cannot see the potential for radical change in the organization of the global economy due to a collection of new technologies, something we'll come back to later.

The introduction of steam power to factories was neither immediate nor smooth, as factory owners had the choice between using existing water power or bringing in the new steam technology to do the heavy lifting. While James Watt patented the improved steam engine in 1769, it took until 1830 for there to be as much installed steam power as water power across the U.K.[18] Costs for both water and steam power fell significantly through the 1800s but it wasn't until the 1850s that steam was more cost effective than water to install and use in production. As a GPT the steam engine had more uses than just providing factory power. The growth of the railways was completely dependent on the arrival of the steam engine and highlights how one technology can pervade many different sectors.

The impact of steam power on productivity in the U.K. from the Industrial Revolution through to the start of the twentieth century shows how the impact of a GPT plays out over a long time period after the invention and initial diffusion of the technology. Steam had a small impact during the Industrial Revolution and peaked toward the end of the 1800s. As new technologies become available, they initially tend to have lower performance than existing alternatives and demand either new means of working or new models of industrial organization to reach their potential. This is

a pattern some think we have seen across the long history of industry and technology development, with the arrival of a GPT leading after some adaptation to a period of sustained growth.

Spotting the arrival of GPTs usually happens after the fact, but thinking about GPTs forces us to consider modern production processes such as 3D printing and automation in a new way. It is not just what they do immediately at the point of making, they can have much broader implications for how we make and where we make over time.

THE FORD MOTOR COMPANY factory, which opened at Dearborn, Michigan, at the turn of the twentieth century, was one of the first "modern" production lines, bringing together all of the ideas we have discussed to maximize productivity. Each worker did a specific task repetitively through the day, gloriously echoing Smith and the division of labor. The work was completed in a large factory, spread over many buildings and many acres in one location.

However, Ford claims and is credited with another innovation which radically changed factory organization: the moving assembly line. Assembly lines existed before Ford began producing the Model T, but in a stroke of inspiration Ford placed the car on a conveyor so that the production line, not the workers, moved around the factory. The line took the cars past work stations where each component could be added on, tightened up, or finished off, each station specializing in one set of operations.

According to Ford's corporate history, the moving assembly line for the Model T was based around eighty-four distinct steps and this change to a moving production line dropped the assembly time for a single vehicle from twelve hours to about ninety minutes.[19] A change in organization, a change in how things were done, meant a jump in productivity by a factor of eight. This is a massive leap forward.

Go inside most modern factories and the core, the heart of the factory, is a moving assembly line. This pattern of organization has been so successful it has survived for over one hundred years, even as the products and the means of production have become more and more complex.

There is, however, another very significant difference between the Dearborn factory of the early 1900s and the factories that emerged following the Second World War. As a company, Ford did practically

everything for itself. In a classic case of "vertical integration," metal, rubber and other raw materials were pushed in at one end of the factory complex and complete motor cars came out at the other. That is very far from how the world of manufacturing works now—a world in which the individual components of even the simplest of products have traveled a few times around the world before they get to you. But this is where many people's view of manufacturing stops, not realizing that even simple products have a very complex beginning.

TAKE SOMETHING AS APPARENTLY SIMPLE as a tennis ball. At Wimbledon it might be served at over 130 miles an hour, going from one end of the court to the other in less than half a second. But that's nothing compared to the 50,000 miles it has already clocked up before it reached SW19.

For something that appears so simple, a lot of components have come together to make the tennis ball: clay from the United States, wool from New Zealand and rubber from Malaysia, to name but three. Combine the miles those components have traveled to get to the factory somewhere in Southeast Asia with the final journey of the finished product to Wimbledon, and that tennis ball will have traveled the equivalent of twice around the equator.

This is an example of what is referred to as a global value chain (GVC), which is the set of activities necessary to get a product from idea to customer—so it includes the design, production, marketing, distribution and after sales service or support. The concept is not new, tracing its roots back to work on commodity chains in the 1970s, which then became global commodity chains in the 1990s and finally in the 2000s expanded to become global value chains.[20]

The classic example of a global value chain, where the lead company controls how the product is designed and made but is using suppliers for many of the tasks right up to assembly, is Apple. A much-used study of the value captured by all of the companies involved in making an iPod in 2007 showed that of the retail price of $299, Apple made a profit of about $80 per unit after taking care of its distribution and retail costs.[21] For Apple's suppliers the absolute profits of their involvement is much lower, as the most expensive component to Apple was the hard drive from Toshiba

which cost Apple just over $73, leaving Toshiba with an estimated gross profit of just over $19 per unit. At the time, with its 60,000 employees in the United States, the profit per employee was around $400,000 whereas workers at Foxconn in China, where iPods and iPads were assembled, were earning less than $400 per month.

Other studies have highlighted the extent of Apple's supply chain both across the world and specifically in China. Of the 759 subsidiary companies involved in Apple's supply chain, 44 percent are located in China. However, "Apple has been reluctant to involve many Chinese companies in its supply chain, with the majority of suppliers, even many of those located in China itself, being foreign companies."[22] The key is that the elements of the iPod or iPad are sourced globally and assembled in China, with the final finished products shipped around the world to be sold to you and me.

Unfortunately, there are few examples that really show how value creation and capture play out across a global value chain, and so the Apple example is extrapolated further than it should be. Claims that companies in developed economies hold on to the design and branding (the kinds of things that were referred to as core competencies by management consultants through the 1990s), and so can extract the most value, are based on this and one or two other examples, without referring to other factors such as the R&D investment, aggressive intellectual property strategies or the value of having a dominant market position.

This kind of extrapolation has also led to something referred to as the "smile curve." As a piece of shorthand it is an interesting idea—that the valuable activities are at the start (R&D) and the end (sales and brand control) of the chain of activities that links an idea with the product in your hand. Production in the middle is thought of as low value, not important, hence the "smile" with a curve high at the start, dropping in the middle, and back up again at the end.

The problem? As ever, there is little to no data to back up the smile curve, but it is quoted as proof that you don't need to worry about the making or the assembling. That's easy, low value. Many countries have based their strategies toward manufacturing on this model, targeting "good" jobs at either end of the value chain and worrying if they feel that they are taking on too many of the "bad" jobs in production in the middle of the chain.

The sketch of the smile curve was introduced by the founder of the Taiwanese computer company Acer, Stan Shih, in 1992,[23] but there has been surprisingly little work to back it up. We're still at the stage of intuition, ideology and narrative and this model ignores the connections between the activities. There are reasons to have manufacturing activities in a country that go beyond direct impacts on jobs or GDP, none of which are accounted for in the smile curve. The smile curve may now be blinding strategy makers to the choices they need to make. What might be clogging up the view for the poor consumer?

A SOURCE OF CONFUSION for the general public about how industry organizes itself is the geographic cross-dressing that happens with the labels and brands we buy. The truth of the extent of global value chains is hidden behind the label "Made in X." As outsourcing and offshoring have taken hold the "Made in" designation means less and less, with parts and subassemblies from across the world meeting and being assembled in another country. Somehow "Assembled in X" doesn't have the same punch and would only lead to difficult questions for the companies trying to sell us American-, Korean-, or German-assembled products.

Brands with a national identity such as Burberry, with its deep cultural connection to the U.K., have operations globally and a complex shareholder-ownership structure. In the case of Burberry, its largest market is Asia, it manufactures largely in China and at least a third of the shareholding is controlled by large U.S.-oriented investors such as the Capital Group (originally based in Los Angeles) and the Massachusetts Financial Services Company. So it may be branded as British, but how British is it?

This confusion of identity, structure and ownership has been exacerbated by how companies are bought and sold. With the American Kraft buying the iconic British Cadbury chocolate makers in 2010,[24] the German BMW taking ownership of another iconic British product, the Mini, and the Chinese company Lenovo taking over production of all-American IBM PCs, are Cadbury chocolate bars American, Minis German or IBM PCs Chinese now?

Again, these changes are not visible to most consumers and so have skewed their view of how the manufacturing world is organized. They complicate the media reporting of manufacturing and create another

barrier to a clear view of what is going to happen in the global economy moving forward.

WE NEED TO RECOGNIZE that some industries have remained explicitly local in their organization. The clearest example is the automotive industry, which has significant anchorage in home and regional markets.

The car industry is still relatively concentrated at the global level, with a small number of large companies in control of the industry. These companies such as VW, GM and Fiat through many mergers and acquisitions have maintained their roles as dominant producers over the past twenty years. However, in terms of sales, up to the crisis of 2008 they were selling the majority of their cars in their home markets.[25]

These sales are based on a regional pattern of production which comes about because of a mix of technical and political factors. Car parts can be heavy or fragile, which makes transporting them to the location of final assembly costly and potentially risky. Historically, many countries have had strong local content rules which forced the final assembly to be in the country where the car will be sold.

So before we think of the hyper-globalization story as having taken hold in every industry and in every part of the world we should stop and think again. For reasons both technical and political, automotive industry supply chains (to take just one example) tend to be contained within a region, and this should make us stop and question the standard narrative straight away. At the very least it shows that regionalized production is possible, and in many cases desirable. It remains to be seen whether that will become the case for more and more industries as the context for making continues to change, as we'll discuss in Chapters 7 and 8.

HOW FAR CAN AND SHOULD the fragmentation of the making of a product go? From an idea in a design sketch, through the development process and on to the making of the thing so that the actual product can be sitting in your hand is a long journey. Is there some optimal level of breaking up or separation of all the design and production tasks that allows a company to make at the lowest cost possible?

For consumers there are other factors at play. Some believe, for example, that the environmental impact from the making of our phones

is important. Others may want to support the enforcement of labor laws in order to protect child workers. It is an open question whether we consumers are willing to pay a significantly higher price for products which don't have a global footprint, are environmentally neutral or have greater protections in place for their workers. But decision makers who don't consider the potential impact of the consumer's values may be blindsided as these views convert into purchasing decisions.

Over the past three hundred years changes in technology and in organization have constrained or enabled what we can make and where we make it. Two different aspects of company organization make this story hard to tell, especially now as companies' supply chains have become more and more fragmented. First, how much of the making does the lead company do and, second, where in the world are the elements of the final product being made?

The amount of actual work the company is doing is a question of how much and what has been outsourced to other companies. Is the company doing everything itself (as in the case of Ford's vertical integration with the Model T), or is it getting other companies to source materials, make the pieces and assemble the final product (what is sometimes referred to as virtual manufacturing), or is it doing something in between? The generic answer to this question from strategy consultants from the 1990s was to focus on "core competencies" and to strip out anything else. These competencies should be things that differentiate you from other companies and are hard to copy.[26] It is unclear whether this kind of answer fits in a deglobalizing world.

The second aspect that causes difficulty is the geography of all those different activities, owned by the company or not. It is clear that companies have elements of themselves (foreign affiliates or subsidiaries) around the world and their suppliers can also be global. Are the different parts of a company's supply chain in one location or in many? Have the company's main activities been held in the home country or have they been moved to another country to take advantage of labor costs, specialist skills or access to a market?

Putting ownership and location together gives us four options or boxes, as it were. These are for an activity to be undertaken within the company at home, outsourced at home, owned by the company in another country,

or outsourced to someone abroad. Most companies are spread in some pattern across all four of these boxes. Remember the Apple supply chain? The R&D that feeds into the development of the Apple Watch is based in the U.S., much of the semiconductor work is completed there as well, while subsidiaries from a number of companies operate in China to service the Chinese elements of the chain. The days of massive vertical integration as represented by the Ford factory in Dearborn are gone.

The question is how the geography of making is changing and how the location box is being filled up—is it at home, nearby or far away? Or, to put it another way, is it domestic, regional or global?

Context, as ever, is king. How we can make determines where we will make to a large extent, adjusted for the size of markets and the actions of governments. How we make impacts the amount of labor involved in the production of a product, which in turn changes the relative costs of making in one country versus another. New production technologies change the output level at which a factory becomes viable (referred to as minimum economic scale), reducing the need for huge factories in a single location. The number of places and their location in which it makes sense for a company to produce continues to change because we keep changing how we make practically every product.

So, to have any sense of where the global economy is heading it is crucial to think about how we will make in the future. The next three chapters will look at different aspects of how technology, organization and transportation are changing and what this implies for how we may make into the future, whether we are going hyper-global or hyper-local.

3

"Tea, Earl Grey, Hot," or How We Will Make

PATRICK STEWART'S VOICE IS a thing of wonder. For the many fans of *Star Trek* it is a joy to hear him exude the sense of leadership needed to fill out the role of Jean-Luc Picard, captain of the USS *Enterprise*. At least once an episode, Picard makes a cup of tea. Not a kettle in sight, he simply utters the words "Tea, Earl Grey, hot" into the "replicator" built into his wall and it creates the tea, the cup, the whole thing, apparently out of thin air.

That one line issued from Patrick Stewart's lips is one of the clearest expressions of the holy grail of making—to be able to control and assemble atoms and molecules directly to make whatever you want, with just a shimmer and a few seconds to wait. No more factories, no more waste, no more shipping of things around the planet—or the galaxy, for that matter.

So when Stewart gravels, "Tea, Earl Grey, hot," he is expressing the ultimate future, in which making occurs once, at the point of need, under the complete control of the consumer. This is a future devoid of want or shortage, a future in which, if you can describe it, the replicator can make it.

It is also, of course, fantasy. We are far, far away from this future, if this is even in our future at all. However, you would be forgiven for thinking otherwise, given all the hype and hoopla that 3D printing (or, to give it its more technical name, additive manufacturing) has attracted recently. The media has been full of breathless stories which claim that all you need

to knock out a gun or a turbine blade are a printer and some powder or plastics and you're done. If only it were that simple.

While this high-fantasy end of making is seductive, other changes already happening in how we make are themselves close to what many may think of as science fiction. In particular, the point at which biology and engineering are coming together, especially in the manufacturing of replacement body parts, is where some strange and wonderful things are starting to happen. At the same time, simple everyday items such as shirts and television screens are being made in new ways, challenging the logic of outsourcing every element of production to the other side of the world.

Our future of making will indeed use new techniques like 3D printing to make existing products in new ways and make new products that we could not have made before. However, a number of companies who are still using traditional production methods—and who may well continue to do so—are organizing themselves in some surprising new ways to maintain their competitive edge. These are changes that are being made from within manufacturing. And it is the coming together of these changes in *how* things are being made, both technologically and organizationally, which will make a significant difference to *where* things can and will be made in the future. This in turn will become a major element in reshaping the world economy, trade patterns and international relations without a single bullet being fired.

STEP OUT OF THE T STATION in Harvard Square, just outside of Boston, Massachusetts, and directly across the street you'll see the autumn red signage of the Coop bookstore. Located in one of those huge comfortable buildings with lots of nooks and crannies, places to hide and spaces to read for free, the Coop has sold textbooks to thousands of stressed Harvard students over the years. Slightly behind you is the Yard. This is the heart of the university for undergraduates, where there are lots of red-brick buildings, the bronze figure of John Harvard in his armchair surveying it all, and the ridiculously imposing Widener Library. Strangely, the *Titanic* has a connection here as well, for the library was built with a gift from Eleanor Widener in memory of her son Harry, who perished aboard the ship. When it was originally built it could hold over 3 million books on fifty miles of shelves. Now there are over 6 million items

in the library, enough to keep most of us in reading matter for quite some time.[1]

The last thing that you would expect to find among the university buildings, trees and narrow streets running off the square is a factory. But head away from the Coop down Mass Ave, wander past the old guys playing intense chess outside the Holyoke Center and just before you hit Bartley's Burger Cottage you'll see the Harvard Bookstore. Comfortably triple fronted and more manageable than the Coop, it's been around since 1932. So, what does this very conventional-looking bookstore have to do with world trade and how things are made?

Nestling at the back of the store between its towering bookshelves is a great example of how making is changing. It looks like an oversized printer and has prosaically been named Paige M. Gutenborg (the top choice from 500 suggestions provided online to the owners Jeff Mayersohn and Linda Seamonson).[2] This rather unassuming machine is a beautiful example of what is likely to happen to many products over the coming decades. Gutenborg will print and bind a production-quality book in about the time it takes to make a good cappuccino and for not much more than a large paperback costs. If a digital file exists for a book and the author and publisher will allow it, then you can have a copy in your hands within five minutes.

This is an extreme example of the trend toward localization of manufacturing that is already happening. The book travels all of a foot to get to you, not halfway around the world from a volume producer in another country. Suddenly books are no longer out of print, they just are waiting to be conjured up from a digital file. To paraphrase On Demand Books, the company who makes the Espresso Book Machine (which is what Paige M. Gutenborg is under the covers), this gives the customer the ability to "search globally and print locally."[3] And the book is still warm when it comes out, like it has been gently heated in its own little book oven, cooked up especially for you.

So instead of printing thousands of copies of a book, publishers can have an individual copy printed at the point of sale at a time when the customer definitely wants to buy it. No pulping of remaindered books, no need for inventory, just print as many books as are needed, when and where they are needed. The basic processes of printing and binding are

supported by the internet and digitization, enabling the source material to be shared and used in a great coming together of the physical and digital worlds.

The book industry hasn't exactly jumped in and embraced this as the way forward yet. Maybe one disruption at a time is enough, given that the publishing world has only recently come to terms with the e-book. But it is a neat example of how the *process* by which something can be made will change *where* it is made and *how many* are made.

Books are hard to write but they are not physically the most complicated of products to make. That's not to disrespect the amount of thought and creativity that goes into making hardback books in particular look and feel as beautiful as they are today. But some paper, some ink and then some way of putting the ink onto that paper in a structured way, that's a book in its simplest sense. And the technology is already here to do this at the point of purchase.

So, if books are relatively simple and easy to make, how about something almost incomprehensively difficult to make, such as replacement body parts for you and me? Strangely, they may be nearer to a reality than many people think.

IMAGINE IF EVERY TIME your phone rang it could signal the difference between life with or without a debilitating disease. For anyone waiting for an organ transplant, each call could be the one that brings the news of a donor, a match, an opportunity to move forward. But everyone on a transplant waiting list is in a race against time, and each has a deadline before which they must receive a donor organ if their condition is not to worsen or, in many cases, become untreatable. Unfortunately, many on the list will run out of time before a donor can be located.

At the end of 2012, 57,903 people were on the waiting list for a kidney transplant in the United States.[4] However, over the course of that year only about 18,000 kidney transplants were carried out—that is, over two-thirds of the people on the waiting list did not receive a transplant. The waiting list for kidneys is the longest; almost four times longer than for liver transplants (12,774) and over twenty times that for heart transplants (2,493). According to the American Transplant Foundation, over 6,500 people on waiting lists in the United States die each year before a transplant can be

found.[5] That's roughly eighteen people per day dying for the lack of organs to transplant.

Why are there not enough organs? There are many reasons, but the main one is that there are too few donors. Not enough people are willing to act as living donors, in the case of kidney transplants, and there are insufficient numbers of these and other organs available postmortem.[6] Numerous programs have been run, outreach efforts from government and from charities, but still the number of organs offered is not big enough to meet demand. Even though the number of registered donors has risen, bereaved relatives can be too distressed to understand and comply with their loved one's wish to donate.

What if we could make a kidney, a liver or a heart instead of relying on one tragedy to alleviate another? What if we could make the organs we need on demand? This is one area of additive manufacturing in which the hype and the reality blur a lot, as significant advances have already been made.

Anthony Atala comes across as a rather modest, almost shy man. Dressed in standard academic garb of chinos and a blue-and-white striped shirt, he looks fairly unremarkable. But this trained doctor, originally from Peru and now at the Wake Forest School of Medicine in North Carolina, is anything but unremarkable. He is one of the leading figures in regenerative medicine, a field which uses the cells in your body combined with biological scaffolds (either man-made using ceramics or polymers, or reusing human tissues denuded of cells) in an attempt to cure rather than treat.[7]

He gave a famous TED talk in 2011 in which he produced a printed kidney structure made using a patient's cells and presented it to an audience that is usually very hard to impress.[8] Here was a piece of the future presented for all to see. What Anthony Atala is working toward at Wake Forest is solving the problem of transplant waiting lists permanently. And he is attempting to do this by making artificial bodily organs.

There is still a long way to go. The structure that Atala presented at TED was just that—a structure. It didn't have the functional elements of the kidney. Also, probably the greatest barrier to making organs in this way hasn't been cracked yet. This is vascularization, the process by which a network of veins, capillaries and arteries are embedded into the organ so that cells don't die due to a lack of blood supply.[9] But even to be thinking

in these terms shows how far the science is developing—and is moving from the realms of science fiction into a possible future.

So, what can we do now? It is early days in the science of whole organ manufacture, but printing skin and simpler structures is already within reach. One of the companies moving into this space, Organovo, is preparing to print strips of liver tissue to be used in testing drugs.[10] Several bone transplants have already been made using 3D-printed pieces. For example, in the Netherlands in June 2011, an eighty-three-year-old woman suffering from a chronic bone infection had her jawbone replaced with a 3D-printed titanium substitute.[11] Replacement ears[12] and noses[13] have also been produced, and in one case in Wales doctors at Swansea's Moriston Hospital managed to reconstruct a man's face after a serious motorbike accident in 2014.[14]

The base technology is moving on as well, with many different techniques being developed under the rubric of bioprinting[15] with significant sums of money being invested in research and development. The core idea is simple—to use an additive approach, printing or placing biological material piece by piece onto a scaffold to make a complex artificial biological product. Much of the technology looks a bit rough at the moment, with old desktop inkjet printers being hacked about to allow cells to be used in the printer cartridges instead of ink and improvised holes being made to move platforms up and down instead of taking paper left to right. As this research pays dividends, however, the scientists behind it are beginning to understand how to create and handle different cell types and how to make three-dimensional structures with different cells placed precisely where they need to go. They are also moving toward solving the intricate problems of vascularization, key to making a replacement organ on demand.

Even though much of the hype is focused in the U.S., the advances being made in this space are not owned or controlled by America. One of the first attempts to solve the problem of vascularization was made by the Fraunhofer Institute in Stuttgart, using bioinks, which remain fluid until cured with UV light.[16] Other groups sinking a lot of research effort into 3D bioprinting include NTU Singapore, the Utrecht Biofabrication Facility in Holland and the Pohang University of Science and Technology (POSTECH) Intelligent Manufacturing Systems Lab in South Korea.

Where the breakthroughs will come from that will lead to whole organ printing is unclear, but all these countries and their researchers want to be part of the race.

Some influential and famous people are becoming seriously interested in bioprinting. You know you're on the cutting edge of a technology if will.i.am wants to get involved. The polymath early adopting musician and producer describes himself on his website as "a multi-faceted entertainer and creative innovator."[17] In a recent interview he claimed we need "new morals, new laws and new codes" to deal with the possibilities of 3D printing, especially when it comes to printing organs or even, in the far future, whole people.[18] The idea of printing whole people is heading back into hype land, but one of the oldest companies in this space, 3D Systems, who invented many of the first processes for additive manufacturing, is taking will.i.am seriously enough to have made him their Chief Creative Officer.

The serious point, though, is how challenging this new production technology is to us technically, scientifically and societally. It has opened up a new set of possibilities for what can be made, where it can be made and who can make it. In terms of making, bioprinting has important long-term, indeed life-saving implications; in terms of trade, however, this is a whole new type of product that is never likely to be shipped around the world in the traditional way. Products made using human cells will always tend to be made pretty close to where the end user is, usually in the facility in which they are being treated. As we already know from experience of organ transplants, moving these kinds of biological products about is expensive and complicated (for example they need very reliable refrigeration). Sending your cells to another country to have the new tissue or organ printed and then sent back to you isn't going to make sense, either medically or economically.

So this is a production technology for a particular product that will not rely on trade to reach its end user. As such it is at the extreme end of our story. But what of 3D printing in more conventional manufacturing?

THE HEADLINES IN TWO very different magazines sum up where we are. The first, which comes from the venerable *Harvard Business Review*, claims that "3-D Printing will change the world," while the second, in the *Architectural Review*, tells us that "3D printing will destroy the world."[19]

3D printing is a process of making based around adding small layers of material over time to build an object. This is in contrast to a lot of traditional manufacturing, which starts with a block of material and takes pieces away to make the object (subtractive manufacturing, in the jargon) or presses materials together to make a new piece (formative manufacturing). What has made many people very excited about 3D printing, though, is that it is a process that can be used to make with fewer constraints, thus many shapes that more traditional manufacturing cannot accommodate are a breeze in the 3D-printed world (for example shapes with central voids, such as the air intake for an engine). Different techniques have been developed,[20] but they all essentially come down to the same thing—creating a digital file of the shape you want to make and then adding or combining materials to build it.

It is this digitization of the inputs to the machines, the ability to take a digital version of a shape and make it appear anywhere in the world where there is a connected 3D printer, that could impact company organization and supplier relationships in a fundamental way. 3D printers act as the bridge between the physical world and the digital world, creating a link between the two. As long as the data specifications are clear and agreed in advance, this allows designers to be remote but to iterate and update designs for parts and products much more quickly and simply. Any changes require simply a download of a file and the machines do the rest. This is a huge attraction for many producers, using the backbone of the internet to allow for remote control of the production process. We'll see more of this later when we discuss what has been referred to as the fourth industrial revolution.

Another advantage of 3D printing techniques over traditional methods of making is that you don't need to create specific molds or rigs first in order to make a new product. This reduces the time needed to make a new part and also eradicates the cost of tooling, which can be very expensive. And because the product shape is formed from a polymer or a powder there is no constraint on the type of shape or form it can take.

When it comes to making specialized parts at low volumes, for example in the Formula One industry, 3D printing is already saving money for the manufacturer by reducing both the time they take to make and the cost of raw materials. Even in more traditional automotive manufacturing there

are advantages to be had. For instance, Ford uses 3D printing extensively in its prototyping and research. Whereas an intake manifold prototype made using traditional manufacturing methods can take up to four months and cost $500,000, the same prototype made using 3D printing can be ready on-site in four days for about $3,000.[21]

Making things in this way can seem almost like magic. A box hums and chugs to itself and slowly an object appears—an iPhone cover,[22] a piece of jewelry[23] or a turbine blade for a jet engine.[24] Research into how to make additively, using lasers to fuse powders and/or liquids, has been going on for over thirty years, but recent advances in manufacturing have taken the scale and cost of an entry-level machine to the point where hobbyists can afford to buy one and print at home. A bare-bones entry model like the Printrbot Simple Metal will now set you back just under $600.[25]

The ability to print metal, building up layers by using a laser to sinter together powdered metal "inks," is a huge advance. If the 3D printing world were constrained to polymers and plastics alone it would be a depressingly dull and structurally limited place to be. However, metal printing, which has been available for over twenty years, has recently started to be adopted more widely for industrial use. The number of metal capable industrial 3D printers sold in 2015 was more than double what was sold in 2013 (808 versus 353).[26] One of the lead adopters is General Electric (GE), which has broken new ground as the first company to have received clearance from the Federal Aviation Authority (FAA) to use a 3D printed metal part in their engines.[27] This part has been retrofitted to 400 engines that power Boeing 777s but GE hasn't stopped there. They now make a fuel nozzle using a 3D metal printer, meaning that a part once made by welding eighteen pieces together can now be printed off in one go and is 25 percent lighter as well. There are nineteen of these nozzles in a GE aircraft engine, and it looks like they will be making 10,000 of them each year to keep up with demand.

It is the availability of cheap home 3D printers that has been one of the main reasons for the growth of public awareness of their properties. Being able to produce something at home has also sparked the imaginations of thousands of people around the world to become Makers, designing and printing their own items. The so-called "Maker Movement," which started on the west coast of America, now has Maker Faires at which people can

show off their creations in what the organizers refer to as part county fair, part science fair.[28] And in case you thought this was just a small bunch of hobbyists meeting in a town hall on a Saturday afternoon, according to Maker Media (the owner of the Maker Faire brand) over 215,000 people attended the main faires in San Francisco and New York in 2014.

Even President Obama got in on the act. In the 2013 State of the Union Address he promoted the first of the new manufacturing innovation institutes that his administration funded to provide support for advanced manufacturing. About halfway through the speech he namechecked Youngstown, Ohio, saying that "A once-shuttered warehouse is now a state-of-the-art lab where new workers are mastering the 3D printing that has the potential to revolutionize the way we make almost everything."[29] You know that something is in the zeitgeist when it is mentioned in the State of the Union speech.

The United States government is not the only one putting some bets down. Toward the end of 2014 the South Korean government revealed a ten-year strategy for the development of 3D printing, specifically linking it to the internet of things (IoT).[30] With a history of rapid industrialization, deep electronics and ICT capabilities and as the home of leading multinational companies such as Samsung, which changed the nature of electronics production, South Korea could be a real challenger in the race to develop the next generation of 3D printers.

Is the attention and hype surrounding 3D printing warranted? Should we be seeing 3D printing as the foundation of another industrial revolution, a general purpose technology (GPT) to use the phrase from Chapter 2? Every new technology, especially one with such broad application, will attract its boosters and its detractors, both wild optimism and deep skepticism. The precise path and impact of such a technology is impossible to plot at the moment, but it has already changed how we make. Prototyping is easier and faster to do than with traditional manufacturing, the ergonomics of a product can be iterated, and new shapes can be made that could not have been dreamt of, using traditional molding or subtractive processes. As 3D printers become better and cheaper they will be used more and more by companies to produce finished products for you and me. This in turn will have a very significant effect on company organization and, as a result, trade.

One side effect of the increase in additive manufacturing techniques such as 3D printing is that there will be fewer pieces (referred to as assemblies or subassemblies) in any given product. Indeed, as we have seen, it has already started to happen: a piece of the F-18 fighter jet that used to be put together from sixteen separate parts is now being made as a single piece using additive manufacturing. The implications are huge. Intermediate trade, that is when unfinished goods such as chips for smartphones or engines for cars are moved from country to country, accounts for approximately 60 percent of current world trade. With a reduction in the number of production steps for many products, the volume of pieces being shipped around the world in intermediate trade will drop. And this will have an immediate knock-on effect on global trade volumes, as we'll discuss in Chapter 8.

But when it comes to Picard's replicator from the start of this chapter printing everything we want on demand, there are still quite a few stumbling blocks. The most important of these is that, while 3D printing does shape very well and is good for creating the frame or the casing of products, printing the electronics, the motors and all the other pieces that make machines actually work is a whole other world. This isn't to say that printed electronics can't be done; indeed, they already exist.[31] But integrating these processes into a flexible, multifunctional machine that can make more than one product without significant modification each time is still a long way off.

We've seen the front edge of bio-printing with Anthony Atala's printed kidney, a product that would resist trade from its inception. Printed food can already be made, mainly for high-end patisseries and cutting-edge chefs, although companies like Hershey's are also getting involved with printed chocolate.[32] Artists are entering the game as well. For example the young German-born artist and product designer Markus Kayser has taken a new approach to making glass sculptures using the sun and the sand in the Sahara desert on a modified 3D printing platform.[33]

But what about more traditional sectors like clothes or food, where these technologies have less purchase? Any changes that happen here will have more to do with the organization of manufacturing, based on the business model being deployed and the demand profile that is being served, than on cutting edge production technologies. And it is these

changes in the patterns of making and moving of existing products that will have the stronger impact on trade in the near future.

IT USED TO BE that you had to take a shoe designer's decisions as final. In the 1990s the release of a new design of trainer, in particular, was a big deal for the fashion-conscious, as there were only so many designs on the market at any one time. Not anymore. Want that shoe with a purple inner? Not a problem. Finding the contrast shade of orange not to your liking? You choose. You've just entered the world of mass customization. On the Adidas website you can choose a base design for a trainer and then customize every color, texture and style for each element, even adding in some text or a photo print if that's what you fancy.[34] The lead time on a new pair of trainers designed by you for you is four to six weeks—not bad for something that is essentially a high-kudos fashion item. But the key here is that those shoes were never going to be made unless you clicked the purchase button on the website, linking production directly to actual demand.

Apparently you don't buy a Rolls-Royce anymore, "you commission one, like a piece of fine art," according to one dealer.[35] That's because Rolls-Royce understand the power of customization, especially at the high end of the automobile market. A base Rolls will set you back over £200,000 and then you can choose pretty much everything else about the interior of the car. The color palette you're working from is not a standard one of eight choices, either; for your new Rolls you can choose from 44,000 colors. And if you're feeling particularly flush you can embed diamonds into the interior or create a star field with fiber optics in the ceiling. The one-off "Celestial" Phantom, made in 2013 to commemorate the car's tenth anniversary, took this to the extreme with 446 diamonds implanted carefully in its interior and LEDs arranged in its roof lining to replicate the night sky over Goodwood, where Rolls-Royce is based, on the night in 2003 when the company delivered the first Phantom to the first customer.[36]

We started this chapter by looking at how new processes are being developed to make in different ways, and on different scales. But something more abstract than that is changing how making is organized—the philosophy that is driving it. The hacker and maker ethics are seeping into the mainstream. The hacker philosophy emerged out of the Massachusetts Institute of Technology (MIT) in the 1980s and was brought into

the mainstream by the journalist Stephen Levy.[37] His codification of the hacker ethic stated that information should be free, that access to computers should be unlimited, and centralization and authority were to be mistrusted. Fast forward to the 2000s and the maker movement emerges in the United States, slowly spreading to other countries. This is a loose collection of people and organizations who believe in making, repairing and reusing at the level of the individual, many times sharing collective spaces. Until recently the movement has been very much associated with 3D printing, driving the improvements in the machines' capabilities to print finer and finer objects. The philosophy of makers is in many ways the next generation of hacking focused on making, sharing, playing, learning and changing the world.[38]

As these ideas move from enthusiasts to the mainstream, multinational companies are getting more and more involved. Levi's started a "Levi's Makers" label that claims to promote makers like Alice Saunders who makes bags from recycled army textiles.[39] General Electric has supported the development of what they refer to as a co-creation space called First-Build.[40] The biggest companies are trying to link at least to the spirit of the maker movement, if not actually to the potential that it represents. This is instilling in ordinary customers the idea that they don't have to settle for mass-produced items, identical to millions of others that fill the shelves around the world. They want to get involved in their own making.

Mass customization is not a new idea. As a concept it has been around since at least the 1970s, long before the emergence of 3D printing. There have been a number of attempts from large brand names to kick-start mass customization in their industry, but they have been less than successful. The oft-quoted example is that of Levi Strauss and its Original Spin jeans, launched in the late 1990s, whereby you went to a store and had your measurements taken and then the made-to-measure jeans were sent to your home in two to three weeks.[41] Unfortunately for Levi's the customers didn't flock to their offering, as they were not prepared to wait three weeks for made-to-measure jeans when there were plenty of other brands on main street and that old favorite of sitting in the bath shrinking your new jeans to fit was always an option. Other attempts at providing some level of mass customization have also passed into history, such as Dell allowing you to spec up your laptop before ordering.

Versions of mass customization keep coming, though. Trek bikes have started to allow you to build your bike from scratch[42] and Brooks Brothers are encouraging you to design your own suit.[43] No matter the difficulties in making mass customization work, companies keep attempting to make it happen. Why? There is a huge market opportunity here. A Bain survey in 2013 found that 10 percent of us had bought a customized product, but over 25 percent of us were interested in buying products made to our own specification.[44] If 25 percent of footwear were sold in this way, that would amount to a $2 billion market every year. Add to that the potential savings from not having to hold stock that doesn't sell, since each customized order is confirmed before it is ordered, and it is not difficult to see why companies find it so attractive. They no longer have to guess the demand profile, they let it emerge from the input of their customers as they choose paint colors and trim for their cars, or multicolored insoles for their trainers.

The other big reason to make customization more widely available is to generate loyalty. Those customers who have taken the time to work up their own product have invested significantly even before they have received their goods. Depending on your target audience, that can lead to a lot of time spent on the website generating advertising revenue and click throughs.

This brave new world of production is one in which production runs are shorter and customization is encouraged. This is made possible by a tight integration between the physical and the digital, as the physical production in factories is connected through dense digital links across the supply chain to the consumer either in store or online. And this organizational change has been enabled by advances in communication and the internet rather than by radical changes in the production processes themselves.

Over the longer term, providing such customization will impel companies to maintain reach and control through their supply chain rather than outsourcing almost every step, as would have previously happened. For only through direct control of the production processes can they effectively implement shorter production runs and customization of either form or function for their products. But what if a company decides to do this from the start?

. . .

IN ZARA STORES around the world the clothes ranges are updated every two to four weeks. For an industry that used to plan collections up to a year in advance this is an incredible change enabled by rethinking how the manufacturing of clothes is organized.

Zara had a very difficult beginning in 1975.[45] Its founder, Amancio Ortega, already had a small clothing factory in northwest Spain but the entire enterprise was put under threat when a German customer canceled a lingerie order. That single customer was life and death for the company, as all of Ortega's capital was invested in that order. Faced with no real choice, he decided to open a store of his own and, having learned from his experience of losing his wholesale customer, he developed an approach to manufacturing and the supply chain that entailed understanding and controlling the product's path right through from the designer's drawing board to the customer in the shop.

Well before onshoring and nearshoring had become fashionable terms, Ortega and his company Inditex, the owner of Zara and a number of other brands, was developing the means to connect and communicate along every link of the supply chain. This communication allows store managers to order more of what sells, to include items based on the comments of their customers and to feed back quickly what is happening in their area in terms of trends and demand. On the production side, Zara produces new lines initially in small batches, shedding those that do not sell and increasing production of those that do sell to meet that demand. The turnaround time from design to delivery in store is between three and four weeks and each store receives deliveries of new items twice a week.

How does Zara manage this blinding speed of design, production and delivery? First and foremost, it has a clear philosophy about what it is trying to do—provide clothes on trend at the fastest speed possible. The company is ruthless in looking to increase speed at every point in the supply chain. Beyond its organizational philosophy, though, the most important thing that the company does is to have the majority of its production in Spain or in nearby (cheaper) Portugal, Morocco and Turkey instead of following the herd and outsourcing everything to Asia. For a company that grew up through the 1980s and 1990s, when the tide was flowing so strongly toward China, this was a very brave and completely counterintuitive thing to do.

The shipping time from China to Spain is anywhere between three and four weeks, which is the same as the whole cycle time that Zara is aiming for between designing a piece and having it in-store. That shipping time is dead time that the company cannot afford to lose. Having a business model of constant change, based on sales and the opinions of customers, riding the waves of trends in real time and focusing on what some refer to as "fast fashion," means that for Zara it makes more sense to have most of its factories close to home.

Going against management trends has been remarkably successful for Zara, Inditex, and the company's founder Ortega. From that one store in La Coruña, northwest Spain, in 1975, Zara has expanded to 6,500 outlets in eighty-eight countries and counting. Between 1991 and 2014 sales for Inditex went from €367 million to €18.12 billion[46] (based mainly on Zara) and the founder of the company is reported to be the second richest man on the planet.[47] Following the management and organizational advice of each decade would probably have been a disaster for a company with such a clear vision of what it wants to do.

Cycle time—specifically, having a very short cycle time in the iteration and production of new clothing lines—has driven Zara to have most of its production close by its headquarters, bringing together design and production and eliminating time on the water to get its products to its core markets as quickly as it can. The next part of this story will be whether Zara will fragment its production in this way into its main markets, for example re-creating the type of organization of production it has in and around Spain again in the United States as that market grows for the company.

In the future, the needs for centralization in order to maintain control and fragmentation in order to obtain market access will increasingly find themselves fighting against one another. The trends that Zara is both creating and riding imply shorter expected time between a customer ordering a product and receiving it, with that product likely to have some element of customization such as a changed color or image. However, companies will still need to have some scale of production to make a factory economically viable. This fine balance is what companies will struggle with as these changes occur and not every company will be able to manage the transitions well.

What of other fashion houses and clothes manufacturers? Are they

morphing and taking on the model that Zara uses? In Chapter 2 we raised the question of what "Made in X" means these days, commenting on the structure of the leading luxury brand Burberry. Having closed factories in Wales and England in 2007 and 2009 with the loss of 500 jobs, the leaders of the company have implemented a significant change of strategy. Christopher Bailey, originally from Yorkshire where the remaining British Burberry factory is located, became the company's creative director and then CEO in 2014. He and the company have decided to invest £50 million into a new U.K.-based factory, responding to the pressures they face to maintain the brand and the skills of the company's U.K. workers.[48] While Zara is close for time, Burberry is close for brand and access to skills they cannot get elsewhere. The answers are similar but the reasons are very different.

What will solve the tension between centralization for economies of scale and fragmentation for market access? If new production technologies allow companies to make economically in smaller volumes in or near a specific market, rather than trying to produce very high volumes in one place to keep production costs down, the pattern of location will become more dispersed. The business model choices that companies make will have a direct impact on how they organize their supply chains and links to their customers, which in themselves will have a knock-on effect on the patterns of trade we see across the globe.

ONE OF THE REASONS that Zara and other companies are able to control their supply chains so tightly is that they have exceedingly good data on what each store, factory and supplier are doing. Imagine if you could understand what every single machine was doing—what could you do if the factory spoke to you as it made each piece and each piece of product also spoke to you in some way?

That is the vision for what has been called the smart or connected factory, the internet-enabled factory or the industrial internet. It is a vision that brings together the digital world of the internet of things (IoT), where everything has a sensor attached to it and can communicate via the internet and the physical world of production. Here is the love child of the internet and Adam Smith after a serious night of drinking and dancing made real.

The Siemens factory in Amberg, Germany, is an early example of what can be achieved if all the production machines can talk to one another and to the products that they are making. This factory produces control devices for use in other factories or processes, and has to deal with a very high number of parts, product variants and fluctuations of demand over time. It does all this with about three-quarters of the machines working automatically and human hands touching the product only once—right at the start of the process when the bare circuit board is placed onto the line. The factory has around 1,000 workers in over 100,000 square feet of productive space supporting and maintaining the production machines. The really impressive numbers from this factory? It has a reported defect rate of just fifteen per million units produced with 100 percent traceability across all its production lines.[49] That is pretty close to a zero defect rate made possible by connecting all the elements of the production process, including the product itself. Each day the factory generates 50 million data points tracing the production process, so the making of a board can be reviewed and seen in great detail after the fact. This is a factory making physical products that has a dense digital life.

In industry circles the idea of a factory or series of factories kitted out with sensors on everything and linked through the internet has become as hyped as 3D printing. Klaus Schwab, the founder of the World Economic Forum, didn't hold back in his piece in *Foreign Affairs*: "We stand on the brink of a technological revolution that will fundamentally alter the way we live, work, and relate to one another. In its scale, scope, and complexity, the transformation will be unlike anything humankind has experienced before."[50]

New technologies are being introduced to the production and delivery process all the time, changing the nature of work and our expectations of what can be made for us. A more measured version of the vision has been written into the German government's plans for the future, referred to as "Industry 4.0" (or, in the German reports, "Industrie 4.0").[51] The German vision is one where customization is the norm, last-minute changes can be flexibly incorporated and resource use can be optimized to minimize waste and maximize efficiency. The overall goal is a little less Hollywood compared with Klaus Schwab's efforts, but they are probably more realistic. "If this is done successfully, Industrie 4.0 will allow Germany to

increase its global competitiveness and preserve its domestic manufacturing industry." Written in this way, these changes appear to be less earth shattering, but they could herald another move away from global value chains and a further pressure toward physical deglobalization.

EACH PERIOD OF TECHNOLOGICAL CHANGE leads to new opportunities for companies, new options for how they organize themselves and new products that make it to market. We've seen this happen again and again, from the introduction of interchangeable parts in the making of rifles in the United States in the 1800s, through the move to the mass production of cars at the beginning of the 1900s and on to the boom in offshoring through the late 1990s enabled by new information and communication technologies.

It shouldn't come as a surprise that the tools and techniques we use to make the things we carry around every day keep on changing. As they change, the ways in which we organize that making—be it where things are made, who makes them or how many of them are made at a time—will also change. Where we will end up will be nothing like *Star Trek's* replicator, but nor will it be anything like how we are making today.

If 3D printing were the only change occurring right now we would not be seeing an immediate challenge to the current modes of making, and existing patterns of trade and growth would continue along their current path over the short to medium term. However, as we have seen in this chapter, that is only one part of a new story that points toward higher levels of customization, customer involvement in design and new modes of making. Changes in production techniques and company organization will alter substantially how we can make and therefore where we will make.

Rather than having outsourced high-volume production all based in Asia, companies will move toward having smaller production facilities in each of the markets in which they are selling. So it is not really a case of inshoring, offshoring or nearshoring. Companies will make as near to the market as they can, and around this will arise a complicated pattern of foreign ownership that governments and companies will have to address. (See Chapter 8 for how this could play out.)

However, as well as having new methods for making our consumer products, we're seeing changes in whether humans are involved at all. The

key word here is automation—taking a process that used to require human input and using robots, sensors and lines of computer code to remove the need for human hands in the making of cars or phones or computers. Will increasing automation of production make the costs of labor irrelevant in companies' calculations of where to put their factories? That is what the next chapter will investigate.

4

All Hail Our Robot Overlords

MOST STORIES THAT INVOLVE ROBOTS tend not to go so well for us, the humans. When you hear the ultra calm voice of HAL in Stanley Kubrick's *2001: A Space Odyssey* refusing to let Dave back onto his spaceship floating somewhere between the earth and the moon, you know that Dave is in serious trouble. He's trying to shut down the computer after a serious malfunction, one that has led HAL to kill the rest of the crew. But the computer knows what he is trying to do and takes all measures to protect itself. HAL's response—"I'm sorry, Dave, I'm afraid I can't do that"—has become a shorthand for any computer that won't do what you want it to do.

Go through the catalogue of films since then and the story repeats again and again. The 2004 film version of *I, Robot* has the U.S. Robotics machines attempting to violently take control; the sentinel robots in *The Matrix* are hunting the humans who have escaped off grid; and the self-named *Terminator* has traveled back in time to kill off the leader of the human resistance to Skynet before he is born. A pattern emerges of the machines becoming too intelligent and deciding that we weak humans are no longer needed, our hubris in trying to act like gods in creating these new metal children catches up with us. There may be happy endings of a sort bolted on to modern movies for the sake of the audience and ratings, but the message is clear—fear the machines.

So when newspaper stories are written about robots in the real world

being able to walk and run or about computers being able to drive or play chess there is a pervasive sense of doom lurking in the background. When it comes to manufacturing and the structure of the global economy the rise of robots and automation poses very real questions. If companies cannot or will not use human hands anymore, replacing them with robots, what will happen to the people who once worked in their factories? Are these changes leading to the arrival of technical unemployment across sectors and countries? And with fewer and fewer people needed, what does this imply for where making will occur? This chapter looks at the current state of industrial automation and gives some perspective on whether the robot uprising has already started in factories around the world.

THE RELATIVE SILENCE of electric cars is disconcerting, especially when you're on a bicycle and they sneak up on you at the traffic lights. The styling on one of the best electric cars, the sleek and elegant Tesla Model S, makes a stretch to the future without breaking the elastic. It's still recognizably a car but so much has changed under the hood. This is an all-electric car that can go from a standing start to sixty miles an hour in under three seconds. This car is a very distant relation of the electric golf buggy most people think of when you say electric car—so distant it's hard to see the connection at all.

What is more interesting, though, is how and where the Tesla is made. First things first. It is manufactured in the U.S., in Fremont, California. Retailing at somewhere in the region of $70,000 before any government subsidies or rebates are applied, this is a high-value product made in one of the highest-cost economies in the world. And there is one thing that has made it possible to manufacture it here—robots.

When Adam Smith wrote about the pin factory in *The Wealth of Nations* he had ten people making the pins. That is a lot of human hands for what is a relatively simple process. Over two centuries later, new machines and new processes have lowered the number of people required in most manufacturing processes. However, until recently, the machines needed operators to make sure they were fed raw materials and to handle any problems that came up on the line. Worse than that, most industrial machines have had to be caged, separated away from the human workers for safety reasons. These machines have been in the main large, heavy

and difficult to move or repurpose to another part of the production line.

Now that is changing, too, and automation is taking off in a very real sense. Automation, as the name implies, is where the processes have been made automatic, self-driven by onboard computers, sensors and many lines of computer code. Whereas before, each machine might have needed an operator, now we have factories that need just one operator to run the complete process. The end point of this? What are called "dark factories," in which robots cheerfully make the goods without the need for light or heat. Are we heading toward a world of darkness in manufacturing, with a very small supporting cast of humans and a new army of robots to make all our things?

IF YOU LOOK FOR IMAGES of actual robots (not those lovingly designed in Hollywood to be all dark and sinister) you're as likely to see a robot that's mimicking the structure of human anatomy as you are to see one that is shaped like a box, a truck or a large dog. Pretty much anything goes when you're designing to get things done and not focusing on the aesthetics of the thing that does them.

Industrial robots in particular come in many shapes and sizes. Some are fixed in place, with a defined maximum reach and a tightly controlled field of operation. These tend to be single-arm robots, able to do pick-and-place operations or a set of welds on a car body. If you look into most car manufacturing plants you'll see a long row of these robots in the body shop, taking the elements of the frame of the car and bringing it all together in double-quick time in a shower of orange and gold welding sparks.

A number of robots are now being made to be autonomous, to be able to roam where they need to be and to interact with the world in a more open manner. One version of such robots, sometimes called tugs, is being used in hospitals to ferry lunches or to take samples from the ward to the laboratory and back again. Automatic pickers in the warehouses and distribution centers of companies like Amazon have started to change the dynamics of how our products are sent to us when we click to buy. Using a small robot from Kiva Systems, Amazon has set up a system where the humans remain at their packing desk while the shelves that hold the products they need come to them. Watching them move about the

warehouse is almost like a techno-version of *Harry Potter,* shelves flying about of their own accord.[1]

Many pieces of more traditional industrial automation by contrast are contained in cages (each referred to as a cell in the production line) to reduce the risk of injury to the few humans on the factory floor. These robots have little to no sense of what is around them, they cannot see you if you walk into their field of operation. Step in front of a standard robot trying to move a piece of metal from A to B and you'll end up feeling very sore and bruised as it won't know it should stop and will keep on doing what it is programmed to do. These caged beasts remind me of scenes from the early *Alien* movies, with lots of gray walls and amber flashing warning lights above the exoskeleton loader that Ripley wields to save the day.

Outside of the factory even more radical robots are being built. Boston Dynamics created the BigDog[2] with funding from the Defense Advanced Research Projects Agency (DARPA) in the United States (there's that military drive for innovation again), a four-legged robot to carry up to 340 pounds of gear across rough terrain. Handy to have a pack mule with a battery on the battlefield. There are brothers and sisters of the BigDog, like Cheetah, who is built for speed rather than simple carrying capacity. Where BigDog wanders along at a stately four miles per hour, Cheetah has been clocked on a treadmill zipping along at over twenty-nine miles per hour—or, as the company puts it, just a little faster than Usain Bolt.

Possibly the cutest robot to be developed for general use is Honda's ASIMO (Advanced Step in Innovative Mobility), built to be a non-threatening image of a small person standing just four foot three inches tall. Their program started in 1986 in an effort to be the first company to have a bipedal robot—one that could walk on two legs.[3] Having solved the walking problem in the mid-1990s, recently Honda has been working on making ASIMO more autonomous. They want it to be able to interact with people, aiming in the long term to make this robot useful as a personal assistant or as a worker in hazardous situations such as a fire in a nuclear power plant.

Making these robots and the automation in production lines useful means bringing together many different technologies including sensors, actuators (the pieces that move), machine learning and vision, to name just a few. This integration of technologies is what is really moving automation

forward and, as we've hinted at in Chapter 3, this is the real heart of the Industry 4.0 movement.

TESLA MOTORS CAME INTO BEING in 2003 when Martin Eberhard bought the domain name teslamotors.com and incorporated the company in Delaware.[4] Eberhard started from the desire to have a sports car (apparently after his divorce), but he said, "I couldn't bring myself to buy a car that got eighteen miles to the gallon at a time when wars in the Middle East seemed to somehow involve oil and the arguments for global warming were becoming undeniable." His previous work on battery technology for the company he sold in 2000, NuvoMedia, pointed toward electric vehicles. But large car makers like GM had tried and failed spectacularly in this space. So he, Marc Tarpenning, and a small group of Silicon Valley engineers with no previous experience making cars set out to upend the traditional automotive world with an electric car that you could be proud to own.

By 2008 the company was able to launch their flagship product, a two-seater sports car called the Tesla Roadster. The Model S, their version of a sports sedan, hit the market in 2013 and was awarded Motor Trend Car of the Year.[5] There is a lot of sleight of hand here, in terms of what is new and what is different. The chassis of the car is based on a Lotus Elise, the small U.K.-based car manufacturer that has managed a Formula One team. Elements of an earlier car, the AC Propulsion's tzero, the car that convinced Eberhard that their dream of a competitive consumer electric sports car was possible, were also included reusing as much existing technology as possible. Not exactly standing on the shoulders of giants, but the industry version of reuse and adaptation that happens day in, day out.

The factory space Tesla Motors acquired in 2010 in which to make the Model S had previously been used for making Toyota Corollas. So far, so not terribly surprising. There are car plants in most countries in the world and, from the outside, this one doesn't look very different from any of the others. Inside it has some of the same feel as other high-end plants with fresh paint and clean walkways, floors color-coded to define the working spaces, the noise of making happening all around you. Although with its skylights everywhere to let in as much natural light as possible and bikes provided for workers to get around the plant, it has—unsurprisingly, given where it is—a touch of "Silicon Valley" about it.

What a first-time visitor really notices, however, is who is doing the making. This is a factory that has been invaded by robots—around 160 of them, to be precise, so possibly more of a raiding party than a full-on invasion. They come in many shapes and sizes, from single-arm robots used to place the seats into the bodies of the cars to larger robots that look a little like forklift trucks which can lift a whole car and place it wherever it needs to be. All the robots are painted a gorgeous deep red in strong contrast to the white floors and walls and it is as if they are dancing around the car bodies that are moving through the assembly space. There is a beauty in the rhythm of the work and the interaction between the human and the robot workers.

This space represents much of what is to come in terms of making, blending together the human and the machine, allowing for the making of things in countries where the economics used to say it just wasn't possible. While the company and its growth have been enabled in a significant way by their current charismatic CEO Elon Musk, who joined as chairman of the board in 2004, that's not our real interest. This is about how automated machines of all shapes and sizes change the economics of making, both in terms of location and in terms of scale. This is one of the key reasons it is possible for companies to choose a different story from that of hyper-globalization—because the cost of labor matters less and less.

WHEN YOU MEET BAXTER you'll be struck by the size of his arms and his eyes. He's relatively light, coming in at 165 pounds, but will look you straight in the eye at around six feet tall.[6] He's not the strongest, he can lift only just over two kilos, but he's a very flexible robot. Just take his hand and you can show him how to move and work with whatever is in front of his cameras.

The company that makes Baxter, Rethink Robotics, was founded in 2008 by Rodney Brooks, an emeritus professor at MIT and former director of the MIT Media Lab. He was struck by how narrow developments in industrial robotics had become, with everyone looking for ways to make existing approaches faster without allowing for the messy nature of the world. With many existing robots, if the tray they were working on was slightly out of alignment, or if they dropped a piece, they could not recover. They had a path and they would follow it no matter what.

Baxter uses image processing and some intelligent programming to gracefully deal with pieces that have fallen over or to recover from a mistake. Instead of depending on a predefined path it uses a vision system that can see in a defined area and search for what it needs. If you take a piece out of the "hand" of Baxter it will stop and restart what it was doing, understanding that it has been interrupted.

Another element of the Rethink Robotics philosophy is that robots are collaborators with, not replacements for, the human. They refer to their products as collaborative robots or cobots, emphasizing their flexibility and that they can work next to humans without placing them in danger. Gone are the cages, flashing warning lights and black-and-yellow tape marking out areas for the human and the robot. Using sensors embedded into the arms of Baxter and programming movement to be slow and precise, with a cutout if it touches anything that shouldn't be there, the claim is that the risk of working with a robot like Baxter has been taken away. Brooks has a novel way to demonstrate the safety of his robots—by putting his head in the way as it is operating. All he gets for his trouble is a soft bump and then the robot stops, retreats and waits until it senses that the offending article, the rather large brain of its creator, has been taken out of the way.

These cobots, these companions to production-line workers, are a small fraction of the total sales of industrial robots to this point. Around one in twenty new industrial robots falls into this category, so they have not taken significant market share yet. However, in developing these kinds of robots Rethink Robotics has shown what is possible at a much cheaper price, one that is much more accessible to smaller companies who may not have thought that this kind of automation was something they could access.

And this is really important, as the vast majority of manufacturing firms are small companies, not multinationals spread over many continents. It is these companies, the subcontractors to the main manufacturers, who are the backbone of supply chains. These companies could reap the rewards of automation and because of it could be competitive without needing to be in low-cost economies.

THE EXTREME OF THIS TREND of automation is to create places where humans rarely go, where the robots do have control. So-called "dark factories" where the line runs without direct human intervention and there

is no need for lights or heating or air conditioning, have been a goal for many companies. Now we are seeing the building of facilities that are approaching this state. They need some inputs delivered, combined with a low level of monitoring and maintenance, but they work twenty-four hours a day producing as ordered with very little oversight or intervention.

China Daily reported in 2015 the building of the first robot-led plant in Dongguan by the Guangdong Everwin Precision Technology company, in which it planned to use 1,000 robots to reduce the labor needed for the factory by 90 percent.[7] The gearing is interesting, as the assistant general manager of the company indicated that sixty robots could take an assembly line that needed 600 workers in the past down to 100. So, not fully dark, but a significant reduction in the number of hands involved in the production process.[8]

This story is repeated in factory after factory, across sectors and companies around China. The Cambridge Industries Group (CIG) wants to replace two-thirds of its workers in a factory making optical networking equipment in Shanghai because labor costs have doubled over the past seven years and they face competition from automated manufacturing in Germany and other traditionally high-cost economies.[9] According to Gerald Wong, the CEO of CIG, "It is very clear in China: people will either go into automation or they will go out of the manufacturing business."[10]

The main driver for these changes? A lack of workers. Hiring is difficult in the region, with estimates of a shortage of 100,000 workers from the local government. It may seem counterintuitive to those outside China that there is a labor shortage in these areas, as the narrative was companies moving east to access the lower labor costs where hands were abundant. That has changed, as wages in manufacturing have risen and China's working-age population begins to shrink. According to some estimates, between now and 2050 China will see the number of its population aged between fifteen and fifty-nine shrink by 212 million.[11]

For the planners and factory owners across China, it looks as if they are hoping to pivot from labor-intensive manufacturing to robot-intense manufacturing, leaping forward to become a high-tech center for making. Their aim is to maintain the country's existing dominance in production for many types of product. However, there is an alternative scenario: that these changes may bring a severe reduction in the ability of China and

other previously lower-cost manufacturing centers to be cost competitive, providing an opening for the West to have its production closer to home.

IT MAY BE AN OBVIOUS POINT to make but robots have a number of advantages over human workers. One is strength. The strongest robot of them all as of mid-2016 is the KUKA KR 1000 Titan (the names never easily trip off the tongue with too many contractions and numbers thrown in).[12] The hint as to how powerful this beast is is in the name—it can take payloads of up to 1,000 kg. That's more than eleven of me being lifted at the same time.

Beyond pure grunt, robots if programmed properly and well built will do what you ask of them again and again with a ridiculously high level of accuracy. They don't get bored, they don't daydream and they won't have the need to call home to check on the kids. This repetitive accuracy is a key element of success for most manufacturers as it reduces defects and faults, which in turn reduces the return or failure rate of its products. Having high confidence in the quality of the making and assembling of cars, TVs and phones protects companies from customer complaints and the costs of either repair or replacement for units that don't behave as they should once they are in the hands of the customer.

As long as you are able to provide your robots with power and materials, barring a fault, they will keep on doing their thing. Forget shift work or rotas, complaints about being made to work through a lunch break or, heaven forbid, someone calling in sick. The machines are relentless and will produce as long as you let them produce. This can smooth out production volumes, making the planning of both production and delivery to the customer much more certain. Companies and consumers hate uncertainty, and if yours can be the organization that always delivers as promised, that counts for a lot in a manufacturing world that has become used to doing everything "just in time."

All this also adds up to faster production. The actual time it takes to take a product down the line, completing its various elements and having it ready to go is reduced when automation is implemented well. The lack of pauses from a robot as compared to a human worker combined with the lower probability of a fault means you have a greater volume of finished products coming off the line every hour.

But if everything is so much better with automation and robots flying about the factory, why will there be any workers left in manufacturing plants at all? If the news is all positive, surely this is the end of employment in manufacturing.

IF YOU'VE EVER SEEN an early industrial robot making a mistake you'll know that there are disadvantages to automation that can outweigh the benefits. Imagine a robot that needs to put milk in a teacup with a conveyor belt of cups coming toward it, one every four seconds. Each cup is supposed to stop in a precise location and wait for the required time of two seconds for the milk to be poured before it progresses on its way. Now imagine that your supervisor accidentally and without noticing nudges the belt feeding the cups into the system and it puts each cup out of place by two inches. Instead of being nice and politely in the right place to receive the milk each cup is just short. What happens from then on?

If the factory is still using an early industrial system that doesn't have vision systems, image processing and adaptive software, the machine will just keep on trying to fill the cups, creating a large milk spill that will continue to grow and grow until that clumsy supervisor returns from lunch and notices what is happening on the line. That's a lot of waste, a mess to clean up and a reduction in output for the day as the machine will not be able to catch up. The repetition that is a strength in terms of having the same action performed again and again without complaint is a massive weakness once there is an error. Without some intervention the system doesn't know when to stop and repeats the error again and again.

People, especially trained engineers and technicians, are good at adapting and learning a new process. Most industrial systems are built to task, that is they are built to do one thing and one thing only. The opposite of such repetition and uniformity is flexibility, one of the holy grails of manufacturing. Flexibility in this sense means being able to make different products, or at the very least customized products, using the same production line, without having to go through the time consuming and expensive process of retooling and reorganizing. Some production lines manage basic customization, for example in car manufacturing having specific interior colors for specific customers, but most do not. And so if there is a variant or a new product, either a new production line is needed or the existing

production line needs to be taken apart and reassembled to make that product. Each time a production line is changed or upgraded it then has to be revalidated—essentially, tested to make sure that it is actually doing what it is supposed to do. All this costs the company time and money, neither of which they can afford to lose in highly competitive markets.

Remember that Amazon distribution center with its shelves moving to the humans packing the boxes for distribution? Well, it begs the question as to whether the robots could do everything including the packing. It turns out this is a harder task than you might have thought. Amazon is trying to crack it and have set up the Amazon Picking Challenge (APC)[13] with a prize of $25,000 for a team that can provide a robot that can manage a defined set of pick-and-pack tasks. At the first competition in 2015 teams could score a maximum of 190 points for picking and handling twelve target items from twenty-five placed in twelve bins on a standard shelf. Of the twenty-six teams that took part half of the teams scored either zero or a negative score, as points are deducted for drops and damage to the items.

The winning team was from Berlin and managed a very impressive 148 points. This, however, is a much simplified version of what the actual Amazon employees are doing day in, day out. Currently "A human is capable of performing a more complex version of the same task at a rate of about 400 sorts/hour with minimal errors, while the best robot in the APC achieved a rate of about 30 sorts/hour with a 16 percent failure rate."[14] There is a long way to go before the whole of the distribution center can be automated so that the lights can be turned off. Human hands in this context for now are far superior to what can be yet done with automation.

Getting into the automation game is hard for many companies as the initial investment costs can be high and you need to have a different skill set to be able to automate a manual process effectively. A rule of thumb for the total cost of bringing a robot into the production line is to multiply the cost of the robot by three.[15] We'll talk through the economics below, but these are not insignificant numbers, especially for small companies. At the same time, depending on the robot and the complexity of what is being produced, the programming of the robot can take a long time, time during which production is not happening.

So, do the advantages outweigh the disadvantages for companies thinking about introducing automation? There is no universal answer to

that question as manufacturing is so diverse and companies face different challenges depending on their size, their products and their markets. Most will be looking very hard at the economics, so we should too.

THE ARGUMENTS FOR AND AGAINST using an industrial robot over a human for a specific task on a production line inevitably turn to the issue of cost. All else being equal, the decision depends on the relative costs of the person and the machine. These can be difficult to assess accurately, as the tasks that may need to be completed will change over time. If either the soft human or the overdetermined robot cannot adapt, the cost calculations get thrown out of kilter as the upfront sunk cost of the robot (around $100,000 to $300,000, depending on the size) has a different interpretation and so-called variable costs of people appear attractive.

With that caveat in place, there is one important thing to notice about the relative costs of metal and wires versus skin and bone. While the cost of labor tends to increase over time, the costs of technology tend to fall. The intelligent part of automation, the computer that controls the robot, has been increasing in power and declining in cost since the 1950s following the invention of the transistor in 1947.[16] Moore's Law has the benefit of both being very well known and broadly correct. Writing in 1965, Intel's co-founder Gordon Moore noted almost as a throwaway comment that the number of transistors on a chip was roughly doubling every year or so and he commented that this would hold at least for ten years.[17] While the multiplier is now considered to be around eighteen months, the basic shape of the prediction has held for over forty years. This means more processing power available to engineers with a massive decline in the costs of the computing used to drive the automated systems in factories.

The costs for people are heading in only one direction. Between 1997 and 2011 the hourly compensation for manufacturing workers went up pretty much everywhere. Granted, there is a wide range to the scale of change (increasing in real terms by roughly one and a half to four times what the cost was in 1997), but labor cost increases magnify the impact of falling technology costs. There is a feeling of inevitability in the air as the machines become cheaper and more productive each year.

It's very important to project these cost changes out into the near future, as what looks in favor of labor today will probably be even in five

years and decidedly against the human in ten. The dynamic nature of costs means most projections will be off, by a little or a lot, but the shape of the trajectory is the important thing—automation will continue to get cheaper while, barring very significant social and economic changes, labor will continue to become more expensive.

So, how much on average does automation cost when compared to human workers? These comparisons are hard to make as the hourly compensation of workers around the world is highly variable and the types and extent of automation varies as much again. On the whole, though, it looks as if automation has now become cheaper pretty much everywhere, with an all-in cost per hour of around five euros for automation compared to nine euros for manual labor in China, or forty euros per hour for human workers in Germany.

This is the key. If automation can now work at the scale required, from the very small to the very large, working with rather than separated from humans, and at a cost that is less than that of employing people, automation will win every time.

IT IS NOT AN ACCIDENT that the sector to have embraced automation most rapidly is one in which the final product has a relatively high price tag. One in every two industrial robots sold is working making cars. According to some estimates, over 80 percent of the work done in making a car is done by machines—so, while not completely replacing human labor, at the very least automation is complementing and enhancing our ability to make.[18]

The International Federation of Robotics (IFR)[19] estimates that the size of the market for industrial robots reached $32 billion in 2014 from sales of over 200,000 units across the world. There are early signs of a significant change in the growth path of installations, jumping by 15 percent between 2014 and 2015—a change that would lead to a doubling of the yearly number of industrial robots being installed by 2018. The invasion looks like it might be picking up pace.

However, economic constraints remain at the level of the company, in that if the volume of production is low or the value of the product is particularly low, it may not yet make financial sense for a company to invest in large-scale automation (and they may not have the necessary cash available

to make the necessary capital investment). Even with our friend Baxter, some companies will not be able to afford to get him into the factory and working on the line.

The leader in the rise of the robots in factories around the world is South Korea. According to the IFR, South Korea has the highest robot density in the world, with 437 robots per 10,000 employees in manufacturing. This is leagues ahead of Japan (323), Germany (282) and the United States (152), and a world away from countries like the U.K. (71). For example, the LG Display factory in Paju has 16,000 workers, none of whom carry the six-foot glass plates that become television or smartphone screens. These are all handled by robots to ensure that they do not break as they make their way through the production process.[20]

Given the advances that we've seen in the past decade and how many things that were supposedly impossible for computers and robots to do, it would be a brave person who said definitively that specific tasks were out of the reach of robots. So what do we think are the limits to the things that can be handed over to our robots and what will remain the domain of the human?

THE USE OF ROBOTS or automation generally in manufacturing is not new. However, there is now an unsettling sense that there is a greater penetration of these technologies into the world of work. The impact of automation across the labor market has been modeled by two Oxford academics, Carl Frey and Michael Osborne, creating a risk ranking for how susceptible your job is to automation into the future.[21] Their 2013 analysis projected that 47 percent of the current U.S. workforce is at risk of their work being automated. The conclusion is sobering. Based on these models, just under half of the U.S. labor market is susceptible to automation (or computerization, to use the phrase in their paper). If your job is about to be automated it may be cold comfort that the post at the top of their list to be automated is that of telemarketer, closely followed by insurance underwriter and tax accountant. At the other end of the scale, and so least likely to be automated, are recreational therapists and social workers.

Frey and Osborne have also looked at China and India, where the results show even higher levels of possible automation,[22] with 77 percent and 69 percent of current jobs in China and India at risk of being automated. This

is not a surprise, given the relative density of manufacturing in the U.S. and Chinese economies, but it highlights that these changes are occurring in all economies at the same time.

The labor impacts of globalization were experienced in the West as deindustrialization. There was an initial flatlining and then a ski slope of decline in manufacturing employment in the United States, the U.K. and other leading economies over the past twenty years.[23] The impacts of deglobalization are harder to model as the effects pull in both directions. Increases in production in or close to the final market for consumers indicate an increase in employment, while the reduction of labor and the increase in automation indicate a fall in employment.

Which will win out is unclear, but any grand pronouncement that deglobalization will automatically lead to a significant increase in manufacturing employment in countries such as the United States or the United Kingdom are probably off the mark. Depending on whether you're interested in consumers and their access to cheaper products, in companies and their ability to thrive, or in society as a whole and the availability of a diversity of jobs, you'll have a different take on whether this is a good or a bad thing. But any discussion on this should include a range of indicators as it is impossible to capture the complexity of the changes that are occurring by telling just a trade story or an employment story.

There is a real concern from economists that what is called technological unemployment, where technical advances occur so deeply and rapidly that a portion of the workforce is made permanently unemployed, is happening now and we're not adapting fast enough. The speed at which machines are being developed to take on new tasks looks to be faster than the speed at which we humans are able to adapt to that and upskill, reskill or find something new to pay our way. As Frey and Osborne's work points out, the changes in artificial intelligence and automation mean that this is not just putting manual jobs under threat. Some researchers think that entry-level lawyers, some doctors and translators are already under threat. The robots are coming for us all, white collar or blue collar.

Technological unemployment has been a concern for some economists for a long time, even if many during the postwar era seemed to forget this. Keynes, writing in 1930 at the time of the Great Depression, was trying to understand the long-run path of change for the global economy. He wrote:

We are being afflicted with a new disease of which some readers may not yet have heard the name, but of which they will hear a great deal in the years to come—namely, technological unemployment. This means unemployment due to our discovery of means of economising the use of labor outrunning the pace at which we can find new uses for labor.[24]

While he acknowledged the problem he remained defiantly upbeat, claiming that economic pessimism was unwarranted as we "are suffering, not from the rheumatics of old age, but from the growing-pains of over-rapid changes, from the painfulness of readjustment between one economic period and another." Are the next twenty to thirty years going to be a relatively brief but painful adjustment phase for the global economy? Nobody knows for sure either way.

The concern for developing and emerging economies is a "premature deindustrialization" where the path of growth that ran from agriculture to industry to services has broken.[25] The dominant element of most economies has shifted from agriculture to industry and then to services over the past decades, and in some cases centuries. This movement can be seen in terms of the share of the economy in these macro categories or in the number of people working in each sector, with a rise, a peak and a fall off of employment. The peak of employment in manufacturing for each country as it industrializes has been happening earlier and earlier. "This means countries are running out of industrialization opportunities sooner and at much lower levels of income compared to the experience of early industrialisers."[26] Or, to put it another way, modern manufacturing is less labor intensive, so growth through manufacturing may provide some benefit at the macro level, but it does not provide the jobs benefit it might once have done.

This strong move to automation should not have come as a complete surprise. We are entering what Erik Brynjolfsson and Andrew McAfee have called the "Second Machine Age" in their recent book of the same name.[27] Here is a world in which machines, robots or artificial intelligence can do more and more of the tasks that we thought were the preserve of humans. The recent encroachment of machines into human tasks started with a computer that could play chess to Grand Master level, has expanded

into winning games of *Jeopardy!* and now includes driving cars around the freeways of California. Time and again since the Industrial Revolution we humans have worked out how to make machines that have both taken over repetitive work and improved on human inaccuracy. Now we are developing machines that can do both the repetitive and the more creative work.

Overall that's been a good thing, releasing people from difficult, dangerous and/or boring roles and allowing them to pursue other careers. Much of the social progress we've seen in releasing people from domestic chores is based on some form of automation. You might already have joined in the automation drive yourself without thinking about it very hard. If you've got a Roomba or other domestic room cleaner, you've automated away that tedious task of getting the vacuum out and trying to get everyone's feet off the floor so you can chase all the dust bunnies away. This is a small, domestic version of automation and is only one example (think washing machine, dishwasher) that has become so commonplace that we don't even see it anymore. In some ways the robots are making a silent invasion, slowly becoming accepted as helpers at home and at work. We probably won't realize the depth of the shift until we can't imagine a world without these extensions of ourselves surrounding us every day.

THE REALITIES WE FACE in this aspect of making are not binary, it is not all robots or all hands. The examples from Tesla in the United States to CIG in Shanghai point to robots both replacing many but not all workers, acting as a complement to a smaller workforce. The general sense will be of fewer and fewer people working on factory production lines even while those lines produce more and more. The introduction of cobots and the demands for workers to be adapted to working with rather than controlling or avoiding the robots is a significant change in the nature of the workplace. It also means that while macro indicators like GDP and production output increase, there is a decoupling from employment in manufacturing. We won't get a significant increase in employment even if the majority of things consumed in a country are made in that country into the future.

Is technical unemployment now real? Or will the people who would have worked in factories be able to find work elsewhere? At this point it is difficult to know, as it depends on how fast the changes are occurring and

both how flexible the workers are and what other occupations come into being in the future. However, the speed of change appears to be running ahead of the adaptation possible for many people who have been trained into a specific profession and who are now being asked to retrain in areas far from their interests and/or abilities. The concept of basic universal income has come to the fore in response to these and other changes, to provide a version of a safety net in the midst of such rapid and far-reaching technological changes. Whether we will have to provide universal income is an argument for another book, but the fact that what was once thought of as outlandish has started to become mainstream shows the extent of the changes we are facing in the world of work.

IN THE CONTEXT OF MAKING THINGS, automation is now crucial. Most production processes are highly repetitive, broken into many small steps and tend not to change rapidly. All these characteristics mean many manufacturing jobs are likely to be automated over time. The likelihood of an increasing level of computers and robots as opposed to hands and brains in factories changes the economics of factory location, specifically taking out the costs of labor and replacing them with capital investment in new machinery. Automation, by dramatically reducing that aspect of the overall production cost that derives from labor costs, can take wage rates out of the economic equation. And any discussions about a factory's location based on the cost of local labor become irrelevant.

Key here is that such machinery faces a more global price when compared to labor—there is a smaller spread of prices for new industrial robots compared to the spread of hourly wages in manufacturing around the world. This means there are fewer possible advantages to be gained by moving around the world looking for cost differences based on those doing the work—the robots.

Foxconn, the company that makes the bits that go inside iPhones, raised some eyebrows when it said that it would replace a million Chinese workers with robots. Eyebrows went even higher when it was reported in early 2014 that the company had decided to move its display manufacturing to the United States. Yes, that's right, from China to the U.S. It used to be an advantage to have a large captive workforce so that you could flex production, changing the process for iterations of a product and

ramping up output for popular product launches. But if the robots can adapt quickly and produce endlessly, even that advantage is taken away. It looks as if we are at a tipping point where the labor element of the landed cost of a product is being replaced by the cost of automation.

As companies begin to adapt their locations to the new conditions of deglobalization, what impacts might be seen in terms of employment? Unfortunately, production or manufacturing in this mode is probably not going to provide as many jobs as policymakers might have hoped for.

A key argument for manufacturing being able to return to high-cost economies as we have discussed is that labor costs are becoming less and less of an issue. The introduction of dense automation into manufac-turing companies in China appears to have a gearing of 10:1, that is the automation being introduced is reducing the required employment on a production line by a factor of ten.

Are the current indicators showing any early signals of these changes? Manufacturing employment in the United States at the start of 2010 dipped to 11.5 million: its lowest point in the modern era. Since then there has been a small but steady increase, so that by the end of 2015 there were 12.3 million manufacturing workers in the United States.[28] Over 2016 that number barely moved, with a loss of around 70,000 jobs in aggregate over the year. There is no short-term major increase in manufacturing employ-ment and so, in relative terms, as the population continues to increase, manufacturing employment as a share of total employment will continue to drop, no matter the rhetoric of Trump, Farage or any other nationalist politician.

As machines are rapidly taking the place of people in the manufactur-ing process and the costs of labor are removed from the cost of making and delivering a product, what other parts of the landed cost calculation are important? The next element that needs to be examined is transport— the actual act of trade whereby goods made in one country sail across the ocean or fly through the sky to get to you. The following chapter asks whether it will still make sense in the near future to have factories on one side of the world and consumers on the other, or whether the death of distance has really occurred.

5

Getting from A to NA
in a Hilly World

ONE OF THE BEST-SELLING BOOKS of recent years on the future of the global economy has been Thomas L. Friedman's *The World Is Flat.*[1] When it appeared in 2005 it garnered lots of attention and positive press. As the Nobel Prize–winning economist Joe Stiglitz commented: "One mark of a great book is that it makes you see things in a new way, and Mr. Friedman certainly succeeds in that goal."[2]

The central thesis of the book is that there were and are forces in the world today that are making the global economy a level playing field of sorts, in that there is little impediment to having production, design, research and services broken up and placed around the world. In its simplest form, distance doesn't matter.

Friedman opens the book recounting the story of his visit to Infosys in Bangalore to discuss what was happening in India with their then CEO Nandan Nilekani. For him there was a eureka moment after their interview and chat about outsourcing and the disaggregation of digital work. He breathlessly recalls, "As I left the Infosys campus that evening and bounced along the road back to Bangalore, I kept chewing on that phrase: 'The playing field is being leveled.' What Nandan is saying, I thought, is that the playing field is being flattened . . . Flattened? Flattened? My God, he's telling me the world is flat!"

Whether Friedman was right even at the time of his book's publication more than ten years ago is debatable, but the image has stuck and his

term "The World Is Flat" has become shorthand for what many think of as globalization. So, what made the world appear to be flat, and what might make it spiky rather than smooth?

YOU PROBABLY HAVE NEVER HEARD of Malcolm McLean, but he and his company may have had more influence over the unfolding of recent globalization than anyone else.[3] McLean was a self-made trucking magnate who grew his business in 1934 from one old, rusted truck taking oil twenty-eight miles from Fayetteville to a gas station in Red Springs where he was the manager, to, by 1954, one of the largest trucking companies in America, ranked eighth by revenue. His next move was to take things to a completely different place.

The engine of our most recent globalization, the force that since the 1960s has appeared to flatten the earth, is a box. Just a box. Shipping containers are standard-sized boxes that can be loaded and stacked in ever more efficient patterns using massive cranes that stretch over the now enormous ships that move along the ocean trade routes of the world. Very little attention was initially paid to this innovation. The original containers were seen as a slight change, a rather dull improvement to the way in which freight was moved. But this change had a transformative impact, not just on shipping but on the geography of production, which plays out to this day.

In order to avoid crowded highways between American coastal cities McLean decided to use ships, taking the truck trailers on board and having other trucks collect those trailers at their destination. While the initial plan was to drive the trucks on, unhook their trailers and then drive off, he realized that this would waste space and changed the concept so that the trailer bodies could be detached onshore and placed on board. Even better, they could then be stacked, making for easier handling.

The first voyage of what would become the modern container vessel took place in April 1956. The *Ideal-X* sailed with fifty-eight containers from Newark, New Jersey, and five days later arrived in Houston. Changing how cargo was handled and loaded had impacts on how long and how much it cost to load each ship. The proof of this approach was in the numbers. Loading loose cargo cost roughly six dollars per ton at this time. McLean's managers estimated that the loading of the *Ideal-X* cost

just under sixteen cents per ton. The company had not merely lowered costs for loading—they had destroyed them.

The shipping industry initially standardized on twenty-foot containers (referred to as twenty-foot equivalent units or TEUs), and the most common container in use now is twice that at forty feet in length. Since this small beginning, with just fifty-eight containers, the global container fleet has grown and grown. As trade has increased based on the rising demand for physical products from a growing global population, by 2012 the estimated number of containers in the world was thought to be in excess of 32 million.[4]

So, while the places and the making of things have become invisible to most of us in the West, there are many symbols of globalization still around us. Containers have become so commonplace that once they can no longer be used for shipping they are regularly turning up recycled as various versions of housing, offices and even a swimming pool. But as signifiers of globalization to the max the shipping container has nothing on the ships that carry them.

IT MAY SEEM PERVERSE to argue against the rise of global trade when you see one of the world's largest container ships blocking out the sun. One of these behemoths, carrying over 19,000 standard-size containers or TEUs, docked at the U.K.'s busiest container port, Felixstowe, for the first time in January 2015. As it docked it set a new record as the largest ship ever to have visited the U.K. The *CSCL Globe,* registered in Hong Kong, looks ultra blocky, as pixelated as a 1980s video game, as the stern is made up of the back ends of rows and rows of containers stacked ten high above the deck. Another stack ten deep reaches below the deck with cars, computers, clothing, parts and all sorts carefully packed into each of the containers.

It all looks too square, too hard edged to be able to float, let alone sail all the way from China to Europe. From a distance it looks almost like a Lego model that you might have made for your children instead of being the cutting edge of shipping technology.

While there are so many things packed into the containers, there are very few people needed to keep everything shipshape. The crew is usually fewer than thirty strong, each doing multiple jobs and trying to find ways

to remain entertained on the slow steam from Asia to Europe. That means there are more than 600 containers of goods for every member of the crew.

Ships like this are one of the reasons why arguments for a coming fall in trade feel counterintuitive for many people. Having lived with nothing but increasing globalization, what they see around them screams that globalization is continuing apace. As physical symbols of how the world moves its shopping about, such ships are hard to ignore: the largest ships today, the Triple E class developed by Maersk, can carry at least thirty times as many containers as the original container ships from the 1950s. These monsters of the ocean are not about to become extinct, but their role in the global economic system is going to change, with fewer ships plying fewer trade routes.

As containers became the primary method of shipping, in contrast to what is called breakbulk, where items are stored around one another in the hold of a ship rather than packed into separate containers, did it change the overall economics of shipping? The answer is again a surprising one.

HOW MUCH DID CONTAINERIZATION actually change the costs and the practice of shipping products around the world? Frustratingly, there has been a lack of comprehensive work on this question, so it is hard to get a clear picture of the changes that have happened in terms of shipping costs. One of the researchers to focus on this is Professor David Hummels, now the Dean of the Krannert School of Management at Purdue University in Indiana. He has worked on international trade for twenty years and has attempted to bring together the very disparate data on trade costs, shipping methods and actual prices faced by companies moving goods around the world.

Economists such as Hummels talk of ad valorem costs, which are the costs in this case of shipping expressed as a percentage of the value of the goods being shipped. In ad valorem terms shipping costs fell from roughly 10 percent to 6 percent of the value of the goods being transported between the early 1970s and the 1990s. However, since then these costs have remained stubbornly constant, fluctuating around 6 percent of the cost of the goods being shipped.

His work looks at the two main modes of shipping—tramp and liner. The tramp market is for the movement of bulk commodities like oil, grain

or coal and is based on charters. In contrast to this, the liner shipping market is for general cargo, the large majority of which is containerized, based on a fixed set of routes and a fixed timetable of movements.

His research indicates that "The price of bulk shipping measured in real dollars per ton has declined steadily over time so that it is now half as much as in 1960 and a third the price in 1952. However, when measured relative to the commodity price deflator, there are large fluctuations but no downward trend." Essentially when adjusted for their price, there has been no decline in the cost of moving bulk commodities over time. A similar index for liner transport shows an increase in costs of shipping, especially through the 1970s, and again no actual decline. Containers do not appear to have reduced the relative costs of transport.

The reality here is that while containerization may have enabled faster movement of goods through ports, with higher levels of certainty of when ships would be able to sail, other factors have kept prices from falling off further. Issues including port costs and variations in oil price mean that the cost of international shipping up to the financial crisis had not fallen as much as you may have been led to believe.[5]

HOW MUCH WILL IT COST you to ship a container today? Well, it's hard to tell, as depending on what you want to ship you'll have to call around and speak to multiple freight forwarders to get quotes, try to haggle and negotiate in an attempt to get the best price, and through it all you have to hope that the prices haven't shifted as they tend to move on an hourly basis. There is no simple way to compare and predict what the freight costs will be in most cases for shipping by sea, which represents 90 percent of world trade.

There are start-ups, however, trying to simplify this part of the process of getting things from one side of the world to the other, the finding and the booking of space for containers to be taken from A to B (or, as the chapter title hints, from Asia to North America). One such usurper company is called Kontainers, which sprang into being in January 2015.[6] According to one of the two founders, Charles Lee, they gather a million trucking rates and twenty-five million shipping schedules and rates so that Kontainers can use their website to provide a quote immediately.[7] They liken it to Expedia or Skyscanner, although they have a very long way to

go before they can claim to have disintermediated the existing freight for-warders in the same way that travel agents have largely been taken out of the flight-booking process.

So how much does Kontainers think it will cost me to get one standard container from London to Shanghai? On a wet May day in Cambridge the fastest transfer that their search shows is also the cheapest—a voyage for the container of twenty-seven days with Maersk costing £463 including fees. What about from Newark to Bremen? Well, that's just fifteen days but it'll cost you the thick end of $2,500 for the pleasure. Be careful not to spend too much time playing about with this, but if you hang about and check the routes over the space of a day you'll see the prices moving about. There is volatility in the costings as spaces come and go on board the giant ships gliding between the ports of the world. So far Kontainers has a U.K. and a U.S. presence, but it is not too much of a jump to see that this may be how freight forwarding will be handled in the future. If, like travel agents, the freight forwarders are taken out of the process of shipping, there will be strong competition to remove as much of the intermediate costs of the process as possible. But we're not there yet.

Will these changes lead to a new, lower level of ad valorem costs for shipping? That is unclear, as again the other costs associated with the shipping of goods such as port costs, tariffs and the cost of oil continue to contribute to uncertainty in the long-run price of shipping. And it is these uncertainties that are a real problem for companies as well as the overall costs themselves.

A KEY INDICATOR of how much it costs to ship raw materials around the world is the Baltic Dry Index. This number, which only came into being in 1985 but traces its roots back to the coffee houses of eighteenth-century London, provides a gauge of the costs of shipping by combining reported costs across a set of routes for different types of large container ships. When it was introduced it was set to 1,000 and until the end of the 1990s the index generally hovered around the 1,500 mark.

Following a brief elevation to 6,000 and back in the early 2000s, in 2006 the index began to rise sharply, and on 20 May 2008 it peaked at 11,793, which for many was a clear signal of the end of the world. However, a new century and the shipping bust following the financial crisis changed

all that. Between July and December 2008 the index fell 95 percent and since then has been extremely jittery, jumping around as demand and ship availability have come and gone.[8] What was going on to make the index move around like this? Well, one part of this is a shipbuilding spree in China, providing a lot more capacity in trading routes around the world. The other major factor was what happened to the price of oil.

OIL IS STILL WHAT MAKES the global economy tick. We use oil in a massive range of products, from fertilizer to tires, tennis racquets and pretty much anything plastic. But its role as the source of power for most forms of transportation, powering 95 percent of the logistics that get our products from A to B, is our key concern here.[9] As the price of oil is a major determinant of the cost of shipping products around the world, what happens to the price of crude oil impacts heavily on what can and will be moved around. But it is not just the price itself. How volatile or uncertain the price of oil is into the future also has a significant bearing, as many companies are trading in the futures market to try to offset the volatility they see in the oil price. Rather than accept the market price on a given day, and with that the unpredictability of events around the world, companies can buy futures that give them access to a volume of oil at a preset price. Get it right and you may avoid a price hike that others will suffer, get it wrong and you lose out on a possible cost saving. But whichever way the futures contract goes, you at least have the certainty of the price agreed in the contract.

Before the financial crisis in 2008 the price of oil was high, in real terms almost at an historic high. For much of the run-up to the crisis oil was north of $100 a barrel and at one point was priced at around $140. Much of the commentary and debate at this point was about whether we now had permanently high prices. This was based on whether the moment of "peak oil" had already passed and so assumed that we were now working with an ever dwindling supply of oil.[10] This narrative is set up to be one of increasing constraint based on the premise that we're starting to run out of oil. The simple version of the economics then says the price of oil will only increase as demand will still be rising. And with prices climbing it will become less and less cost-effective to be shipping products thousands and thousands of miles.

The financial crash changed this discussion rather abruptly. After the crash the subsequent contraction in world trade wasn't a huge surprise. That meant that there was a surplus of both oil and shipping capacity as the demand for products fell. Fewer products being bought means fewer ships moving products and the oil that they depend on being used less. So oil prices fell. The graph of the fall in price at that point in 2008 looks like the side of a glacier, bottoming out around $30 a barrel.[11]

As the world tried to right itself and as trade began to grow again the price of oil started a climb back to where it had been into the neighborhood of $100 per barrel, a gentle hill climb back to normality of a kind. But then a strange thing happened as 2014 unfolded—the price of oil collapsed again, dipping below $30 for a while and hitting $26 at its lowest point. Increased oil supply, weaker demand and an unwillingness of oil producers to limit production was pumping a constant excess of oil into the market.

Since then there has been a mini-rally but the price has remained in the doldrums, wavering around $50 a barrel. Will it stay there and, if so, for how long? This is an incredibly difficult question to answer as the role of countries within OPEC and beyond in setting production targets, and hence the world's supply of oil, is relatively opaque. The current oversupply is likely to keep prices low but volatile during the coming years.

These movements in oil price have led to significant uncertainties in transportation costs as a lack of pattern makes planning very difficult. When prices could remain low or equally could double, how do you decide what to pay for a futures contract for the oil you're going to use to power your ships?

The volatility in oil prices and in the Baltic Dry Index are an indicator that we're in uncharted economic waters in which no one is quite sure what is going to happen next—and this is likely to continue. Uncertainty in shipping costs creates another barrier to moving goods around the world. If you cannot forecast your shipping costs, how do you price your goods accurately? This leads to an important question that every manufacturer has to answer—if you can remove uncertainty from your supply chain and manufacturing process by not having to ship as many parts around, why would you not?

. . .

THE ACTUAL COSTS of shipping extend beyond how much you'll be charged for the loading, moving and unloading of your standardized container. How important are shipping costs when compared to other costs such as tariffs around the world? To answer that question it is necessary to look at how tariffs have changed over time and whether there is a general pattern to how much we charge one another for the privilege of exporting to our respective countries.

At the end of the Second World War twenty-three countries came together and negotiated the General Agreement on Trade and Tariffs (GATT) which set the basic template for how international trade would be governed for these countries and began the process of tariff reduction. By the 1950s average tariffs, which had been above 40 percent of the value of the goods being imported, were now below 20 percent in many of these countries. Eight rounds of negotiation later, the Uruguay Round in 1994—by which time 128 countries had come into the GATT process— saw GATT replaced by the World Trade Organization (WTO).[12]

Why this focus by developed governments on tariffs and the extreme levels of effort expended to reduce them? The institutional memory of many governments seems to have been set by their experiences leading up to and following the Great Depression. It was at this time that the most infamous episode of tariff imposition occurred—the introduction of the Smoot–Hawley Tariff Act in the United States in 1930. Representative Willis Hawley was a long-serving Republican congressman originally from Benton County in Oregon. For such a historic mistake it is interesting that the principal co-sponsor had been for sixteen years a professor of history and economics at Willamette University.[13] When Congress voted for the Act, which raised the average tariff on durable goods from 40 percent to 48 percent,[14] it probably didn't think it would contribute to a decline in world trade of over two-thirds between 1929 and 1934 or that the world average tariff would reach 25 percent.[15] Over the two years following the introduction of the Act imports into the United States fell by 40 percent, although the Act itself was not responsible for all of this fall.[16]

While the early rounds under GATT were primarily between developed economies, as the scope of negotiations expanded, more and more countries at different levels of development became involved. So the

complexity of the negotiations has increased significantly and it has been harder and harder to accommodate vastly different needs and agendas. The latest round, the Doha Round, has died a death. The last rites were administered at the end of 2015, fourteen years after its inception.[17]

So what of the comparison between shipping costs and tariffs as multilateral negotiations have come and gone? It used to be that tariffs had a greater impact on the landed cost of a product, being double the cost of shipping for many products coming into the United States at the end of the 1950s.[18] However, by 2004 the situation had completely changed, with shipping costs for U.S. imports on average three times higher than tariffs paid.

Essentially, while tariffs remain contentious, especially in relation to developing countries and their access to the world market, and continuing multilateral negotiations following the Doha Round appear to make less and less progress, the direction of travel has been clear. Tariff costs have not been volatile in the same way as the price of oil and the implied costs of shipping. That may be about to change if the rhetoric of political campaigns around the world are to be believed. The campaign of Donald Trump was a signifier for such changes. His main statements on trade included a 20 percent tariff on all imported goods, which would reverse the changes made since the start of the GATT process.[19] The United Kingdom's vote to leave the European Union has opened up many questions on what tariff schedule it would operate under, as it is not clear early in the process of Brexit whether the U.K. can adopt existing WTO schedules or not. Depending on how its politics continues to evolve, the U.K. may change lanes on trade, putting even greater pressure on global value chains and again increasing the likelihood of greater regionalization.

SIZE CAN BE YOUR FRIEND or it can be your enemy. Companies are told by leading business thinkers and researchers to be agile and nimble in the dynamic global economy. But they are also constantly told that there are economies of scale that they need to achieve to give them cost advantages. The shipping industry obviously took that advice to heart as Maersk and others bought larger and larger ships, each now costing in the region of $200 million to build and deliver. However, by the middle of 2016 it looked like that was a bad bet.

In the summer of that year a French shipping company announced that, having operated an 18,000-TEU ship called the *Benjamin Franklin* from the west coast of America to Asia for just five months, it was suspending the route.[20] This was the largest ship to ever have docked at a U.S. port, a ship that took nearly sixty hours to unload all its containers. Five more ships of that size were in the works for the company, but the lack of demand on the route stopped the order before it could happen. Now it is unclear what this monster of the sea will be doing with itself but it is surplus to requirements at the time of writing.

Given the time lag between ordering a new ship and having it available to operate a route, there has been an ongoing problem of backlog for shipping companies. When the global economy was ticking along before the financial crisis and trade was growing at twice the rate of global GDP, the signals all pointed to the need for more and more shipping capacity. That forecast was wrong.

Another problem with ships of this size is risk, or rather the concentration of risk. The size of these container ships has raised the potential loss from a shipping accident or piracy to new levels. How much stuff can you get into a container? Of course, that depends on what you're shipping, but to get some sense of what it means in human terms, shipping companies estimate that a twenty-foot container can hold everything from a two-bedroom apartment, while a forty-foot container can take all the belongings of a three-bedroom house.[21] Look around your house and start to add up the retail value of everything you see and you get a sense of how much value can be packed into one container. Now multiply that by 18,000 and that's one hell of an insurance claim if the ship were to be lost.

Since its publication, Friedman's book has been heavily criticized for being too simplistic and in some instances flat wrong. One of the most prominent critics is Richard Florida, director of the Martin Prosperity Institute at the University of Toronto's Rotman School of Management, who in 2008 published his own take on the structure of the global economy with *Who's Your City? How the Creative Economy Is Making Where You Live the Most Important Decision of Your Life*.[22] His response to writers like Friedman is that the world is spiky, with dense concentrations of innovation and power in a small number of cities such as London and San Francisco. For Florida, instead of place being unimportant it actually

may be the most important thing of all. And, worryingly, the high ground is getting higher and higher, leaving behind valleys in which lie megacities and their slums, such as Nairobi and Kolkata, and vast tracts of agricultural land on which there is little economic activity.

In a flat, frictionless world most if not all things would spread out and cover the globe evenly. There would be few discontinuities caused by borders or extreme differences in wealth or health. That is clearly not the case. If the world were truly flat, why is it that, even now, three-quarters of everything bought in the United States is made in the United States?

It is obvious that variations in climate, economic circumstance and governmental control mean that the world is not flat to all people, or even most of them. Freedom of movement around the world is clearly not a reality, when over the past five years we have seen the desperate flight of refugees from the war in Syria and others coming through North Africa, all trying to get to Europe and a new life. Is everyone allowed to move to wherever they want? Clearly not. The pictures of refugee families held at various border crossings and constrained by the refusal of other countries to accept refugees in any significant numbers highlight how mountainous is the task some face in moving from one region of the world to another.

In their mid-year report for 2015 the UN High Commission for Refugees (UNHCR) estimated that over 60 million people were forcibly displaced across the world, 15 million of whom were refugees mainly driven by the war in Syria.[23] Most countries have controlled immigration, with limits to the number of people accepted each year and in many cases a focus on accepting those with skills that are in short supply in that country. Clearly not a level playing field.

If people find the world to be difficult to move about in the transnational sense, there is more freedom of movement within most states. The expression of a spiky or rough world is seen in the distribution of where people are living. The rise of the megacity is a key trend, impacting on how families are structured, the kinds of products that are demanded and generating logistical challenges to feed and water that many people in such a dense environment.

As reported by the UN by 2014, more people in the world now live in cities than in rural settings, with 54 percent of the world living in an

urban environment. Less than one-third of the world was in cities in 1950 and it is projected that the share in cities will be over two-thirds by 2050.[24]

Most cities remain small, with fewer than 500,000 inhabitants. But the populations of the megacities are difficult to comprehend. Mexico City, Mumbai and São Paulo each have 21 million, Delhi has 25 million and far out in front is Tokyo with 38 million people together in one urban landscape. It appears that Florida is more on the money than Friedman.

SO, IF PEOPLE AND THINGS are not moving smoothly around the world, what about ideas? How is spending on research and development (R&D), both as a proxy for and as an engine of growth, spread around the world? The picture here up to the turn of the century was one of dominance by the West, with companies holding on to R&D in their home countries due to advantages in accessing highly skilled researchers as well as their concerns about weak intellectual property rules in developing and emerging economies.

The current picture is more complex, as China and other Asian economies have significantly raised their R&D investment levels. Currently three regions account for just over 90 percent of global R&D spending—North America (29 percent), Europe (22 percent) and the part of Asia that includes China, Japan, South Korea, India and Taiwan (40 percent).[25] At the country level the United States performs just over a quarter of the world total, followed by China at one-fifth of the world total and then Japan with one-tenth. Barring Germany at 6 percent of R&D investment, everyone else is below 4 percent and in most cases much lower than that. This is a highly concentrated market with no signs of becoming flat anytime soon.

While the world has not flattened in terms of R&D investment there has been a definite change of shape. The growth rate of R&D investment in China has averaged just under 20 percent per year between 2003 and 2013, almost doubling the amount it spends on R&D as a percentage of GDP (from 1.13 percent to 2.08 percent of GDP over the ten-year period). In relative terms, this has moved it past the U.K. and in absolute terms makes it the second largest spender on R&D. South Korea has put significant effort into raising its R&D spend as well, growing on average over

11 percent per year, and putting it top of the charts when looking at R&D spend as a percentage of GDP at over 4 percent.

The breathless claims for a flat world don't appear to stack up against the actual numbers. The distribution and flow of people, ideas and things are not in any sense flattened in the current context of the world economy. So why did the image take hold? Why were so many commentators, academics and politicians convinced that the world had become weightless, frictionless, flat? If the world is patently not "flat" with such significant discontinuities in terms of people, money and things why did the idea become so entrenched?

Toward the end of the twentieth century two crucial things were thought to be moving in the same direction. Telecommunications costs and transport costs were both falling, making it easier to connect both physically and digitally. Both moving in the same direction at the same time created a narrative that masked what was actually happening. The changes as the world became digitally connected rolled out over a generation, meaning many had only one experience of the world as the digital and physical headed the same way. But this has created an expectation that cannot be fulfilled in the longer term—that all prices will fall forever.

Between 1950 and 1997 the cost of a three-minute telephone call from the United States to the United Kingdom, Germany or Japan fell by around two-thirds, dropping from $12 to just over $3 in each case. The introduction of dense fiber-optic communications and the arrival of Skype and FaceTime have now made these costs negligible for the average user.

Shipping costs fell in absolute terms, even if they were not falling as a percentage of the value of the goods being shipped. The reporting of these changes was based on the absolute cost changes and so the public did not see the relative changes. It may seem like a technical point, but how these changes are framed has had a large impact on the public interpretation of what has happened and will happen to the global economy.

Friedman's claim that the world was flat seemed to catch a particular moment when concerns about how the global economy was evolving were particularly high in Western economies. At best it described elements where there were real changes in how easy it was to outsource and offshore production and some services such as call centers. At its worst it created a narrative so strong it has clouded our view for a decade, getting in the way

of discussing the complex, messy and rough nature of the interconnections between countries and regions.

RICHARD FLORIDA'S WORK ON CITIES is in some ways an urban version of industrial clusters, working at the level of the individual rather than the company or an industry. Such work on how different industrial activities cluster or agglomerate stretches back through Michael Porter to Alfred Marshall and his work on industrial districts. The change in the unit of analysis is interesting, though, as again it raises the point that if we look at the evolution of the global economy from only one perspective, for example through the nation state as much trade theory does, then we'll miss interesting changes and effects.

One of the open questions is whether the massive collection of companies making so many things in southern China has become a self-reinforcing cluster, a location with its own internal gravity binding manufacturers to it for a significant time into the future. The benefits of having many producers close together range from the ability to find workers with the requisite skills to the sharing of knowledge between companies trying to solve design problems. However, given the rise of automation and the desire of lead firms to retain design and intellectual property control over their products, some of the clustering forces for places like Guangzhou and Shenzhen may not be as strong as might be thought at first glance.

The Florida view of the world as spiky and urban has its own problems when applied outside of the developed country context. His argument within countries such as the United States implies that there are centers that will continue to aggregate power and influence and other places simply will never have a chance to catch up. But when taken into the heady world of Shenzhen or other centers of manufacturing, do the same rules apply? That's unclear.

THERE ARE OTHER REASONS why moving products around the globe three or four times before they are bought and used will become less at-tractive. One of these is time to market. A recent study by the Boston Consulting Group looked at the labor cost savings of having production in China for the U.S. market. The average cost saving was around 10 percent,

which is too low when you take into account the extra time taken in shipping and the risk in managing operations overseas. The clothes manufacturer and retailer Zara, which it is claimed can get a clothing line from development to store in just one week, needs to be able to change its designs, production runs and destinations at very short notice to keep its high-diversity business model working. Headquartered in Spain, approximately half its production is located domestically or in nearby countries such as Portugal or Morocco. For Zara, cost is less important than control and speed. The three to four weeks it takes to ship a container from China to Spain is the complete cycle time that Zara is trying to work within. Time on the sea is time the company cannot afford.

Toward the end of his history of containerization, Marc Levinson acknowledges one key thing—that "the trade patterns that containerization has helped to create are not immutable."[26] He is discussing late entrants in terms of ports such as Busan, Le Havre and various others across Asia in the 1990s. But it also applies to the global pattern of trade itself. There is no reason to believe that the ways we organize how we make and deliver to the final customer have become fixed and constant.

Beyond the rap sheet that we've outlined above there are greater and greater pressures on producers to reduce emissions in an attempt not to overheat the planet. Manufacturing is part of this process in two ways—in the emissions from the making of products and the emissions from the movement of goods from one side of the world to the other. The next chapter will discuss the possible impact of tighter controls on transport emissions, as well as looking at whether there is a positive environmental story that can be told about manufacturing in the future to replace those dark satanic mills of the Industrial Revolution.

6

Manufacturing the Environment

DANNY BOYLE'S OPENING CEREMONY for the 2012 London Olympics was a truly amazing spectacle that used a thicket of references to Britain past and present. When you get to show the Queen jumping out of a helicopter ahead of James Bond you know you've pretty much nailed it.

At one point in the ceremony the hymn "Jerusalem" rang out over the pastoral idyll created in the stadium. "And was Jerusalem builded here / Among these dark Satanic Mills?" Blake's words floated over the green landscape, then, right in front of the 80,000-strong crowd and the millions watching all over the world, industry was shown destroying the land. The green fields were pulled up, smokestacks sprouted from the ground belching out ugly black clouds and workers in gray and brown rags spewed from the earth to feed the machines created there.

As a statement on how the Industrial Revolution is often viewed it was pretty powerful stuff. The image of the dark Satanic mill, churning smoke and foulness into the air, is a hard one to shake. The history of the Industrial Revolution, which happened at a time when regulation was nonexistent and before there was any concern over the impact factories were having on either the health of the workers within them or the environment outside, is written into the fabric of life in the U.K.

We live in different times. The environment and the future of the planet more broadly have become one of the battlegrounds of modern politics and debate. The emergence of the science of climate change, argued and

denied for many years by powerful voices, now appears undeniable. Manufacturing in its processes of making, how it delivers products to us and what we collectively do with those products when they are no longer desired, is under great pressure to have a positive rather than a negative environmental effect. How will this change the nature and organization of manufacturing? Are these pressures pushing toward the global or the local? But first we each need to ask ourselves why we buy so much stuff.

HOW MANY TIMES have you had to upgrade your laptop or tablet before you wanted to, replace your washing machine because of a simple fault or throw out what appears to be a perfectly good phone just because there is no easy way to replace the battery? On the flip side, how often have you abandoned your latest phone or TV because something newer and sexier has come to the market?

Welcome to the world of planned obsolescence, where design on the inside or the outside of products is used to attempt to make you have to or want to buy the next iteration of the same product much faster than you might have otherwise. Instead of built to last, we have built to be replaced with another version of the same thing.

It wasn't such a dirty phrase when it began its life back in the 1930s. Then the world was reeling from the Great Depression and any and all ideas were being tried to stimulate the world economy. Bernard London, a Russian-American real estate broker, wrote a pamphlet in 1932 with the glorious title of *Ending the Depression Through Planned Obsolescence*.[1] He argued that productivity had so increased that it was a problem of plenty destroying prices rather than the specter of Malthus and scarcity driving the Depression.

In the midst of the crisis "people generally, in a frightened and hysterical mood, are using everything that they own longer than was their custom before the depression." In a proposed intervention far beyond the scope of what we would consider possible in modern Western economies he argued that:

> the Government [should] assign a lease of life to shoes and homes and machines, to all products of manufacture, mining and agriculture, when they are first created, and they would be sold and used within

the term of their existence definitely known by the consumer. After the allotted time had expired, these things would be legally "dead" and would be controlled by the duly appointed governmental agency and destroyed if there is widespread unemployment.

London's pamphlet shows the extremes that people were willing to go to in their thinking in efforts to overcome the devastation of the Great Depression, no matter how impractical and strange the proposals would have been to carry out.

Through the fifties and sixties the tone and meaning of planned obsolescence changed. Instead of being an out-of-left-field broad attempt to stimulate growth the practice became a way for individual companies to increase their turnover and their profits. In the relatively benign version of this strategy, instead of letting poor souls such as us languish with a perfectly adequate phone or television, companies could nudge us to buy a new television with improved aesthetics or minor changes. The more forced version pushes you ever forward, with software upgrades that stop working with the old device and will only work with the new device. The most explicit version is when the parts and assembly of a product are designed to last a specific period of time, say eighteen months or so. Soldering in batteries or using plastics that will eventually crack and break are classic examples of design explicitly setting a lifespan for products and forcing consumers to buy more if they want to continue to have that phone or computer or desk.

Leading industrial designer Brooks Stevens is credited with introducing the phrase in this more modern sense. As an industrial designer Stevens shaped many of the iconic products of the postwar period, including the first clothes dryer and the Oscar Mayer Wienermobile. In a 1954 speech at a marketing conference he is claimed to have defined planned obsolescence as "instilling in the buyer the desire to own something a little newer, a little better, a little sooner than is necessary."[2] For Brooks this was a valuable mission, not a negative. It wasn't, however, a stance that was universally shared.

The classic text exploring the downsides of planned obsolescence is Vance Packard's *The Waste Makers*.[3] He begins with the dreams of a marketing executive, wishing for Cornucopia City, where "all the buildings

will be made of a special papier-mâché. These houses can be torn down and rebuilt every spring and fall at housecleaning time. The motorcars of Cornucopia will be made of a lightweight plastic that develops fatigue and begins to melt if driven more than four thousand miles." It is based on a simultaneously optimistic and depressing picture, one where all the essentials we need are available and accessible to all while, driven by the need for growth, companies force the making and buying of more and more. Packard comments that future historians may label this, the 1960s, as the "Throwaway Age." If only he had seen what the velocity of product development and iteration would become by the turn of the century, especially in consumer electronics.

It is unclear whether planned obsolescence strategies are still a staple of leading companies around the world. Companies like Apple have been accused of having intentionally planned obsolescence strategies for many years and have in some cases been taken to court. At the end of 2013, as the new iPhone was launched, the operating system was upgraded as well. According to many users, some of whom tried to sue through a class action, there was no warning that the operating system upgrade would make the old iPhone so slow as to make it to all intents unusable.[4]

The existence of planned obsolescence as a strategy for companies and our collective inability to act is one of the reasons we have an ever increasing mountain of electronics waste. Companies want you to buy the upgrade. There is little incentive for them not to make each product obsolete quickly when we as consumers are willing to make the shift to the next iteration or the next version of essentially the same product. Since its launch in 2007 we've gone through six major and a few minor iterations of the iPhone (although there is now talk that we've reached "peak phone") and the first quarter of 2016 was the first time since its launch that iPhone sales have fallen.[5] Nine years with ever-increasing sales for a product that is incrementally improving is incredible. Especially when at its core it does the same things, admittedly faster and with more pixels (I can hear the screams of the Apple devotees from here).

But will we as consumers continue to play along? Are we unaware of the strategies that are being used on and around us and will we begin to change our relationship to upgrading? Each country and culture will have different answers to this question but there is evidence that consumers

generally have come to expect products to have short lifetimes. For example a survey of over 800 Brazilians did not find that product longevity was a concern when consumers were buying products, even though two-thirds of those surveyed felt that the actual lifetimes of products were shorter than they would have reasonably expected.[6] A set of focus groups in the U.K. also indicate that we have low expectations of how long products, especially mobile devices, will last and we don't have significant guilt about that yet.[7] There does not appear to be a link made yet for the general consumer between the products they buy and the environmental impact their production, use, and disposal may have.

We create the demand side for the ever-increasing volume of global production. How those products are made and shipped to us creates the core of their environmental impact. Is there another way to think about industrial organization that can by design be less environmentally harmful but to the benefit of companies and consumers?

TRY TO IMAGINE how much stuff, how much raw material, the world uses every year. Have a number in your head for the amount of water, oil, or wood we get through? Let's see if we're even in the ballpark of correct.

The headline figure is pretty shocking. Each year we dig up or extract and then use 60 billion tons of raw materials.[8] Our demand for the basic building blocks of our manufactured world has soared over the past fifty years. The demand for cement, steel, paper, aluminum and plastics has increased five times over since 1960.[9] Even though we have become much better at generating economic value using less—a dollar of GDP uses a third less material than it did at the start of the 1980s—increasing population and economic growth mean we keep on using more and more.

It's too hard sometimes to be thinking in terms of the planet. Where I'm sitting in the U.K. the average single-person household uses 149 liters of water per day, so to put that into perspective that's three hundred standard bottles of water from your local shop.[10] Cross the pond and that number doubles, with the average person using over 300 liters of water per day in the United States.[11]

As the global population increases and we add more consumers to the world economy the pressure on our resources is only going to increase. The United Nations monitors population numbers and regularly updates its

forecasts on how many of us are standing on the planet. There are more than 7 billion of us here now and by 2050 it looks like there will be well over 9 billion people trying to meet their basic needs of shelter, security and food.[12]

At the same time we are seeing a growing middle class in China, India and other countries with disposable income who will also be looking for something to do. Especially for China the emergence of a younger upper-middle class will drive consumer spending, regarded by many as the most Westernized of buyers.[13] This is the generation born after Deng Xiaoping famously visited the south in 1992, touring Guangdong and the now major cluster of Shenzhen as part of his signaling of major economic reforms. According to some estimates, and the numbers are open to debate on many fronts, the middle class in China now exceeds 500 million people. That's quite a market, and how Chinese consumers act into the future, what culture of buying and owning they follow, will determine whether we see the same speed of consumption in Asia as the West has experienced over the past decades.

As ever, there are those who take the technology optimist's position—innovation has always found a way forward, technology will save us. We will find new sources, new ways to trade off any shortages that we may run into for the materials that go into our products. The problem is that as products become more and more specialized, the materials used in them are tuned or chosen to be as effective as possible. It is not just the overall amount of each material that is the problem, it is that our products and their performance depend on very specific chemical and physical properties to achieve their speed, durability, or lightness. Our products are materially complex and highly specific—computer chips now use sixty different minerals in their production, up from twelve in the 1980s.[14]

This issue of complexity in material use was the focus of a recent study that looked at the use of sixty-two metals in various products and the potential for substitution with another material.[15] The results were sobering—none of the sixty-two had a clear substitute that could match the performance of the original material and twelve had no adequate substitute at all. What does that mean? Without transformative breakthroughs in materials technology, if we keep using materials at our current rates we will have to use substandard alternatives. And that will probably

mean computers getting slower, not faster, engines decreasing in power and anything computer based falling backwards in terms of performance. For a world used to constant improvements, seemingly infinite upgrades and the fruits of Moore's Law this would come as something of a shock.

The message is pretty clear. Acting in the same mode as we have in the recent past will put incredible pressure on the raw materials we need to make the products we want to sell. Most materials will never run out, there will be some of it somewhere in the world, either buried in an extremely out-of-the-way place or embedded in products in use. But without some change, some revolution in the linear model of making, we're heading toward a difficult future.

SEVENTY-ONE DAYS, FOURTEEN HOURS, eighteen minutes, thirty-three seconds. That's how long it took Ellen MacArthur to sail alone around the world, becoming the fastest person to solo circumnavigate the world in 2005.[16] It was a massive achievement, given that it was her first attempt at the record—a record which had been destroyed just one year previously by Francis Joyon. He had lowered the record by an incredible twenty days and few in the sailing community thought that this new benchmark could be touched in their lifetime.

MacArthur was a very experienced sailor by the time she set out on 28 November 2004. She had been part of a failed attempt at the Jules Verne race, which is for full crews circumnavigating the globe, and had been second in the Vendée Globe, possibly the toughest race there is as it is a solo, non-stop, unassisted race around the world.

The fragility of her seventy-five-foot boat and the possibility of disaster are best explained in her words from the logbook toward the end of the race:

> I saw a whale very, very close to the boat . . . it was just in front of us, and we sailed right over it. It went underneath our starboard float and, as it went underneath us, it blew its air tanks out and its nose came out of the water. I didn't see its tail, but it must have been about 30ft long. I braced myself for a collision, to be honest, because it was so close.[17]

The sailor turned campaigner has claimed that her experience of sailing alone around the world gave her the perspective she needed to see the world as finite, itself a kind of boat floating in space. MacArthur was obsessive about planning, ensuring she had properly prepared her meals and medical supplies so that they would last the trip. If she ran out of powdered milk there wouldn't be a convenience store to restock from—she had to make the best use of whatever she took on the boat with her.

This hard, finite limit to her resources for her circumnavigation stuck with her. You can see how easy it is to extrapolate from her journey to that of the planet circumnavigating the sun every 365 days and running out of materials at a shocking rate. The Global Footprint Network, an international think tank, calculates when each year we have used more resources than the earth can regenerate.[18] That day has been creeping forward ever since it was first calculated in 2006. Then overshoot occurred in October. By 2016 it had moved back to the middle of August.

Having taken time to step back and think about what she wanted to achieve after claiming the record, MacArthur brought together B&Q, BT/Cisco, the National Grid and Renault to be the founding partners of the Ellen MacArthur Foundation. Its mission—to accelerate a transition to a circular economy.

THE SIMPLE CARICATURE VERSION of making products has manufacturing run in a fairly linear fashion. Take some raw materials out of the ground, put them together in some process that may or may not be hazardous or polluting, and then once that product is either unwanted, obsolete or broken, bury it in a landfill. At that point the assumption is that as it's run out of use for the consumer and has been thrown away it doesn't have any other value and so we need more resources to make more things. A conveyor belt moves from extraction through making and use and on to disposal, with nothing used more than once.

This is, of course, the extreme version of unsustainable production and use, but unfortunately it appears to not be far from reality. According to Annie Leonard's work for the *Story of Stuff*,[19] for many products the amount of the materials used to make that product that are still in use six months after it is bought is 1 percent.[20] Just make sure you've thought about that—99 percent of the materials that were used in the making of

the product are not in use half a year after you bought it. They have been used, wasted, binned or whatever phrase you want to use.

This linear version of making—summarized as take, make, dispose—is contrasted to the circular version of the economy.[21] Conceptually, the circular economy is easy to understand. Instead of buying a new car, refurbish the one that you have. At the end of your laptop's life, instead of just throwing it all into a landfill, strip out the useful components and recycle the materials as much as possible into other products and other industries. Think of all the waste from one industry as being the inputs to another. The core idea of circularity is to close the loop on materials use as much as possible. So rather than consuming materials in a one-time deal when making something, you make the materials go around again and be used as many times as you can.

The furniture juggernaut that is IKEA is working toward having circularity embedded in its design and manufacturing processes. The company was started by the seventeen-year-old Ingvar Kamprad in 1943 and it appears that some of the values of frugality that come from growing up in a poor rural region have embedded themselves in the mythology of the company. Its initial steps into sustainability were relatively traditional—less waste, materials sourced from sustainable sources, and a focus on having energy from renewable sources.[22] So much, so traditional, but now it is beginning to offer mattress take-backs and is creating a market for selling second-hand IKEA furniture. Then, at the start of 2016, the head of sustainability for the company, Steve Howard, stated that their aim was to have a circular IKEA where you could repair and recycle products easily.[23] He may also have let a different cat out of the bag when he said, "If we look on a global basis, in the west we have probably hit peak stuff. We talk about peak oil. I'd say we've hit peak red meat, peak sugar, peak stuff... peak home furnishings." It doesn't appear that the comment has applied to purchases of the IKEA flat pack just yet.

There is a long tradition of second-hand clothing, from the properly vintage end to bags of unwanted clothes donated to charity stores around the world. Fashion retailer H&M has moved into the circular space through an in-store collection program.[24] Customers are encouraged to bring their unwanted clothes into the store in exchange for money-off vouchers. The clothes are then sorted and the majority are sent into the

second-hand clothes market. However, much of the clothing collected is used as cleaning cloths or as insulation material. Some is even used as the source material for new fabric. Since the program started in 2013 H&M have collected over 28,000 tons of clothing in this way, which is the equivalent of the material in 120 million T-shirts.

Where are we starting from in terms of the level of circularity in the economy? It is one thing to say that we use so many tons of steel or liters of water, but how much are we recovering and renewing into the economic system of the planet? Unfortunately it looks like the level of circularity at the scale of the planet is very low, around 6 percent in 2005 measured as the share of recycled materials in total processed materials.[25] A full two-thirds of processed materials left the economy as waste or as emissions and just under a third were embedded in long-life goods like buildings and infrastructure and so are not available for reuse for an extended period of time.

A more recent study is no more encouraging. Looking at Europe as an integrated economy, what can we say about how much the continent uses and reuses per year? Each European uses on average sixteen tons of materials and the level of reuse and recycling is depressingly low.[26] Sixty percent of discarded materials were either incinerated or thrown into a landfill. In terms of value it appears that 95 percent of the material and energy value is lost for products through their life cycle.

The idea of a circular economy, with materials being used again and again in different products and different industries, is a powerful one. However, we seem to be very far away from anything resembling the concept, stuck with a linear take, make, dispose approach to our products. Even though many of us talk the talk when it comes to protecting the environment, we may unwittingly be contributing through our love of the new.

GETTING MATERIALS BACK OUT of a product is not a simple process, passing it through a sieve or unbolting each component. We design and make products hard to recycle and that's a problem. While the broad sense of the concept of a circular economy is relatively simple, making it happen is another thing altogether. Technically difficult, under supported by established interests and out of step with our culture of the new, the circular economy has not yet taken off in the way its proponents hoped.

It looks like there was a turning point in the mid-2000s when electronics companies took on a set of manufacturing processes that made it almost impossible to repair and in many cases recycle their products. In the middle of 2012 Apple released a new version of the MacBook Pro and in their report *Wired* referred to it as "the least repairable laptop we've ever taken apart."[27] This was because the display was fused to the glass, the memory was soldered to the rest of the electronics and the battery was glued to the case. Nothing in here could be upgraded or repaired (bar sending the machine back to Apple for a battery replacement costing $200) and the possibilities for recycling were minimal.

These were all design choices. They were taken for many reasons—cost and ease of manufacturing being the two most likely targets. But this is also a reflection on us as consumers. We are buying and demanding thinner products while knowing at some level that this means they have a very finite lifespan and cannot be repaired and upgraded.

ALL THIS TALK ABOUT CIRCULARITY and linking industries together might sound nice in theory but surely it will cost companies enormously to make this a reality. If there were cost savings to be made, managers of multinationals would already be doing this, wouldn't they? It can be difficult for companies to take on radical new structures as they are running so hard to stay competitive within their existing environment. Also, many of the changes that need to be made are at the system level—you only get the benefits if you can see the whole system and start to connect the inputs and outputs of many companies and many industrial sectors.

If we could make circular the new linear, what would the benefits be? Well, each element of the circular economy represents a different level of direct value and potentially impacts on employment as well. The World Economic Forum's work on the circular economy includes examples such as the U.K.'s opportunity to create income of $1.5 billion from recycling mixed food waste, or that each ton of clothing collected can generate a gross profit of $1,295.[28]

Modeling how this comes together at the national or international level is incredibly difficult as so many assumptions have to be made about how different countries and companies will react. The Ellen MacArthur Foundation in partnership with the McKinsey Center for Business and

Environment created a detailed scenario for Europe for 2030 to contrast growth under business as usual and with a strong commitment to a circular economy.[29] If all the assumptions made in the scenario hold true, for example on the impact of driverless cars, or the advent of the sharing economy, there is an opportunity to increase resource productivity by 3 percent annually with total benefits per year of €1.8 trillion. Compared to their modeling of business as usual, this would mean GDP would be 7 percent larger in the circular economy scenario. As part of the report a systematic review of research into the employment effects of the circular economy was carried out, and over sixty-five studies the consensus is that, while it is hard to put a number on it, there would be positive employment effects from the adoption of the circular economy.

This scenario for the benefits to be gained by Europe through a strong adoption of circular across the economy feels instinctively to be too generous an estimate. Using these numbers with certainty is suspect, especially given how many unknowns are in the scenario and how much depends on individual and collective action across the member states. However, individual companies are seeing positive returns from moving toward circularity and it does appear that the net outcomes are positive if the changes are carried out fully.

The direct economic benefits to companies are one thing, but there are reasons to move to circularity that go beyond the immediate economic benefits. There are significant risks baked into the existing extended supply chains that we use to make our products, the timing of which is very hard to predict.

The 2011 earthquake and subsequent tsunami that hit the Fukushima prefecture of Japan was horrendous. At magnitude 9.0 it was the largest quake in history to hit the Japanese mainland. The waves from the tsunami reached forty meters in height and moved ships and houses inland as they broke across miles of shoreline. Alan Taylor's photographs from *The Atlantic* show some of the devastation, including a picture of a ferry stranded on top of a building in Ōtsuchi, Iwate Prefecture, as the waves receded.[30] In one of the saddest moments of recent Japanese history over 16,000 people lost their lives. At the time the Japanese government estimated it would cost ¥25 trillion (over $300 billion) to rebuild and recover.[31]

In the face of the human loss it feels inappropriate to talk about supply chains and the risks to companies. But this disaster highlighted how vulnerable global supply chains can be, at least in the short term. As the disaster unfolded GM had to stop making in its Louisiana factory owing to the shortage in Japanese parts, and others such as Nokia and Sony Ericsson saw disruptions in their supply chains.[32] Rolling power shortages following the tsunami meant factories in areas not directly affected also were disrupted. Companies building their supply chains to be lean or just in time, working with low levels of stock and depending on the efficient functioning of all the elements of the supply chain, are exposed when events such as this destroy the capacity of a part of the system.

Whether natural disasters are increasing in frequency or not is a highly charged debate. However, there are many who believe that climate change, and specifically our role in increasing emissions and increasing temperatures, is increasing the frequency of weather-related disasters.[33] If our inability to curb emissions and global warming continues, it is more than likely that global supply chains will face increasing disruption from extreme weather and natural disasters and companies will have to build greater resilience into their networks in order to maintain continuity of production.

DIFFERENT COMPANIES HAVE RESPONDED to environmental pressures in different ways. Some, ever conscious of their image, have tried very hard to be seen to be green. Others have just chugged along, letting the heat and fury of the climate debate pass them by.

The early days of companies engaging with the environmental agenda saw many firms attempting what was referred to as green washing.[34] Putting on the appearance of taking action to meet environmental goals but not actually committing to them in the long term has been a problem and many companies struggle to overcome skepticism from consumers that they are really making changes.

That charge is unlikely to stick on Nike. It has taken a clear turn toward becoming eco-friendly and has stated that it intends to double its business while halving its environmental impact.[35] This breaks down into multiple targets, such as using 100 percent renewable energy by 2020, and many of the targets are scheduled for the future rather than already achieved.

However, on a per-unit basis, that is per product made, Nike's claim is that they reduced their emissions by 18 percent in 2015. It is also clear that the message on the circular economy has reached the top of Nike as a section title of the report baldly states, "The future will be circular."

On the other side of the world, LG in South Korea has introduced a same day walk-in repair service so that instead of throwing away your phone that has been damaged you can get it mended. Rather than depend on a disposable economy, the LG example shows how it is possible to return to longevity in products as part of this circular story.

So, how serious is the threat of environmental regulation and are companies just trying to get ahead of prospective constraints? That depends on the coercive power of governments around the world and whether they are willing to constrain how companies can act within their borders. As emissions don't respect borders, that implies the need for collective action, something we've struggled to achieve on this and many other issues up to now.

DECEMBER 2015 MAY GO DOWN as one of the most important months in the history of the planet. On 12 December, following four years of global negotiations and two weeks of back and forth at the COP21 meeting in Paris, 195 countries adopted the first universal, legally binding climate deal.[36] As president of the conference, the French foreign minister Laurent Fabius took obvious pleasure in being able to strike his gavel and declare the Paris agreement adopted. He then was able to bask in the warmth of applause from the hundreds of delegates in the conference hall, usually restrained civil servants and officials hugging in recognition of how far they had come.

Controversies about climate change aside, there appears to now be a consensus across the globe that there is a need to reduce emissions if there is any chance of limiting the increase in global warming to less than two degrees, with the hope that it can be constrained at one and a half. However, the Paris agreement is about voluntary contributions from all the countries involved, and does not become legally binding until fifty-five countries, accounting for 55 percent of global emissions, sign the agreement. As Kumi Naidoo, the former executive director of Greenpeace International, commented after the events in December, "The Paris

Agreement is only one step on a long road, and there are parts of it that frustrate and disappoint me, but it is progress."[37]

The agreement was deposited at the United Nations in New York and opened for signatures on 22 April 2016. The fresh-faced new leader of Canada, Justin Trudeau, the rather more craggy-faced President Hollande of France and U.S. Secretary of State John Kerry with his granddaughter were among 175 who signed the agreement on the first day possible. As UN Secretary General Ban Ki Moon said at the press conference afterwards, "This is by far the largest number of countries ever to sign an international agreement on a single day."[38] While signing is not ratifying, surely this is a sign of the movement toward the reality of a global agreement on reducing emissions.

As countries commit to harder, binding targets for emissions reductions, the ideas of reuse, remanufacturing, circularity and zero waste will all gain more currency and increase the uptake of these ideas across industry. It does not seem feasible for manufacturing to ignore these trends and to remain a globally organized activity. Will we be able to create industrial ecologies that feed into and from one another across sectors and products? Can we make the majority of products closed loop and zero waste? Possibly not, but as we move in that direction it looks as if our factories will be moving closer to us.

THE ENVIRONMENTAL IMPACTS of making our products go beyond the moment of making and the consumption of materials. There is an environmental price to pay for moving so many pieces around the world multiple times to deliver you a phone or a bike. It may not sound like a lot when you say that shipping is responsible for about 3 percent of total global emissions, but when you know that's a billion tons of CO_2 every year then you take some notice.[39] This is roughly the same as the total emissions for Germany.[40] The costs of shipping are not just felt by companies and the consumers who buy their products, they are felt in the effects of the emissions from the ships, trains, cars and planes that are linked together to get our products from where they are made to where we buy and consume them.

It is interesting to note that there is a very broad range of future scenarios for the growth of maritime transport emissions, reflecting the

uncertainty on growth in different parts of the world and how each region will relate to others in terms of trade. Estimates for the increase in shipping emissions range from 50 to 250 percent by 2050, or a jump to between 1,500 million tons and 2,500 million tons of CO_2. This breadth of possibility points to creeping uncertainty about global growth, the pace of technology change and how companies will or will not adopt emissions-reducing kit. This at a time when every effort is being made to reduce emissions to keep the average temperature rise due to global warming below one and a half degrees.

In an attempt to really understand what is going on in terms of the emissions from ships passing through their ports, the European Union adopted a monitoring, reporting and verification plan in April 2015. Without clear and reliable data it is hard to know what ship types to target, or under what conditions emissions increase. So this regulation states that all large ships "monitor and annually report the verified amount of CO_2 emitted on journeys to, from and between EU ports and also when in EU ports" from the start of 2018.[41] Whether this kind of monitoring, which is not continuous, will have the desired effect of a reduction in maritime emissions of 2 percent by 2030 is not clear.

What is the simplest way to lower emissions from ships loaded with containers plowing across the Atlantic or the Pacific? Make them go slower. Making ships sail more slowly is estimated to reduce emissions by almost a fifth, a far greater impact than any other potential method studied.[42] The phrase now used is speed management, implying a more constant speed to achieve reductions. What that means is a stretching of the time it takes to get the containers and their goods from one port to another. As we discussed earlier, time is one of the things that companies have less and less of. So even if the costs of a carbon tax or other restrictions don't tip the balance in terms of distance, time may be the factor that does.

TO ACHIEVE A CIRCULAR ECONOMY of any description requires action from individuals, companies and governments. The concept is relatively new for policymakers, but there have been many position statements as well as some action over the past couple of years as governments try to understand the issue.

At the end of 2015 the European Union announced a new action plan entitled "Closing the Loop."[43] Their response is arranged along four axes—production, consumption, waste management and the market for secondary raw materials, as well as having some sector-specific elements. Many of the actions are to do with information and standards, seen as critical bottlenecks for companies and industries to be able to operate in a circular manner. For a strategy that hasn't had a lot of media play there is significant money behind it—€650 million from the research budget and €5.5 billion from structural funds.

For China, resource intensity—how much material is used to produce a given amount of wealth—has become a serious strategic issue for the country's development. It takes China roughly five times as much material to produce a dollar of GDP compared to the OECD average (2.5kg to 0.54kg).[44] This level of material use creates a dependence on imported fuel and minerals, which more and more come from less stable parts of the world. Without closing the loops in production China faces a problem of security of supply and an environmental challenge to reuse or safely dispose of the waste from its production processes.

It is not a surprise that China is now racing to solve the implementation problems of the circular economy. It has one great advantage over Western economies as it attempts to move this agenda forward—concentration of manufacturing. The existing supply chains of U.S. and U.K. companies, which include companies in China, are generally spread in terms of both geography and control. However, in China the majority of manufacturing is located within industrial parks and export processing zones.

If governments and companies make common cause on the issue of the circular economy it should become mainstream quickly. However, with significant uncertainty remaining in international markets and margins tight, it isn't something that should be taken for granted.

IS A CIRCULAR PROCESS necessarily one that has manufacturing located closer to the consumer? That is not clear as there are too few case studies to draw firm conclusions and the questions asked of the circular economy concept so far are based on material flows rather than location of the parts of the interlocking supply chains and the associated coordination costs that come with the complexity.

While transport cost uncertainties hamper forward planning and potentially harm the ability of companies to price effectively, the fact that we've moved to containers for shipping has some unintended consequences. The asymmetry of trade flows means that there are empty containers chugging their way back across the world's oceans—many of them to Asian ports—for their next run. These containers are a valuable opportunity if there are circular flows that can use their capacity to close a loop.

A good example is the use of recycled rather than virgin materials to make paper board. In 2014 the cost of a ton of virgin material (referred to as kraftliner) was $1,000 compared to $577 for a ton of recycled materials (referred to as testliner). And so, even including transport costs (at the time estimated at $64 per ton), recycled materials become attractive as inputs, which may explain why there were 30 million tons of recovered paper and cardboard shipped to China in 2012, up from 17 million tons in 2005.[45]

If this kind of model can be replicated, as long as shipping costs are a small percentage of the final cost of a product, the geography of circular supply chains will be complicated. But there is a danger that the short-term evolution of supply chains, even if they are broadly aligned with the concepts of circularity, will be a misstep. Into the longer term, constraints due to shipping costs and shifts in demand profiles as the emerging middle class in Asia flexes its purchasing muscles, will mean current patterns are misaligned. These next steps in the structuring of supply chains need to be analyzed with potential regionalization and localization in mind.

CHAPTERS 3 TO 6 have discussed the changes that are occurring across manufacturing, from new ways of making, through the introduction of robots and automation, the problems of getting things from A to B and the environmental pressures that companies face. Taken together, these pressures make the decision on where to make more likely to be local rather than global. This is not a green agenda or a labor agenda, this is the economic context changing and providing companies with a solution that is more local than global, that is deglobalizing rather than hyper-globalizing.

But are we seeing any signs of this happening yet? Are there some

first movers, companies getting ahead of the curve, or is all still an abstract possibility? The next chapter tries to pick out the weak signals of change, starting with the rise of the reshoring movement to show that these arguments are more than just words. They are the new reality for companies.

7

Looking Through the Other End of the Telescope

EARLY, USUALLY WEAK, SIGNALS of change are both hard to find and hard to interpret. Astronomers have known this for a long time in their search for new planets or in their efforts to better understand the structure of the universe. One of the most famous finds was Jocelyn Bell tripping across pulsars—pulsating radio stars which give out a regular, strong signal—in a field in Cambridge in the late sixties. She almost dismissed the signals as they were too regular, too perfect. As she said, "here was I trying to get a PhD out of a new technique, and some silly lot of little green men had to choose my aerial and my frequency to communicate with us."[1]

The early weak signals of the shift from global to regional and on to local, the deglobalization of the physical economy, are hard to see clearly and possibly as hard to interpret as the first signs of pulsars. There is a lot of noise in the data collected on the international economy, but there are early signs of change that have been seen in the rise of companies deciding to use suppliers from, or manufacture in, their home country rather than overseas.

There are many terms flying around for this—onshoring, reshoring, nearshoring, backshoring. Most of these are slightly misleading as they conjure up images of factories being physically torn out of the ground and shunted about. Like the old man's house in the movie *Up* with the plumbing hanging out of the bottom, the image is of these factories uprooted and placed on some giant ship landing on a beach somewhere on the coast of America or Europe in a triumphant homecoming. The reality is a complex

mix of companies changing suppliers, updating products and investing in new production facilities, as well as shutting down operations overseas either to expand or to create new capacity in their domestic market. The changes are not simply additions made in one country balanced by sub-tractions from another. There are many different things happening within and between companies at the same time, confusing the picture of where the flows of people, things and money are going.

A further problem for this discussion is that the existing international statistics are only capturing glimpses of what is happening. These statis-tics, agreed between countries and usually lagging behind the reality on the ground, are not well adapted to the rapid changes that are occurring. As the United Nations slightly sheepishly admits, "The existing measure-ment frameworks ... do not fully grasp the measurement of economic interdependencies, exposures and vulnerabilities of countries through the global value chains or through operations of multi-national enterprises."[2] In other words, take the conclusions drawn from the macro statistics with a pinch of salt.

This chapter tells the stories of some of the more counter-intuitive changes in how companies are already restructuring their activities around the world and looks at some of the headline statistics. These stories are only the leading edge, the early signals, of the wave of restructuring of the global economy that will take place over the next decades.

COMPANIES DON'T TEND TO LAST for very long. Roughly one in ten of them in the industrialized West die every year and the average lifespan of a company from the S&P 500 index has fallen from over sixty years at the time of the Great Depression to around fifteen years now. So for a company still to be going 122 years after its foundation is testament to a deeply embedded strategic skill and an awful lot of luck along the way. That the founding father of the company I am referring to was Thomas Edison, the inventor of the lightbulb, may have something to do with it. General Electric (GE) was formed in 1892 through a merger between Edison's various electrical endeavors and another electrical company, Thomas-Houston, based in Schenectady, New York. The company is one of the original twelve that formed the Dow Jones Industrial Average and the only one to remain on the index in its original form to this day.

While the long history of GE has many twists and turns, one of its recent moves highlights how the context for global production is changing rapidly, along with the understanding and intention of many executives.

Jeff Immelt became the CEO of GE in September 2001, four days before the attack on the World Trade Center—a moment that for many marks the turning point from comfortable optimism to doubt about the stability of the future of the West. Toward the end of 2013, he and GE held a party at Appliance Park in Louisville, Kentucky, to mark its sixty years of operations at the site. So why hold a party for a site that might well be on the path to full closure in many people's eyes? Why hold a wake where manufacturing had been and left?

At its peak in the 1950s there were 23,000 people working at Appliance Park, turning out washing machines and the like, in a facility so large that it has its own zip code. By 2011 the once enormous plant was almost a ghost town, with under 2,000 workers, the typical story of deindustrialization and offshoring for American manufacturing. GE had tried to sell the whole thing off toward the end of 2011. It failed. No one wanted to take on such a large site in such a high-cost economy.

Within two years, Immelt went from trying to sell off Appliance Park to refurbishing two lines and building a new production line. Part of this change of tack came from the realization that appliances that were being made in extremely high volumes in China could be made in the U.S. at the same cost or even more cheaply. The first product to be reshored was a water heater, which was redesigned and improved significantly, resulting in both reduced costs and improved performance. Incredibly, the design team at GE managed to make a better heater for 20 percent less than the one that had previously been made in China.

The assumed logic of outsourcing was being turned on its head. GE had decided by the time of the party to invest the thick end of $1 billion into the site and U.S.-based manufacturing generally. Maybe the party was the start of something rather than the end?

MANY SECTORS, COMPANIES and industrial processes effectively disappeared from Western economies over the past twenty years as the great wave of offshoring took place. Things that were mass produced and labor

intensive were the most likely to be taken away from the more expensive labor markets of Europe and America and replanted in the emerging industrial cities of China and other low-cost economies.

While the fragmenting of production process led to global value chains, the epithet "Made in . . ." became less and less meaningful, except in China. The imprint of "Made in China" that you could run your finger over on the back of toys, clothes and shoes became almost ubiquitous. The age of plastic in every corner of the house for those with small kids and large toy cupboards was born.

But as the context is changing yet again so companies, even in these types of high-volume sectors, are revisiting their decisions from the 1990s to take their production out of their home country. Spain has a thriving footwear industry which made 95 million pairs of shoes in 2010.[3] Half of those shoes are made for export. But having sent most of the production overseas, since the mid-2000s there has been a steady increase in domestic production and a dampening of offshored production.

Interviews with fourteen shoe manufacturers in Alicante, where the shoe sector is focused, show interesting patterns of offshoring and reshoring.[4] Four of the companies never offshored, holding on to their production at home to maintain quality levels, believing the quality levels they required would not be achievable in a low-wage environment. The other ten companies were part of the wave of restructuring that took shoe production to Southeast Asia through the 1990s, while retaining design and other non-production activities in Spain. Depending on whether the companies were making dress shoes or sports shoes, were high-end or mid-market, the strategy of offshoring took anything from 20 percent to 100 percent of production out of the country.

What is most interesting for us is that, barring mid-range sport shoes, all the companies have reduced their offshored production and in many cases eliminated it altogether over the past ten years. The lower the volume each company produced, the higher the probability that they would relocate all their production back to their home market.

This is not the story that is usually told about globalization for a product like footwear. These industries were supposed to have gone forever, consigned to the history of developed economies and subsumed into the growth of emerging countries. But is this just a phenomenon for

the weaker countries attached to the European Union like Spain or can it happen in higher-cost economies as well?

At the end of 2015 Adidas unveiled what they called the Speedfactory in Ansbach, southern Germany.[5] Shoes usually made by hand in Asia would now be made by robots in one of the highest-cost economies in the world. The rationale for Adidas is based on time to market, but you have to assume that the economics work as well. From an initial run of 500, the factory is going to scale up to produce 500,000 pairs each year. Plans for the company reportedly include opening Speedfactories of similar capacity in the United States and the United Kingdom.[6] The company claims that the focus for them is not reducing the number of workers but increasing the speed of production. Details on how many people work at the Speedfactory are hard to come by, but there were 160 positions created with their partner, Oechsler Motion GmbH, who helped to build and now run the factory.

Given that Adidas makes over 300 million pairs of shoes each year, this is a small slice of their output. However, it is a great example of how the decision on the location of manufacturing is not binary—it is not whether you make at home or abroad. Companies will be making in all their main locations, scaling the production to the market it serves on a regional if not local basis. The question for Adidas is how far to take this change and how quickly, not whether to engage with automation and the changing context of the world economy. Will other companies and, more importantly, other sectors see the value in making in high-cost locations?

THE HANDSETS, TABLETS and controllers we've all become addicted to are some of the most iconic globalized products, produced en masse in Asia. Anything with silicon in it, memory chips and the like, is assumed by most people to be made in the East, where companies like TSMC (Taiwan Semiconductor Manufacturing Company) have flourished. Founded in 1987, in 2015, TSMC produced over 9 million twelve-inch-equivalent wafers (from each of which thousands of chips are cut as the basic building block of consumer electronics) and in the process earned itself $26.61 billion in sales revenue.[7] It is hard to fight against that kind of scale.

So when a group of engineers led by Eben Upton in Cambridge wanted to build a new low-cost computer to be used to teach programming in

schools,[8] it was not really questioned by commentators where they would be made. However, inside the team there was an attempt to find a U.K. manufacturer as the heritage of the product was rooted in past computing-for-schools efforts, specifically the BBC Micro from the 1980s. They felt themselves to be a British enterprise and wanted the computer if at all possible to be made in Britain. However, there were no suppliers that could do the manufacturing in the U.K. at the price needed, and so off to Asia the production went.

Now, the Raspberry Pi is no ordinary computer. Costing just $35 (£25 for the low-specification version in the U.K.) when it was launched in 2012, the credit-card-sized computer allowed children, schools and hackers all over the world to have a dirt-cheap computer, based on an ARM processor with decent memory and an open-source software foundation. As the saying goes, the crowd went wild. According to the BBC, the websites of the distributors of the Raspberry Pi were knocked over within a minute of opening for orders due to the volume of demand.[9] For a not-for-profit foundation with a staff of six people this was pretty amazing stuff.

In the first year of operation over a million Raspberry Pis were sold. The mixture of cost, capability and philosophy hit a nerve and people started to use the Pi to do incredible things[10]—rebuilding old arcade games, controlling Christmas lights, making talking toys and even using it as the foundation for a mobile phone. The Pi had captured the imagination of kids and hackers alike and was going from strength to strength.

The desire to have the manufacturing of this British designed and British led project in the U.K. had not gone away. Over a six-month period the team met with and developed a way forward with Sony and their factory based in Pencoed, South Wales. This factory used to make high-end displays and there was a reservoir of skills and capability that allowed the partnership to develop a high-volume line, with significant automation. Instead of coming from the other side of the planet the Pi would now have the words "Made in the U.K." next to where the power supply plugged into the board.[11] A British computer made in Britain.

Since its launch the Pi has evolved through a number of iterations, been into space with Tim Peake (rebranded as the AstroPi), and now a new version has been produced that may be as big a change as the original. The Raspberry Pi Zero is again a fully specced computer but this time

it costs just £4 ($5). Suddenly there is a computer that costs as little as a fancy coffee.[12] It is still made in South Wales. By early 2015, 5 million units had been shipped and in September 2016 Eben Upton posted on their website that they had just made their 10 millionth Pi.[13] In under five years they have managed to make 1,000 times more units than they thought they ever would—the Raspberry Pi team thought they might sell around 10,000 in total. This British company has come from nowhere and has used its scale of production to learn how to save costs to the point that they can make a computer that can almost be given away. All in one of the highest-cost economies in the world.

THE CLASSIC FINNISH BIKE is a Jopo. Originally released in 1965, it was redesigned and reissued in the early 2000s and remains the most popular bike in Finland. The best description of this glorious piece of design is that it's a chopper with serious style.[14] The maker of the Jopo, Helkama Velox, has been making bikes in Finland since 1953 and remains a relatively small company with fifty-eight employees and a turnover of around €15 million.[15] Through the early 2000s the company was facing stiffer competition as other Finnish bike manufacturers decided to relocate their manufacturing out of Finland to lower-cost locations. Up to 2007 all the Helkama bikes were made in their factory in Hanko but that was about to change.

In late 2008 the management of the company decided to outsource all the production of the fabled Jopo to Taiwan. Even though the relaunch of the Jopo in 2002 had been successful, with average sales growth year to year of over 40 percent, the profitability just wasn't there. The hope was that the company could access lower overall production costs in Taiwan and retain the growth path that they were on with the Jopo.

When making the decision the company compared the costs of production in their Finnish factory to the total landed cost of producing and shipping from Taiwan. In 2008 it appeared to be a simple decision, with the offshored and outsourced production and delivery coming in 32 percent cheaper.

Having made the decision and sent the bike away, the world began to change around them. Exchange-rate volatility after the financial crisis made it almost impossible to hedge currency fluctuations and this was important as they were buying in U.S. dollars. As well as these external

factors the management of the contract manufacturers in Taiwan was more difficult than they had expected. The quality standards Helkama demanded were higher than the Asians were used to and some of the production techniques were new to them as well. This meant that instead of costs continuing to fall after they had taken the decision to outsource, Helkama faced cost increases from its contract manufacturer of 10 percent in 2009 and 15 percent in 2010. That one-third difference in costs was disappearing into the air.

Between 2008 and 2010 the Helkama management had reduced their staff and taken the opportunity to improve their production processes at the same time. This meant that when they ran the numbers again in 2010 the difference in production cost between Finland and Taiwan had completely shifted in the home country's favor. Now it was 4 percent cheaper to make in-house. The Jopo was coming home.

Was this a set of bad decisions on the part of Helkama? Did they make a mistake in offshoring, given that they had to repatriate their production so quickly? Overall this has ended well for the company, as they have reduced their costs, reduced their time to market and, using new methods in Finland, been able to increase their product offerings (though whether it has been good for their workers is a different question). Key to the changes that occurred were volatility in international currency markets and an overoptimistic view of the costs they would face with their contract manufacturer. It could have ended badly, but this is one case where the pain of taking production out and then transplanting it back was worth it.

THE PROBLEM WITH THINKING about manufacturing location as a win/lose, as companies either coming back or leaving, is that it ignores where the output of those factories is destined to be sold. In a deglobalized version of the world, products are made as close to the end market as possible. So American companies will not be setting up manufacturing in China because of offshoring opportunities and low labor costs—it will simply be the most cost-effective way to service the Chinese market. Again, this is about owning assets in or near to the markets you serve as a company, rather than chasing a global solution.

The U.S. is seeing companies such as GE, Caterpillar and Mars as well as brands like Kangol returning from overseas. Aside from these headline

companies, how many others have changed the balance of their production structure to lean toward their home markets? Over the past four years Hal Sirkin and his team at the Boston Consulting Group have been surveying American companies with large turnover (over $1 billion in revenue) to understand their intentions around manufacturing.[16] In their latest survey toward the end of 2015, 17 percent of the companies surveyed are actively reshoring, meaning that they are currently changing production location from outside the United States to within it. The percentage of companies admitting to actively reshoring has more than doubled between 2012 and 2015. At the same time, the executives surveyed now favor the United States as the most likely place to expand production to serve home demand, ahead of China (31 percent vs 20 percent). This is a reversal of the position from 2012 when China was favored over the U.S. by 30 percent to 26 percent.

The reasons that the companies give for these changes reinforce how much the landscape has changed for these location decisions. The reason to reshore most often cited is the need to shorten supply chains and reduce shipping costs. Of all the companies surveyed, 71 percent believe that advanced manufacturing processes will improve the economics of localized production. If their expectations are met, this would mean more companies coming closer and closer to the United States to service the needs of American customers.

What about in other countries? The latest data from Finland indicates that there is reshoring happening, but that the outflow still outpaces the returns. In a survey of 229 companies, 30 percent said that they had taken production out of Finland in the past five years, whereas 13 percent indicated that they had moved production back home in the same period.[17] Interestingly, given the Jopo story, the survey used the phrase "permanently," asking if the moves were permanent. This may have affected the responses, highlighting again how difficult it is to get reliable and comparable data in this area.

A group of Italian universities have been trying to collect data on the levels of reshoring across the world, looking at the types of companies involved and which countries they are moving production back from. Of the 501 examples within their database, the majority (295, from a broad range of countries) were moving production away from China.

The trend over the past five years in the United Kingdom also points to an increase in reshoring. One of the leading trade associations for manufacturing is the Engineering Employers Federation (EEF), and they have been asking their many thousands of members repeatedly about where they have their production and where their suppliers are located. The EEF have a clear response to the direct question on whether U.K. companies are reshoring or not. "The short answer is yes."[18] In the three years up to and including 2014 one in six of the companies they surveyed had moved production back to the U.K. from a low-cost economy, or had changed suppliers from one based abroad to one based in the U.K.

This move to have companies reshore or expand domestic production isn't just an American or a Western story. Early in 2014 the government of South Korea passed what is referred to as the "U-Turn" law to give significant support to Korean companies to move their manufacturing from China to South Korea. This is a continuation of a trend in which more and more Korean companies are leaving China, seeing opportunities as Chinese wages increase. In the past they may have tried accessing lower costs in India and Vietnam, but now companies are coming back to their homes in Korea. Manufacturing has been a core element of the South Korean economy for many years and now it represents just under a third of total GDP.

What of the great exceptional economy of the United States, the so-called bastion of free trade and openness? Are American companies coming home? According to the Reshoring Initiative, between the start of 2010 and the end of 2015 over 1,300 companies either brought production back to the United States or chose to source from a supplier at home over moving overseas.[19] The claim is that there is a balance between companies moving production overseas and those coming back to the United States, so that we currently have some version of a status quo.

THE PROCESS OF CHANGING the geographic focus for a company's manufacturing is not an easy one. When companies began moving en masse to China and the rest of Asia, some struggled to manage both the transition abroad and the running of factories and relationships at a distance. It should be obvious that the reverse process, bringing production back inside a company and reorganizing to be within its home market, also

has risks. Willy Shih at Harvard Business School, a leading researcher on the problems of reshoring and offshoring, looked at a number of attempts to reshore and saw many common errors and issues.[20]

The first problem is finding the workers who can operate the factories. Even with significant levels of automation large factories need workers. GE's Appliance Park operation had a target of hiring 2,500 people for its facility and it started in April 2012 with 10,000 applicants. So far, so good. Just over 6,000 passed the initial screening and of these 730 were hired. Not a bad start—except that 228 were fired in their first year, a turnover rate of 23 percent.

This pattern was repeated for Google when they attempted to make the Moto X smartphone with Flextronics in Fort Worth, Texas. Even though they used six recruitment agencies, screened people at the front of the application stage and provided training before sending people to the line, the hires just didn't stick. In order to have 2,500 actual employees they had to hire 6,500 people, given the churn they saw after hiring and training new starters.

Beyond hiring and retaining operators for the lines, there is the larger problem of a generational gap in many skills associated with manufacturing. When the wave of offshoring through the 1980s and 1990s was in full flow, there was no incentive for workers to train in welding or in how to operate complicated machine tools. In setting up the facility in Fort Worth, the lack of trained engineers in the U.S. meant they had to call on automation engineers from a sister plant in Mexico.

Companies fragmented their production as part of the process which enabled them to offshore, and in doing so they induced a move of suppliers to be close to their dominant production location. Now there is a problem of a lack of suppliers capable of serving new production in countries such as the U.S. and the U.K. The weakening of the industrial commons, the resources that companies depend upon across the economy, has been significant and may be the greatest impediment to countries like the United States benefiting from deglobalization. Without a revitalization of the commons, countries will be regionally disadvantaged and will not be easy places for companies to invest in and successfully manufacture.

. . .

OTHER BIG-NAME COMPANIES are slowly, in some cases quietly, starting to make their products in the U.S. again, too. Apple closed what was thought to be the last of its American manufacturing bases in 2004, thereby making the etching on the back of iPods absolutely true— Designed in California, Made in China. Again the received wisdom seemed to be holding true: everything bar the design moving east. Fast forward to 2013 and Apple was opening its second manufacturing facility in the U.S., creating 2,000 jobs to manufacture the sapphire crystals that are used in the fingerprint scanner of the iPhone 5S and potentially on screens for their many products.

Even the contract manufacturers that Apple and others depend on are having a change of heart. Foxconn is, unfortunately, well known for the conditions that its workers face in some of its factories in China. However, over the past year, as labor costs there have risen quickly, the company has invested significantly in automation. This started in 2011, when CEO Terry Gou claimed that Foxconn would buy a million robots to take over routine production tasks. Then stories appeared that the company was looking for sites to manufacture in the U.S. Now it has a facility in Pennsylvania and is in talks to open more production facilities in a number of other U.S. states.

So much ink has been spilled on the moves away from countries like the U.S. What about Chinese companies who are investing and creating factories in the United States? Foxconn is not the only one. The trend for Chinese companies to own assets in the U.S. is not discussed much in the popular press, but there has been a rising trend of investment since 2000. In 2015 the level of Chinese acquisitions, new operations and expansions reached a new record of $15 billion.[21] Chinese-affiliated companies in the U.S. now number close to 2,000, employing 90,000 U.S. workers. This is part of a pattern where Chinese outward foreign direct investment is shifting from developing economies to developed economies.

One example is BYD Auto, where the BYD stands for Build Your Dream.[22] BYD started life in Shenzhen in 1995 as a battery maker servicing the companies making mobile phones and other portable devices that wanted a rechargeable battery as their source of power. As mobile phone making and final assembly concentrated in China, BYD, with its focus on lithium-ion batteries, was able to position itself as a key supplier to companies like Motorola. BYD listed on the Hong Kong stock exchange

in 2002, by which time it had become the leading Chinese manufacturer of rechargeable batteries.

At this point the founder of BYD, Wang Chuanfu, began the next phase of his strategy—to turn the company into a maker of electric vehicles. Buying an ailing existing car maker (Shaanxi Qinchuan Auto Company) allowed BYD to quickly enter the passenger vehicle market, focusing on building a car around its existing expertise in battery technology. In 2005, after one false start, BYD launched its first car to the market, the F3, priced at just over $10,000. Five years later BYD had become one of the top three domestic car manufacturers and the F3 was its best-selling model. Riding the wave of political interest in electric vehicles, BYD decided to expand into making buses, selling 200 to its hometown of Shenzhen in 2011. And this is where the story connects back to us—now it was in a position to move into the American market.

While they initially intended to make passenger cars, BYD ended up making buses and selling these to local municipalities in California. It broke ground in Los Angeles on its American headquarters in 2011, and to solve the problem of Buy America provisions, opened two production plants in Lancaster, California, in 2013. This made BYD the first Chinese car maker to actually make in the United States.

This story reverses the motto inscribed on the back of iPods from their early days, instead of "Designed in California, Made in China" we now have "Designed in China, Made in California."

WHAT IS HAPPENING at the global level? According to the latest *World Investment Report* from the United Nations Conference on Trade and Development (UNCTAD), global FDI has been suppressed since the financial crisis in 2008 but has risen to near the peak again, sitting at $1,762 billion in 2015.[23] If global economic conditions continue to stabilize the total flows of FDI should surpass the previous highs by 2017.

In 2015, announced greenfield investment around the world totaled $766 billion, which was an 8 percent rise over the previous year overall. However, the increase was greater in developed economies, jumping by 12 percent, again hinting at a focus on countries like the U.K. and the United States especially as total FDI flows to developed economies nearly doubled between 2014 and 2015. Looking just at the United States this

shift is even more pronounced as incoming FDI flows leapt 250 percent in this one year, albeit from a low base. This reverses a five-year pattern in the dominance of developing economies as the major recipients of FDI flows. This cannot yet be described as a trend, as it is just one year, but it may be hinting at changes under the surface.

The flip side of who is receiving FDI is that someone else must be spending their money. The top three countries sending investment overseas are the United States, Japan and China in that order. Overall emerging and developing economies saw falls in how much they were investing overseas, except for China, which saw a modest increase from $123 billion to $128 billion.

Sometimes the statistics let you down. The United States Bureau of Economic Analysis (BEA) used to collect data on how much foreign direct investors were spending in the country on acquisitions and the establishment of new facilities. The data was really interesting, showing a climb from around $50 billion in the mid-1990s to a peak at the dot com bust of around $330 billion. That led to a collapse back to the levels of the 1990s but was on the rise again, climbing to over $250 billion just before the global financial collapse.

Frustratingly, at that point the data collection was stopped. A gap of five years has been created as the data is now being collected again. So making inferences on the scale and impact of foreign direct investment specifically for expansion of manufacturing is slightly difficult at the moment from the BEA figures. The figures available for 2014 show $241 billion of FDI for the specific purposes of acquisition, establishment or expansion across all sectors.[24]

While the vast majority of this investment (about 93 percent) is for acquisitions, there is a tidy sum of $16.6 billion for greenfield investments in 2014. Buried in the news release for this data there is a very interesting comment on the greenfield investment numbers—"Including expenditures from other years, the largest source countries for greenfield expenditures were China and Japan."[25] This is only one year, but it is pointing toward Asia as the largest source of investment for the establishment of new company facilities in the U.S. based on foreign money.

What is driving some of these changes? Unsurprisingly, the managers of transnational companies believe that general economic conditions,

including the state of the U.S. economy and new trade agreements, will probably increase the level of global FDI.[26] More interesting for this story is that they also believe technological change will increase investment flows and two-thirds of the companies surveyed are looking to internationalize their operations. The early signals for a shift in how companies are organizing themselves seem to be there. Whether they will hold up against the uncertainties in the global economy is another issue altogether.

WHAT ARE THE QUALIFICATIONS that need to be added to this story? First, reshoring and the decisions around where things are made affect more than one company. The continuing changes in how companies organize and manage production involve changes both to the company itself and to its supply chain—those who provide goods and services to the lead company. So when we ask whether a company will reshore or bring its production closer to where the customer is, the question also implies whether it will shorten its supply chain, either using new suppliers in the region or forcing existing suppliers to move with them.

Second, this is not an either/or debate. Companies do not need to shut all their operations overseas and re-create that capacity in their home market to be successful or to qualify as reshorers. In fact a key message is that companies will keep facilities in China or Mexico if they already exist there to serve the Asian and North American markets, respectively. The companies who will see the greatest changes will be those who offshored all or close to all their production and now will need to bring production close to their home market to be able to be competitive in that market.

Finally, the footprint of production into the future is not a zero-sum game. There is not a fixed amount of production, a fixed level of output that is going to be divvied up between the countries and regions of the world. We keep making more and more things at the global level, with manufacturing value added growing at an average rate of over 6 percent per year since 1970 (although current post-crisis growth rates are around 2 percent).[27] This means that many of these decisions are about new production capacity rather than existing production capacity, especially as new industries emerge around new technologies and new products (for example the products of regenerative medicine).

There is a danger that we will fall into the trap of hype, becoming

cheerleaders for reshoring without being critical of what claims are made about these movements and changes. The politics of reshoring and manufacturing in general have switched at a terrifying pace, from downright neglect in the 1990s to a championing that appears out of character for many of our public figures. The former British chancellor George Osborne's triumphalist statements on the coming "march of the makers" which would "carry Britain aloft" in his 2011 Budget speech stands out in particular.[28] This is the peak of a wave of comments on rebalancing the U.K. economy that never grounded itself in reality or detail. The vote to leave the European Union and the confusion over various forms of Brexit leave the U.K. in a weak position to move this agenda forward, even though it may be even more important if the U.K. does eventually leave the EU.

THESE EXAMPLES OF COMPANIES bringing production into the country where the customer is may not sound significant, but it is a sea change in global manufacturing—it means that many companies will swap exporting for owning. Rather than go through the hassle of managing shipping, export licenses and logistics at great distance, companies are more likely to make within the market they are selling to.

The competencies that companies need, especially in terms of management, to manage owning factories in key foreign markets are very different from those needed to manage exporting to those markets. Switching to this model will take time and investment, neither of which is being encouraged at present by governments, who are instead encouraging smaller companies to grow through exporting and are leaving the big companies to manage themselves. The concept of having production in both the home market and foreign markets so as to be close to where the demand lies has not yet reached policy level. Another point where our politics lags what is happening in boardrooms.

With production being more closely tied to the markets it serves, a number of questions are going to be asked that will be very difficult to answer. Government regulations on foreign ownership will become the new trade barrier, as without openness to foreign ownership companies will struggle to access many markets. The structure of companies' tax affairs will come into even sharper relief, as operations in one country may have restrictions on repatriation of profits from that country to the

home country of the company. The whole concept of "home country" may become even weaker and the supposed benefits of having the HQ of a multinational within your own economy may be further weakened.

These are the issues that the final chapters of this book take up, moving from describing why industrial organization is going through an inflection point to what that means for trade, politics and the state of the global economy. So what will the global pattern of trade look like in ten, twenty and fifty years?

8

Mapping the Fracture Between the Physical and the Digital

PREDICTIONS, WHETHER ABOUT THE ECONOMY, technology, or anything else at the world or at the national level, should always come with a health warning (although they never do). The most famous errors in prediction have become the stuff of internet memes and motivational posters. From Thomas Watson in his role as president of IBM in 1943 saying, "I think there is a world market for maybe five computers" to pretty much every single political analyst saying that it was impossible for Donald Trump to become the presidential nominee for the Republican Party in 2016, let alone win the election, our history and our present are littered with very specific predictions that have been spectacularly wrong.

Why is this particularly a problem when it comes to the global economy? Simply put, there is a level of complexity which defeats us when we try to simplify and predict. Just how complex is this thing we call the economy?

Cesar Hidalgo and his colleagues at Harvard have been investigating how to measure economic complexity in the global economy for many years. They have created beautiful network maps and images of how interconnected different countries and products are, based on the available trade data. One look at their maps should leave you in no doubt as to the complex interrelationship between countries and the diversity of capabilities in

countries around the world to produce different products.[1] Key to their approach is to look at the complexity of products that are exported by a country, sophisticated chemicals and machinery, for example, considered to be more complex, while raw materials and simple agricultural products are less so. They combine the diversity of what is exported with how ubiquitous these products are to give an overall economic complexity score (referred to as the ECI or Economic Complexity Indicator).

Rankings for over 120 countries from 1995 to 2014 are provided, and it is interesting to see how different countries rise and fall, as there is a strong link between economic complexity measured in this way and the income level of a country. Top of the rankings across the whole of the period is Japan, consistently being ranked first for economic complexity, followed by either Germany or Switzerland, one home to significant and dense manufacturing industries, the other a locus for the pharmaceutical industry.

Given the focus on product complexity in exports as the measure of economic complexity, how leading economies' rankings have changed may be an indicator of whether their manufacturing base has remained at the frontier of what is possible or if it has fallen behind. So Japan has consistently remained at the frontier of what is possible in manufacturing, while the United States over the twenty years from 1995 onward appears to have fallen off slightly, going from seventh in 1995 to fourteenth in 2014.

The work of Hidalgo's team has provided a way to compare the complexity of countries based on the composition of their exports. As we move into a period where trade is not expanding as quickly as GDP, the measure may lose its validity as the complexity of the economy may become more internalized. How else might we think about the complexity we face?

Another measure of the complexity of the modern economy is how many different kinds of goods and services we can buy. This number was recently estimated by Eric Beinhocker to be on the order of 10^{10} (yes that's 10 billion) unique things we can spend our money on.[2] That's a lot of things being made in thousands of factories all around the world. It may not be a good thing in terms of sustainability that there are more and more products vying for our attention and our cash, but it appears the trajectory has been one of increase. Again according to Beinhocker, there were only

100 or 1,000 products in the market when we were at the earliest periods of development. Since the Industrial Revolution things have really taken off in terms of global wealth and the available number of products has risen sharply year on year.

The world is connected through products, but it is also connected through money. The nonlinear nature of the economy, or at the very least the hidden interconnections between the different parts of the economy, were painfully brought to light with the financial crash of 2008. The boxing up of subprime mortgages and the relabeling of their risk profiles meant that those at one remove and more from the financial services industry missed how risky home buyers in the United States were now linked to pretty much everyone else through the selling of these so called collateralized debt obligations (CDOs).[3] This meant financial problems were exported around the world more quickly than governments could react to contain the crisis.[4]

Notwithstanding all this complexity in terms of both the pure number of things we can buy and the interlinkages between parts of the economy, the future trends outlined in the previous chapters taken together imply a very different pattern of world trade from today's, with strong changes in trade balances and a fundamental restructuring of the relationships between the major economies of the world. This chapter will discuss the regionalized and sometimes localized production patterns that will emerge, what this implies for the gross trade flows between key regions and countries, and what kinds of products are likely to end up in each category.

TAKING ON BOARD OUR WARNINGS on complexity, what can we say about how the trends we've discussed will affect the future of trade and the relationships between the regions and countries of the world?

At the global level we will see a lowering of the relative volume of trade compared to overall economic growth. Since the early 1970s the ratio of world trade to GDP has risen from around 30 percent to just over 60 percent in 2008.[5] As the impacts of the financial crisis have unraveled this ratio has declined, slowly at first but by over 2 percent between 2014 and 2015. The aftershock of the crisis of global capital may have brought forward what is likely to be the new norm for physical globalization with

growth in trade permanently lower than growth in world GDP. Trade will grow more slowly than the global economy, meaning it will decline in relative importance compared with the role it currently plays.

While new production technologies are not going to give us a *Star Trek* like "replicator" anytime soon, they are enabling smaller factories to be economically viable. They do this by lowering what is referred to as minimum economic scale, the lowest volume of production for which the investment in the factory is financially viable.

The simple view of production was that bigger is better: you offset large capital costs by having a factory that produces in high volume with extreme efficiency. The case for ever-increasing sizes of factory hits barriers of coordination if the factories become too large and the level required to be efficient or cost competitive has fallen as additive manufacturing and other techniques have developed and improved their performance. A key implication of techniques like additive manufacturing is that they remove the need for specialized components such as molds or forms to be made specific to the product working its way down the assembly line. As well as saving cost and time by not having to make these specialized pieces, it also means that a factory can more easily make a variety of products. Rather than thinking of the investment in a factory being tied to one product, the costs can be offset against the income generated from a series of products, hence a lower minimum economic scale for each product. With lower scale, the likelihood of having a greater number of smaller factories instead of a small number of extremely large factories goes up. And as that happens the factories are going to be geographically dispersed, lowering the number of trade movements necessary to get a product to customers in different countries.

At the same time the likelihood is that most complex products will have fewer pieces (or subassemblies) as new production technologies allow us to make pieces in one step rather than having to have multiple elements produced and brought together (remember the F-18 fighter jet—one of its subassemblies went from sixteen separate pieces to a single piece because of additive manufacturing). The journey of these pieces or elements of a product between countries in an extended supply chain are represented by the trade in intermediate goods—parts of a product or a not yet completed product making its way around the world to be finished off or assembled.

Between 2000 and 2009 the share of intermediate goods in world exports remained stable at around 50 percent (with a small dip for the financial crisis).[6] Half of what was exported was not a complete product, it was a part of a product. With fewer pieces to be made and assembled because of new production techniques, trade in intermediate goods will fall, and as that now represents close to 60 percent of global trade this will have a very significant impact on the overall volume of trade.

The second level of change is a strengthening of the regionalization of trade. The temptation is to work at the extremes—everything is global or everything is local. This misses the subtleties that are needed in industrial organization and the diversity that exists in manufacturing. Regionalization will be driven by the balance of forces between the scale required to have efficiencies and the desire to reduce time to customer and the costs of being in different countries simultaneously.

It is worth noting that even though the declining importance of distance for trade has been accepted as a stylized fact for many years, distance has always moderated trade.[7] The further away from each other two countries are, the smaller the level of trade we would expect to see between them. A recent review of over one hundred academic papers on the effect of distance on trade indicates that the average effect means that "a 10 percent increase in distance lowers bilateral trade by about 9 percent."[8] Distance continues to matter even with absolute transport costs falling and increasing digital interconnection around the world.

With smaller factories being economically viable and tooling costs falling due to increased use of techniques like additive manufacturing, companies can produce for the different regions of the world independently rather than attempting to have a global product. This enables a regional production strategy, like that employed by Coca-Cola. Some lead products, for example Coke Classic, are available everywhere but some products are only available in a few countries depending on local tastes, such as Kuat in Brazil or Qoo in Japan and China.

In a regionalized scenario a company may not have its supply chain and final assembly all in the country in which it will be selling its products. They can organize themselves and their suppliers across the region. However, in some cases that won't be the best way to be organized, for example if time is really an issue. If there cannot be a lag of, say, a week to get goods from

Mexico to the east coast of the U.S.A., then the company will need to have at least final assembly in the country of purchase, if not more of the supply chain feeding that assembly process for your product.

Our falling expectations of how long we have to wait to receive our products is partly the responsibility of Amazon and other online retailers. The promise of next-day delivery at the click of a button is, for many, too strong to resist. The introduction of Amazon Prime in 2005 allowed customers to pay $79 and have unlimited two-day delivery no matter how many things they ordered.[9] Since then, as well as adding a whole host of extras like online video streaming, the offer on products has improved with one-day and in some cases same-day delivery available. When for a flat fee you can order as many products as you like without any thought for the shipping costs, your view of how the geography of the world works will change. A recent Deloitte report asked over 4,000 U.S. consumers what they thought qualified as "fast shipping."[10] Over 90 percent agreed that anything from two days and less was fast, whereas anything over four days was considered slow by 82 percent of the survey. We are not willing to wait for our products.

At the third level within regions we are likely to see agglomeration or clustering effects. These clusters arise as there are positive effects for companies to be close to other companies in similar sectors. The idea of clusters goes back to Alfred Marshall, who used the term "industrial districts" to discuss the advantages of having concentrations of companies which included a large and skilled labor force, the sharing of knowledge and the availability of specialized machinery.[11]

Manufacturing is regionally concentrated in most countries, some areas having much higher output and employment in manufacturing than others. In the United States manufacturing is concentrated outside of cities in the Midwest and Southern states like Indiana, Ohio and Alabama.[12] Silicon Valley is a concentration of what is loosely referred to as "tech" but is in reality a concentration of venture capital and a mixture of software and hardware companies. The sprawling industrial cities of Shenzhen and Guangzhou are industrial districts on steroids, with huge manufacturing compounds the size of small cities themselves.

Countries hoping to attract manufacturing companies will be compared as a location on a regional rather than a global basis and then

within the country at a local level. Is it better for American companies to make within the United States or to use Mexico as a base to cover all of North America? For companies deciding on the United States as their location, should they be basing themselves in California or Ohio? Should companies looking to access the Chinese market be in China or placed within other Asian economies? Each company will answer this question for itself, but due to cluster effects, where companies tend to colonize an area in order to share skills, facilities and a local labor pool, within regions dominant locations will emerge.

This will play out differently across different products and industries, with most industries becoming heavily regionalized (as the automotive industry currently is, for example, with products mainly shipped within the European Union or domestically within the United States rather than moving across the globe), some becoming localized to the level of the country or subnational region.

So if an American company has an existing or potential large market in China it is likely that over time it will site its production to serve those customers in Asia. At the same time, this same company with customers to sell to in the United States will site its production to service those customers in or near the United States. The pattern of location for companies, rather than being tilted toward Asia based on labor cost and scale efficiencies, will more and more reflect the sizes of the markets they serve based on regional geographies.

TO GET A SENSE of how complicated this can be take a look at Nike's global map of its contract production structure. Most of Nike's products are made by contract manufacturers and as part of their transparency drive Nike provides a map of all their factories, currently totalling 666 locations around the world.[13] The map doesn't tell you which factory supplies which location, but it is interesting to see 170 factories listed in China with just under 212,000 workers as compared to the United States with 62 factories employing just under 7,000 workers. Even though this map blends together different products (trainers as well as clothing, for example) it is clear that this network is not highly concentrated in one country, it is spread out around the globe.

This pattern of having production close to the customer is important

to emphasize as it changes the common interpretation of offshoring and reshoring. Most discussions of offshoring and reshoring mix together completely different effects. The first is the change of location of production for an existing product, which is a true movement, in contrast to the introduction of new production capacity for a new or changed product. For domestic companies, which of the two is happening when they claim a reshoring event is hard to unpick. The second is whether, for example, a U.S. company investing in production in China is doing so to re-export the products to sell inside or outside China.

For foreign companies coming into a country, as long as the statistical agencies collect the FDI data well (as the Bureau of Economic Analysis in the United States has this past year begun to do), we should be able to see what is new and what is an expansion. So, as we speak of realignments and changes of strategy for companies we should take care not just to lump all these changes together as reshoring or offshoring.

To get a sense of the scale of the change that is coming we need a scaling factor to translate the current levels of trade in physical goods into this future context. It is not possible to predict accurately what the level of trade will be ten years from now, but we can estimate the magnitude of the change to understand how significant their impacts will be.

One possible way to do this is to use existing research on the possible levels of automation of work across the economy. Frey and Osborne's study of the potential for automation of work has a headline figure that about 47 percent of U.S. employment is at risk of being taken on by computers and robots.[14] However, that is across the whole economy. What about the kinds of jobs that are directly related to production? How likely is it that they will be automated?

Their scale to measure the likelihood of automation (or, as they say, computerization) runs from 0 (not computerizable) to 1 (computerizable) as a relative probability that each job category could be taken over by the machines. The labels for the job categories feel anachronistic, with clunky groupings that feel more representative of the 1960s and 1970s than the present, a reflection of how out of date our statistical categories have become. Scanning the list, though, we see various machine operators and technicians are rated at 0.97 and welders come in at 0.94. Cargo and freight handlers are right up there at 0.99. Job after job that is related to

making and shipping products scores much higher than the average and generally is above 0.7. The other end of the scale is, as you might expect, filled with occupations that demand significant creativity or human interaction. Psychologists, engineers and fitness trainers all come in at less than 1 percent likelihood of automation. The chief executives of the companies about to face this complex set of trends and decisions are also at this end of the scale, apparently at 1.5 percent likelihood of being taken over by computers.

In a future with highly automated production, many cobots working with very few humans, what will be needed are highly skilled workers capable of adapting to this environment. And, as we've indicated, this will mean a convergence in the labor cost element of production, if you take the humans and the robots together. There is a broad but narrowing spectrum of hourly wages for manufacturing workers around the world (anything from around $10 per hour in Taiwan to $30 per hour in the United States),[15] whereas there is a much smaller spread of costs for industrial robots and automated systems, from Baxter at around $40,000 through to larger systems from KUKA and ABB which run toward the $100,000 mark. But, as wages continue to increase, the price of robots is falling and their productivity is increasing. For example, a spot-welding robot for use in the automotive industry has increased its performance at 5 percent a year since 2005 and fallen in installed price from $182,000 to $133,000 over the same period.[16]

The gearing, or multiplier, we should take from this, however, is not simply a direct pass through. It is not the case that if 70 percent of the jobs associated with production can be automated then we'll see a 70 percent drop in trade. As labor content and labor cost become less and less important within the total cost of production then the decision on where to place each factory will be based less and less on the availability of low-cost labor. The scale of the regional and local market will increasingly determine the scale of production placed into that region.

Bringing the effects of automation and reduction in parts together, it is likely that we will see anything from a 20 percent to a 30 percent fall in global merchandise trade (services are not affected in the same way) over the coming decade. That is an assumption, looking across the varied manufacturing sectors and the rate at which new robots are being purchased

and installed. It is by no means a precision estimate built from the ground up, but it is a reasonable assumption, given the scale of the trends we have been discussing. Based on current trade patterns, what does that imply? For 2014 world GDP was $78 trillion and merchandise exports were $19 trillion.[17] At the lower end of the impact on trade our estimate would imply a reduction or shift in trade activity of about $4 trillion. This would mean merchandise exports as a percentage of world GDP would fall by a fifth, from around 25 percent to 20 percent—a very significant reversal of physical globalization.

IF THESE CHANGES are going to increase the level of regional trade at the expense of global trade it is worth asking where we are starting from— how regionalized is trade now?

The simplest way to measure this is to look at how much of the exports in a region end up as imports in another country within the same region. Taking the regions as defined by the World Trade Organization (WTO),[18] and looking at their yearly review of international trade statistics, one can see how each region's internal trade as a share of its total trade changes over time.[19]

Some patterns emerge (Figure 1). For the big three—Asia, Europe and North America—the level of internal trade is roughly 50 percent or higher as of 2014. This means that at least half of the exports of the countries in these regions are destined to be imports in other countries within the same region. While Europe's position has not changed significantly in nearly fifteen years, Asia has slightly increased the share of trade that is internally focused (up 3 percent) and North America has jumped from 40 percent in 2000 to 50 percent in 2014. This change for North America could be an early sign of the shifts we have been discussing, although the change is not gradual over the years so we should be careful not to over-interpret.

The other regions of the world all have less than a third of their trade landing again within the same region, highlighting how some regions have stronger dependencies on the big three as a target for exports. Southern and Central America has increased its level of internal trade by 8 percent over the past fifteen years and is now seeing a quarter of its trade circulating within the region. Interestingly, there has been a significant shift for Africa as well: in 2000 it had only 7 percent of its trade focused within the region;

Figure 1: Pattern of regional trade, 2000 to 2014

now it is up to 18 percent. The only region to see a decline in the regional focus of trade is the Commonwealth of Independent States (CIS), what was the former Soviet Union and is now Russia plus the Baltic States.

This existing pattern of regionalization of trade which has been a reality for many years is going to deepen. For Asia, Europe and North America, the dominant regions in terms of manufacturing output, spending on R&D and foreign direct investment, the majority of trade happens intra-regionally. This is our starting point, a trading pattern that is already regionalized to some extent and is only going to become more regionalized over time.

A DEEPENING OF THE REGIONAL PATTERNS of trade means a shift of some economic power from the East to the West, a reversal of the trend that many have commented on over the past decade. The concept of an economic center of gravity should be taken with a large pinch of salt, but if it exists, it was located in Asia in the 1500s, moved west till the end of the 1950s, not quite making it to Greenland, and ever since has been heading back toward Beijing.[20]

The shift back toward the West will be because of asymmetric trade flows between the different regions of the world. The changes we are going

to see in trading volumes and destinations are not going to be felt in the same way in all regions. Those who are the largest exporters with large trade surpluses are going to be affected most significantly by an overall fall in trade. Countries whose growth is export-led, such as China, would see a hit in their future growth, whether or not the expected fall in imports that led to a like-for-like replacement in domestic production occurs. At the same time countries such as the United States would see a positive impact on growth as the fall in imports and the implied economic activity that had been reshored would more than offset the losses due to a drop in exports.

A fall in trade of similar proportions between regions would imply a narrowing of the trade deficit between North America and Asia. In 2014 exports of products, either finished or as an intermediate good (referred to as merchandise exports), from North America to Asia were $504 billion (based on soy beans, aircraft and integrated circuits), whereas the physical exports in the opposite direction (furniture, toys and footwear) were $1,065 billion.[21] If both regions see a fall in exports to the other of 20 percent the trade deficit for North America to Asia would drop from $561 billion to $449 billion, with that $112 billion of production activity potentially located in North America rather than in Asia. (Whether all that activity would end up in North America is open to question; some might land in South America.)

What if these changes occur between the two largest players directly? Given the asymmetric nature of trade balances between the U.S.A. and China, any broad reduction in exports and imports would move the trade balance significantly in favor of America. As an example, in 2013 the U.S.A. exported $2.3 billion of electrical equipment to China while importing $33.6 billion, leading to a trade deficit of $31.3 billion for these products alone. An across-the-board reduction of a fifth in terms of exports and imports would imply a revised deficit of $23.2 billion—a swing of over $8 billion in electrical equipment alone.

This is why even a change of a fifth in terms of exports and imports would make such a difference to the global economic strength of countries like the United States. The deficit based on goods traded between the United States and China in 2015 was $367 billion, so a reduction of a fifth would be a drop in the deficit of $73 billion, quite a significant shift of economic power toward the West.[22]

While the assumption of similar falls in trade for each region is simple to calculate, it is unlikely that each region will be affected in the same way. The current pattern of exporting for example from the United States to China is a mixture of finished goods for sale, intermediate goods used in making things to sell in China and in many cases the exporting of intermediate goods to be used in products that will be re-exported and sold back in the United States. If the finished products companies are exporting from the United States have some special properties, for example there is sensitive intellectual property in the integrated circuits or electronics that would be at risk if the production were outside the United States, then the decline in exports from the United States will be lower than the fall in exports from China.

Between Europe and Asia the trade differences are not as pronounced since the trade deficit for Europe with Asia is much smaller ($162 billion). Assuming the same drop of a fifth in mutual exports, this would lead to an implied increase in activity in Europe or elsewhere of $32 billion as the trade deficit narrowed and production occurred elsewhere. The difference in the scale of the trade flows opens up a question for Europe on the strength of its trade relationship to China as compared to that of North America and whether this will be an issue as the context changes.

However, it is important to stress again that this is not about declines in output, falling growth and failing economies. This is relocating the activities of companies among the regions of the world because of the changing context of making, which has knock-on effects on trade flows but in this simple version does not reduce overall output. It is a potential opportunity for new companies to take over in a market, if they are more aware of this changing context and are flexible enough to enter a market ahead of the existing players. These changes are a disruptive moment that companies may or may not see coming.

WE CAN ATTEMPT to get a handle on which products are more and less likely to be made closer to home by looking at manufacturing industries by their levels of labor content, automation, sensitivity to logistics costs and overall product value. So, for instance, food and wood products are very sensitive to logistics costs, whereas high-value electronics goods are less impacted by logistics and are only moderately impacted by labor costs.

This approach was partly used by the Boston Consulting Group when it analyzed the manufacturing parts of the U.S. economy to understand which sectors were likely to remain offshore versus those that were likely to return to the U.S. from overseas.[23] In their work they focus on the costs of logistics and labor relative to the product cost (so they do not consider automation impacts) and so build a matrix of what is in the U.S. and likely to remain, what is likely to stay offshore and what they referred to as the "tipping-point industries" that have a mixed footprint but whose presence within the United States is likely to increase.

In the first category are some of the usual suspects—food and drink and wood products (lumber and plywood, for example). These are the types of products that have very high logistics costs and low to moderate labor costs when compared to the product price and already tend to be made close to their final market.

The second category—the so-called "tipping-point industries"—include finished furniture like sofas and cars and trucks, showing how diverse the impacts are likely to be. On the boundary between this category and offshore are computers with low logistics and labor costs. This is where the BCG analysis starts to break down, since considering logistics and labor without moderating each result with the scale and the potential for automation in production leaves products like computers a little in limbo.

The last category is the industries that it is claimed are likely to remain offshore. Heading this list are textiles and footwear, with relatively low logistics costs and moderate labor costs. However, this may have changed even in the short time since the BCG analysis was completed, as the Adidas Speedfactory in Germany shows. This again demonstrates the impact of automation on the viable scale of production and the costs incurred. Automation fundamentally changes the placement of industries in the BCG matrix as it compresses the labor axis so that there is less variation between industries. Automation raises the likelihood for all industries to be open to regionalization, if not localization, because of how it changes the relative nature of the different costs incurred in making, shipping and selling a product.

So can the iconic iPhone ever be labeled "Designed in California, Made in California"? One estimate of how much more an American iPhone

would cost compared to its current price is $60 to $100 on top of the 2015 retail price of $749, an increase of between 8 and 13 percent.[24] This assumes suppliers would now be based in the United States, with no changes in production technologies and a scale disadvantage for semiconductor fabrication in the United States, given the scale of operations for companies such as Taiwan's TSMC. However, semiconductor factories (referred to as fabs) become obsolete quickly, and so a new fab on mainland America would be as easy as reinvestment abroad. Add to that increasing logistics costs as emissions regulations kick in, and the potential for improvements in automation and production technologies, and there is scope for an iPhone that is cost competitive compared to one made in China. It looks like many high-end electronics goods, the furniture that fills your house and the parts that make up your car, are in future all more likely to be made much closer to where you buy them than they are now.

IS IT POSSIBLE to have local making and what would that look like? Well, one example is the aptly named Local Autos, which started out life in Phoenix, Arizona, in 2007. They now make cars using 3D printing, producing each one as it is ordered by a customer. Their first car, the Rally Fighter, was crowdsourced from 35,000 submissions with many enthusiastic potential buyers contributing to the designs. Now they are heading into production of the LM3D Swim, printed and assembled at one of three so-called "microfactories" in Chandler, Arizona; Knoxville, Tennessee; and Berlin, Germany.[25] They have gone all electric and are betting that urban centers will be the place to be as electric cars make their mark.

The company has grown quickly with 116 employees supplemented by their online community members who now number over 50,000.[26] It continues to expand its product base and introduced in 2016 the Olli, a twelve person self-driving minibus which uses IBM's Watson as its interface to the world. The design is based on the winning entry to their 2015 Urban Mobility Challenge, reinforcing their co-creation model. Made in a new facility in National Harbor, Maryland, just outside Washington D.C., Olli uses a number of different printing technologies and like the Rally Fighter and the Swim it can be made in volumes of one rather than needing to be made in many thousands to achieve cost efficiencies. The time to make is pretty impressive as well—an Olli can be printed in

ten hours and assembled in one hour. Just in time and just in the volume that the customer needs.[27]

Localized manufacturing is happening in other sectors, usually with a little twist. Rishi Bali had been with Goldman Sachs before he started Yogasmoga, a clothing company making performance yogawear.[28] The kick-start for the company was a realization that most yogawear still used fabrics like spandex which had been invented over fifty years ago. This started a search for new fabrics and a steep learning curve for an ex-financer with no knowledge of clothing or textiles. Working with Invista, a spin-off of DuPont, Bali and his team produced thirty new options for fabrics, some of which dry extremely quickly, others that feel like soft wool but are breathable. Next he had to find somewhere to make Yogasmoga clothes.

Because they were using new fabrics it quickly became apparent that their clothes could not be made in Asia. Even to get the fibers milled into cloth they had to work with a speciality mill in California. High-tech fibers meant local manufacturing, to control the quality and to be able to work closely with the machinists. In the end Bali landed at the door of Griffin Manufacturing, based in Fall River, Massachusetts, just sixty miles south of Boston.

The journey has been a successful one for Yogasmoga to this point. In 2015 the company was valued at $74 million and it had opened its twelfth store in the United States. Not bad for an ex-Goldman employee with no prior knowledge of the clothing industry building the headquarters of an athletic clothing company in New York and making in Massachusetts.

How local could we be when making products? Amazon signaled that it was thinking that it might be able to bring the making to the customer when they filed patents for mobile 3D printing on demand early in 2015. To put it another way, Amazon wants to make en route, putting the 3D printer in the back of the delivery truck and printing your product on the way to your house.[29] When it comes to changing the trade pattern, this takes the biscuit, but is, of course, another attempt to have *Star Trek's* replicator on the cheap. While the patent generated a nice set of headlines and grabbed the attention of the techno-optimists, it doesn't look like a serious or feasible move right now.

· · ·

LARGE MULTINATIONALS WITH MANY years of experience at leading global supply chains are in the best position to take advantage of these changes. In May 2015 General Electric's CEO Jeff Immelt was speaking at the Stern School of Business in New York and he made a very large claim: "In the future sustainable growth will require a local capability inside a global footprint... We used to have one site to make locomotives; now we have multiple global sites which give us market access."[30] This is a company with a market capitalization somewhere in the region of $300 billion saying that it was taking a local approach. Now, Immelt's stated reason is the political turbulence and increase in protectionist sentiments around the world—his claim is that the localization strategy will insulate the company against protectionism as they will already be within country boundaries. That may be the headline he's provided, but I would be very surprised if his strategy team has not also concluded that the economics stack up in favor of local over global. Similarly for many other multinationals, which will have the capacity to deal with and potentially prosper in the midst of these changes, local will be chosen over global.

Smaller companies risk being shut out of international markets if they cannot manage the complexity of running multiple operations in multiple geographies. Dealing with the diverse cultural, taxation and ownership issues that can arise from being in many places will be a real stretch for many smaller companies with small staffs and a limited pool of experience to draw from. If they cannot be close to their customers this will place them in an uncompetitive position in relation to companies able to structure themselves to be close to the customer, losing out in terms of cost and time. Exporting, with its costs and delays, will always disadvantage a company vis-à-vis another in the same country if the cost structures of the companies are similar—i.e. if they have a similar level of technology and automation in their production processes.

IF WE HAVE STRONG REGIONALIZATION of production and trade the next question is whether there are going to be dominant locations within each region. Will one country emerge as the place to make for each region for different industries? Regional identities, both economic and political, have been bolstered through a succession of regional arrangements such as the North American Free Trade Agreement (NAFTA) and

the emergence of regional political unions (for example the Association of Southeast Asian Nations, or ASEAN), however successful or unsuccessful they may be perceived to have been. These frameworks should enable interregional trade and make it easier for specific locations within regions to dominate as they remove the need for bilateral trade agreements and they equalize or remove the tariff structures between signatories.

Who might be that dominant power in each region? In Europe this is a very difficult question as there is a much broader set of countries who could conceivably secure regional dominance in a given industry. The most prominent candidate is Germany, owing to its high level of manufacturing retained within the economy (23 percent of GDP in 2013, double the level in France or in the United Kingdom), as well as a complex mix of research, education and transitional institutions that allow new production technologies to be developed.[31] Germany has a strong link between academia and industry through institutions such as the Fraunhofer institutes which were founded in 1949 to carry out applied research with and for the private sector. The Fraunhofer network is made up of sixty-six institutes and research units, with more than 22,000 staff and an annual budget of €1.9 billion. This network of actors has allowed Germany to retain a focus on manufacturing while other leading economies in Europe saw their manufacturing industries shrink.

The German government has since the mid-2000s had explicit high-technology strategies, the first in 2006 and the second in 2010 launched as the "High Tech Strategy 2020."[32] The action plan associated with this strategy identified ten "future projects" which are viewed as critical to increasing rates of innovation and growth. One of the ten is Industrie 4.0, or Industry 4.0, which is fancy labeling for an approach to making that uses sensors on products and production machines and connectivity to allow the system to talk to itself and optimize what it is doing from the level of the individual production machine, to the line, the factory and up to the complete supply chain. "Simply put, this means that industrial production machinery no longer simply 'processes' the product, but that the product communicates with the machinery to tell it exactly what to do."[33]

The Industrie 4.0 future project was awarded €200 million to support continuing research and development and the coalition government that came to power in Germany in December 2014 stated in its coalition

agreement that Industrie 4.0 in its view is key to Germany achieving technological leadership. Chancellor Angela Merkel refers to these industrial changes in most speeches about the economy, pushing for greater private-sector engagement. In a speech at the world's largest industrial fair, the Hannover Messe, she said, "We have reached a critical moment, a point where the digital agenda is fusing with industrial production."[34] For her, though, German companies are not responding fast enough, and she fears any lead Germany has may evaporate: "This period will determine the future strength of the world's leading industrial centers. We have yet to win this battle."

The U.K. would have been seen as a contender for some industries, given its strengths in the automotive, aerospace and pharmaceutical sectors prior to the vote to leave the European Union. The surprise (to some) result of the referendum means its access to the European single market is now in doubt.[35] Many companies will have long-term concerns about using the U.K. as a base to serve the needs of European markets if there is any likelihood that there will be tariff barriers between the U.K. and mainland Europe. Such tariffs would obviously raise the cost of delivering a product to a customer across the English Channel, but it would also increase the time to market for goods that have to clear customs—while goods from across the remaining twenty-seven members of the Union would continue to move with no such extra cost or restriction. Andrew Liveris, the chairman of Dow Chemicals, speaking at the 2016 Financial Times Future of Manufacturing Summit three months after the vote, before any clarity had emerged on the path forward, commented that lots of investments would sit on the sidelines and that he had paused Dow investments in the wake of the Leave vote.[36] The political context has overtaken the economic context and so the U.K. is unlikely to be able to take advantage of physical deglobalization.

Other countries are making efforts to strengthen their position in the European region, but not through scale or based on prior manufacturing leadership. The Netherlands made attempts to get ahead in this sense by promoting itself as a circular economy hotspot as part of its activities during its presidency of the EU through 2016.[37] As a dense, well-connected economy it is a living lab for how industrial ecology might be achieved and an example that other regions may follow. Companies being placed close

together and supported through a strong local network is necessary to allow the sharing of inputs and outputs as the circular model imagines. The Dutch government has stated that by 2050 it wants all its companies to make utilizing reusable raw materials.[38] Given the scale of the country, it may be able to manage the coordination required between the public and the private sector to make this happen and this would allow it to become a target for companies who are attempting to be circular, whether that is for purely commercial reasons or through a belief in sustainability.

The situation in Asia is again complicated by the mixture of political systems and intentions. China, by virtue of its scale and high rates of growth to this point, has attracted the lion's share of attention from commentators and politicians alike. The dense agglomerations of manufacturing in cities like Shenzhen and Guangzhou are hard to ignore. Shenzhen, now seen as the global manufacturing hub for electronics, has a population of over 12 million. Just over thirty-five years ago it was a small fishing village. However, the difficulties of doing business in China for foreign companies, from ownership structures to the risks of intellectual property theft, mean it is not a simple calculation. Japan and South Korea both have significant industrial infrastructure and a focus on manufacturing that should allow them to be at the forefront of the changes that new industrial systems will imply.

AS WE MOVE INTO A WORLD where products have shorter journeys to get to us, where factories are smaller and there are more of them, and where there is great uncertainty about what work we will be doing, the other elements of globalization will also continue to evolve. Nothing in the trends we have described will by themselves reduce or block digital globalization. The mass movement of people, as we are seeing in the current refugee crisis, may be impacted by the availability of work, although the crisis of war is a greater impetus than the lure of employment.

What is certain is that governments will have a major role to play as countries around the world attempt to adapt to this new reality. Companies will make their choices within the context of these large social and technological changes, but governments have the ability to moderate that context to a greater or lesser extent. What are governments doing as physical deglobalization becomes a reality?

9

The Changing Politics
of Manufacturing

MANUFACTURING HAS LONG BEEN a political football kicked about between parties of all flavors, left and right, and with particular relish in the West. It served as the foundation for many parties of the left, as they grew out of the union movement which provided fertile ground to nurture future leaders. And for those on the right it has represented national strength, through what has been referred to as strategic industries such as the defense industry, aerospace and electronics.

But even though manufacturing has been namechecked by all the major party leaders recently, the level of actual support has waxed and waned as manufacturing has gone in and out of favor. The words are there but it is questionable whether they have led to significant action.

A year after narrowly and surprisingly winning the 1992 general election in the U.K., John Major gave his leader's speech at the Conservative Party conference. It was clear that in the wake of a recession he was attempting to boost all parts of the economy. He gave the clearest statement of support for manufacturing for many years in that speech—"Who says we can't make things in this country? Manufacturing industry is one of our great national assets."[1]

In the run-up to the 1997 election Tony Blair, then much less well known than he became, took the opportunity in a speech in Blackpool to criticize John Major and the Conservatives on their support and protection of manufacturing. "Look at the Tories—two recessions, one of

which wiped out a third of our manufacturing base," he blasted, outlining Labor's plans for greater support for industry through funding research and development and better industrial relations.[2]

Through the tenure of Labor in government in the U.K. from 1997 right up to 2010 there was an attempt to revive industrial policy from some members of the party, to provide direct support for a broad set of industries like shipbuilding and pharmaceuticals. However the policies that were being proposed could not be called "industrial policy"; that would have been a step too far. Industrial policy was seen to be a term too loaded with the baggage of failed direct interventions like the creation of International Computers Limited (ICL) by forcing the merging together of the computer division of English Electric and other existing companies in order to create a competitor to IBM.[3] Terms like "industrial strategy" and "industrial activism" came into vogue with Peter Mandelson in the mid-2000s, leading to many position papers but no fundamental change in the support provided to manufacturers.

In a similar vein, the U.K. coalition government, which came into power in 2010 following an indecisive general election, focused on looking to increase the role of manufacturing in a rebalanced economy. In May 2010 David Cameron, in his first major speech as prime minister, set the trend when he said, "Our economy has become more and more unbalanced, with our fortunes hitched to a few industries in one corner of the country, while we let other sectors like manufacturing slide."[4] This term "rebalancing" is now used extensively but it is never properly defined— does it mean rebalancing between manufacturing and services so that there is as much manufacturing as services? Or is this a rebalancing in a geographic sense, to bring the north of England into line with the growth pattern of the southeast?

The peak of rhetoric may have been reached with the changes to the structure of government that were brought in by Cameron's successor, Theresa May, who became prime minister on 13 July 2016.[5] A new department was created that brought various bits of old departments together to form the Department for Business, Energy and Industrial Strategy (DBEIS).[6] Politicians on all sides in the U.K. appear to be torn between an instinctive disregard for manufacturing and an analytical sense that

manufacturing matters more than they understand in both electoral and economic terms.

What about on the other side of the Atlantic? Manufacturing has played a key role in the identity of the United States, especially the Midwest states. But that identity has been challenged through major job losses. For example after the 2001 recession, by 2003 the U.S. had lost 2.7 million jobs, of which 2.4 million were in manufacturing. The U.S. president, George W. Bush, commented that "there's a problem with the manufacturing sector. And I understand for a full recovery, to make sure people can find work, that manufacturing must do better."[7] This effort to support manufacturing led to the appointment of an assistant secretary for manufacturing, quickly shortened to "manufacturing czar." Unfortunately for the president, his first nominee withdrew on the day of the announcement following claims that his company was opening factories in China while laying off workers in Nebraska.[8]

The focus on manufacturing continued into the Obama administration and if anything became stronger. In the midst of talk of gun control, healthcare reform and reviving the U.S. economy after the collapse of 2008, many may have overlooked something important in Barack Obama's 2012 State of the Union address. Whether something makes it into the State of the Union is a key indicator of whether that issue has any chance of gaining political capital in the coming year. And Obama's 2012 address focused on manufacturing as the bedrock of future U.S. growth. Not just somewhere down in the footnotes, but upfront and central there in paragraph three.

The contrast to the financial sector was writ large. "We will not go back to an economy weakened by outsourcing, bad debt, and phony financial profits," he said, calling for "an economy built on American manufacturing." Here was the leader of the free world trying to change people's perceptions in real time. Some of this rhetoric was political—the votes of rust belt states are important to the Democrats—but it was also strategic. Looking forward, there is a sense, if not a clear understanding, that the role of manufacturing is changing and that advanced economies need to have a strategy that isn't simply one of benign neglect.

The recent campaign for the highest office in the United States saw a

lot of talk about trade and manufacturing, so much so it prompted articles wondering why politicians appear to be obsessed with manufacturing.[9]

Donald Trump's key policy appears to be raising tariffs on goods coming from China to the United States, possibly as high as 45 percent of the import value.[10] In his main speech on trade he likened himself to Ronald Reagan, who imposed tariffs on the importation of Japanese motorcycles in 1983 to protect the last remaining U.S. motorcycle manufacturer at the time—Harley-Davidson.[11] The tariff on a Japanese imported bike (British, German and other makers were excluded from the tariff) jumped from 4.4 percent to 49.4 percent for one year and then tailed off over five years.[12]

The problem with the comparison for Trump is that this was a very specific tariff imposition, based on Section 201 of the 1974 Trade Act, which provided an escape clause to impose tariffs if imports were causing serious harm to domestic companies.[13] A blanket tariff on all imports from a country is an easy statement to make on the campaign trail but it is likely to cause significant harm far beyond any perceived positives that would come from it.

Hillary Clinton's campaign team put a different spin on the discussion of support for manufacturing, looking to portray her as anticipating the future rather than trying to hold on to the past. Rather than focus on reshoring existing jobs, her manufacturing plan focused on the technology frontier, forging partnerships between businesses, banks and universities to create new companies based around new technologies. As her adviser Thomas Kochan, a professor of management at MIT, commented, "It's not nostalgic in the sense that we're going to bring back a lot of the jobs that were shipped overseas, but it's focused on the next generation of manufacturing opportunities."[14]

While the rhetoric might be there for manufacturing it is not the case that this naturally flows into action. As we've seen, governments of every flavor like to talk up manufacturing now, but what about the policy framework to support it? Given the perceived decline of manufacturing, what has been happening in the policies of leading economies?

There has long been a decline in the perceived importance of manufacturing, initially gradual but accelerated by the turn toward free market economics and the rise of Thatcher and Reagan. This was the period that saw the effective death of traditional industrial policy in the West, the end

of so-called "picking winners" by government. By the mid-1980s in the U.K. "industrial policy was all but abandoned."[15] The United States had a slightly more strategic perception of government but with Republican control came the realization that "any Republican industrial policy is likely to be 'half-baked'—grudging, halfhearted, flawed by huge gaps, and biased toward investors and financial markets."[16]

Not every government has had to turn on a sixpence, however. Germany has had a strategy of export-led growth for many years and in terms of this debate has been far ahead of other Western governments. However, even the Germans may have problems in the future, as their strategy is directed toward global exports which may come under stress in this new world order.

Most governments are still using an old model for interpreting the economy as a choice between services and manufacturing and, at best, they are looking to port existing factories back to the home country, rather than creating a new industrial system. It is a mess of onshoring, reshoring, nearshoring and rebalancing. There's a lot of political confusion out there about what is really happening and what governments should do next. How did we get into this position?

WHAT WAS ONCE THE STRENGTH of many countries has been perceived to be in decline across the West through the 1990s and into the new century. This perception of decline in manufacturing in the West is based mainly on falling employment in manufacturing and a widening trade deficit between the West and China. But is this the whole story?

Over the past fifty years the developed economies have seen manufacturing employment fall off a cliff and manufacturing as a share of the whole economy decline over that time. Between 1970 and 2005 employment in manufacturing as a share of all employment dropped by between ten and twenty percentage points across the OECD (Figure 2).[17]

The U.K. went from just under 30 percent to around 9 percent employment in manufacturing, compared to a drop from 25 percent to again 9 percent for the United States. The graphs for this are like intermediate ski slopes, a quick descent with a few minor upward ticks to keep everything interesting. This decline in employment is one strong reason why more and more people have less interest in or consideration for manufacturing.

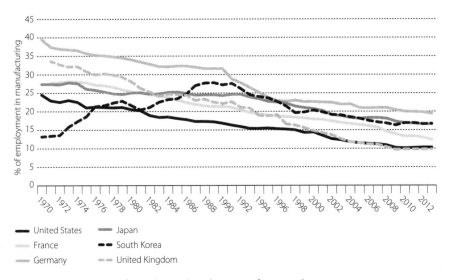

Figure 2: Percentage of people employed in manufacturing by country

Fewer people see the inside of factories, fewer communities have a sense of manufacturing as a source of cohesion for their towns and villages.

Viewed just from the employment perspective manufacturing has collapsed. But this ignores the fact that most countries produce more now than they did at the start of the 1990s. Productivity (the amount produced per hour or per worker) has increased, so with fewer employees factories are able to produce more and more.

As Figure 3 highlights,[18] South Korea has been increasing its production steadily since 1990, whereas countries like the U.K. barring the dip after the financial crisis have maintained their levels of output even with such large falls in manufacturing employment. Manufacturing hasn't left, it has changed its structure and its position relative to the service elements of the economy.

At the same time the trade position for most Western economies went from broadly neutral to very negative in terms of manufactured goods (Figure 4, page 160).[19] The most recent figures for the trade in goods highlight the position of China relative to the rest of the world, but also show how Germany has maintained its export-led growth to this point.

Depending on which indicator you want to emphasize you can tell a more or less negative story about manufacturing in Western economies.

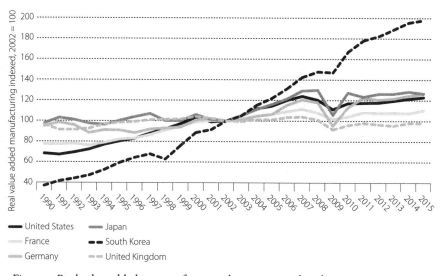

Figure 3: Real value added in manufacturing by country, indexed to 2002 = 100

But cherry picking or giving preference to one perspective on what has happened in manufacturing around the world denies the complexity that exists in manufacturing organizations in each country and region.

SO, SHOULD GOVERNMENTS FOCUS on manufacturing? Many commentators have taken the position that it just doesn't matter and that politicians are obsessing about the past rather than worrying about the future.[20] This argument starts from the position that manufacturing is too small a factor in the wider economy to have a significant effect on the nation's fortunes. The line goes something like this—once manufacturing was half of the economy, so a 5 percent or 10 percent drop in manufacturing was a big deal. Now with manufacturing counting for less than 10 percent of most developed economies (Germany aside), such a change is small in the scheme of the economy as a whole.[21] So no need to worry.

A mixture of ideology and an out of sight, out of mind attitude has created this dangerous position where manufacturing is thought to be unimportant, out of date and unnecessary for future economic growth. This would be a dangerous story to tell yourself if you are a company executive or a leading politician as the context continues to change.

This raw interpretation of the share of the economy ignores any

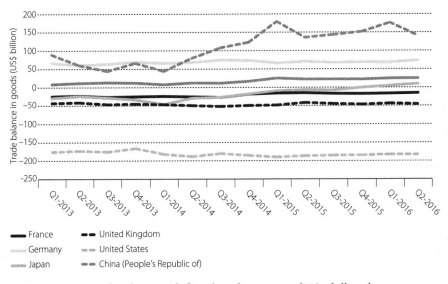

Figure 4: Balance of trade in goods for selected economies (U.S.$ billions)

knock-on effect (referred to as the multiplier) from manufacturing jobs, for example creating jobs in associated services like accounting. Recent estimates for the employment multiplier in the U.K. highlight how different the knock-on impact is for manufacturing industries when compared to services.[22] The average multiplier across the manufacturing industries in this study (based on 2010) is 2.5, that is each job in manufacturing has a multiplier of jobs in the rest of the economy of 2.5. This masks a range of between 1.5 and 5.5 for different manufacturing industries. In contrast, the average for the rest of the economy excluding agriculture and mining is 1.7, with the majority of sectors outside of manufacturing having a multiplier below 2. Manufacturing has a distinct impact on employment beyond the sector itself.

The next plank of the "not important" argument is that putting the products together has little significance; what matters are the high-value parts of the process which are thought to be the research, development and design of products. Just look at Apple—all that income from such a strong brand, thanks to the likes of Jony Ive, their chief designer and interpreter of Steve Jobs. The problem with this line of thinking is that it assumes you can disentangle yourself from the making completely and still be able to design leading-edge products. Ive doesn't give many interviews,

but it is clear that one thing he obsesses about is making, expressed in his love of sketching, carving and being in his workshop.[23] Without having a connection to how things are made or partaking in actual making at some level, it is unclear that designers can effectively design for manufacture.

The danger for many countries and companies is that if they do not have a focus on making they will also suffer in terms of innovation performance and economic growth that requires innovation. Beyond the making itself, a lack of connection to the making of things can lead to an inability to innovate. Adam Smith, when speaking about improvements to the machines of making, gives an example (possibly mythical) of the inventiveness of a boy who was tasked with opening the link between the boiler and the cylinder of a steam engine. By tying a string to the valve he could automate the opening and slope off to play rather than work. Workmen are often innovators. As Smith says, many machines "were originally the inventions of common workmen, who, being each of them employed in some very simple operation, naturally turned their thoughts toward finding out easier and readier methods of performing it."[24]

This concern for the wasting away of the knowledge of making is expressed in the present time as a concern over the industrial commons.[25] The combination of the installed base of different production technologies, the knowledge base embedded in the people working with the machines, and the technical understanding of how the machines, the materials and the systems work, all come together to form the industrial commons. This industrial commons is the stock of people, knowledge and machines that together make it possible for companies to make the products they want to make where they want to make them. The problem for countries like the United States and other developed economies is that we may not have paid enough attention to this as a resource for the future, so have become caught up in a narrative which said that manufacturing didn't matter anymore.

What does losing or degrading the commons mean? As companies depend on suppliers for specialist tasks and parts it becomes harder to source those in your domestic economy as the commons degrades. The commons is the pool of experienced labor that can move from company to company, taking with them their prior knowledge and ensuring that new production facilities can learn from the other companies in the region.

Without a strong commons companies struggle to get the skilled technicians they need to build, qualify and operate the production lines. And the commons is a shared vision, an ethic that is in the background, rarely felt except when it does not exist. Without a critical mass of producers sharing the commons it can feel very lonely for companies attempting to produce in a region.

Two Harvard professors, Gary Pisano and Willy Shih, made this argument clear in their 2009 piece in *Harvard Business Review* on how to restore American competitiveness. Their reading of the 1990s was that companies "were steadily outsourcing development and manufacturing work to specialists abroad and cutting their spending on basic research . . . the outsourcing has not stopped with low-value tasks like simple assembly or circuit board stuffing. Sophisticated engineering and manufacturing capabilities that underpin innovation in a wide range of products have been rapidly leaving too."[26] Because of this fewer and fewer American companies are able to innovate, especially in hardware, as they are so far removed from the production process.

In a short-term perspective that regards manufacturing as obsolete and unconnected to the innovation potential of a country, the commons is not a huge worry. But as pressures make manufacturing abroad a less attractive option, this becomes a real problem. When they wrote the *Harvard Business Review* article Pisano and Shih already worried that the United States had lost and could not recover technologies such as displays, rechargeable batteries and advanced composites.

While the situation may not be as terminal as they describe, regenerating the commons in the United States is not a simple process and requires understanding and partnership between the public and the private sector. That may be the weakness for Western economies as there isn't a good relationship between the two: each views the other as more of an enemy than a partner.

MUCH OF THIS DISCUSSION has been focused on the large economies, the big players on the international stage. However, these changes also herald a potential stumbling block for further development through industrialization for developing economies and in particular African countries. In fact it may strengthen a trend of premature deindustrialization.[27]

Developing economies, aside from those that political economist Alice Amsden referred to as "the Rest,"[28] appear to reach a peak in manufacturing employment earlier than Western economies in their relative economic development path. This is earlier in the sense of both sooner and at a lower level of income per capita. This means that industrialization as an engine of potential development seems to be weakening. This is a real concern as manufacturing, as opposed to services, has greater gains in productivity over time contributing to stronger growth. As Figures 2 and 3 above indicate, manufacturing tends to shed workers even as it increases output, the definition of productivity improvement.

Unfortunately, a future with physical deglobalization may make these trends worse. The combination of the decline in the importance of labor costs along with potential constraints in shipping due to environmental legislation means that there will be little incentive for companies to try to use African countries as a low-cost base for production. At the same time domestic African companies will be disadvantaged in trying to access international markets and may not be able to compete against multinationals with sufficient capital to produce in Africa for an African market, if it is seen as profitable.

Aid-for-trade became a greater focus of multilateral institutions following the WTO's 2005 Hong Kong Ministerial, moving from simply providing aid to intervening in order to support industrial development and new exports.[29] Commitments targeted as aid-for-trade were $19 billion in 1995, reached $23 billion in 2005, and by 2011 were $41.7 billion. The claim is that each dollar of aid committed in this way leads to an extra $8 in trade. But the context is shifting and the path of trade will be less and less accessible to developing economies, especially those in Africa which do not have particular skills or resources.

Can developing economies translate aid flows into investment in domestic production, supporting a step forward in development through industrialization for expanding domestic and regional markets, for example in West Africa? That may be possible if the model of development adopted is one that targets creating and strengthening domestic producers. At the same time if the further expansion of multinationals into developing countries is not met with strong resistance from both the development community and the countries themselves, domestic firms

may still lose out both in terms of servicing their home market but also in being blocked from setting up activities overseas.

There is one caveat on this negative interpretation—access to raw materials. The global map of political influence and power will be redrawn as the power of trade declines, but raw material sources remain strategically important. Countries that have even more domestic production will still need the raw materials to enable that production and, as the Chinese have realized, countries that have control over key raw materials, especially commodity metals, will be in a stronger position. Indeed, in order to shore up their position, the Chinese have made a number of acquisitions (for example China Hongqiao Group buying up companies in Guinea with rights to bauxite mines, the raw material for aluminum) and investment in roads and other infrastructure across the African continent. The U.S. is waking up to this strategic play and held the first U.S.–Africa Summit in Washington, D.C. in August 2014. At this, President Obama announced $14 billion of investment from U.S. companies into Africa and $17 billion of state and multilateral funds, that is, similar levels of investment in Africa to those from the Chinese government. This may be the lever that developing countries with a natural resource base can use, but this will need to be a conscious choice linking raw materials extraction and sale to investment in domestic and overseas industrial capacity for companies from those countries.

FROM THE OPENING UP OF CHINA to the United States in 1971 with Richard Nixon's trip to Beijing and the restoration of diplomatic ties in 1979 under Jimmy Carter, there has been a steady increase in economic ties, with China now seeing America as their largest export market. In the mid-1980s, at the halfway point of Ronald Reagan's time as president, the trade flows between the two countries were essentially equal.[30] With just under $4 billion of goods going each way, the U.S. had a trade deficit of just $6 million with China in 1985 (yes, that's not a misprint, that's million). Since that moment, the movement has been in only one direction. By the end of 1990 the trade deficit for the U.S. was up to $10 billion, $83 billion by 2000, just before China was admitted to the WTO, and at the end of 2015 it stood at just under $366 billion. In 2015 China exported roughly four times as much to the United States as it imported from there.

A critical issue as production moves closer to the customer, relocating where there is demand, will be which companies, domestic or foreign, will serve the local market. Will U.S. companies serve U.S. customers and Chinese customers? Or will the Chinese and other companies in the global value chain, who have taken over production tasks as either original equipment manufacturers (OEMs) or original design manufacturers (ODMs), take control of the channel to Chinese consumers?

China's concern is getting trapped at a specific point in the value chain. "While scholars have pointed to the benefits for emerging economies of integration in [global value chains], they also highlight the pitfalls of the low value-added modularity trap, with Sturgeon and Kawakami (2010) suggesting in 2010 that China's handset sector had already fallen into this trap because of its high dependence on external sources of technology."[31] This comes down to an ability to innovate which implies a different set of skills from being able to manage highly efficient production.

As production localization occurs there will be a land grab of sorts for the emerging middle class of countries like China and India between indigenous companies and multinationals. The former will be trying to convert their roles in existing global value chains into dominance in their local market, whereas the latter will be trying either to maintain their relationship as lead in a value chain that is tightly regionalized or to move into production themselves within these markets.

What are the early signs that external investors are seeing as Chinese companies start to challenge them in their home market? Well, "foreign investor companies in China, which see China's growing domestic market of great significance for their own development, . . . are experiencing growing competition from Chinese technology companies supported by China's government giving preference to local companies, products and services particularly in the public procurement market."[32] It looks like the China–U.S. relationship will be put under further strain as both governments maneuver to give their country's companies an advantage in this changing landscape.

DOES THE SIGNIFICANT VALUE of offshore profits that are currently held by U.S. multinationals give them a significant advantage as production regionalizes? There has been significant debate on how to manage the

repatriation of something in the order of $2 trillion in offshore profits to the U.S. but that debate could become redundant if these U.S. companies decide to use these profits to invest in their own production capacity in overseas markets.[33]

The level of American corporate offshore profits should be contrasted with the rising level of Chinese corporate acquisitions. "Mergers and acquisitions, traditionally seen only as an aspect of the Western economic sphere centered on the U.S. and Europe, has now also gone global as companies themselves—and not just their products and services—are traded worldwide."[34] Since the mid-2000s Chinese companies have joined in the M&A game, with a record $106 billion in deals through 2015.[35] That record was already been equaled before the middle of 2016 and it remains to be seen how far this trend will go.

Countries' approaches to how open they are to foreign direct investment (FDI) will be a key indicator of whether their governments have a preference to have domestic companies serving the domestic market or whether they are comfortable with multinationals coming in and taking the lead. Currently, according to the Chinese Ministry of Science and Technology, "the percentage of actual FDI devoted to the manufacturing industry has been declining since 2006, and the total FDI in the manufacturing industry has been declining since 2012."[36] The current conditions in China appear to show a weakened interest in foreign investment into manufacturing in China and so it will be important to see if domestic Chinese companies are taking up the space of foreign companies and whether this will continue.

As production becomes even more regionalized there is a high likelihood that other functions such as R&D or design will also regionalize. A driver of this will be the availability of funds within a company to carry out such activities, because moving money around the globe is not a smooth process. There are issues of repatriation of profits occurring both in the country of origin (restrictions on moving those profits out of the country) and in the home country (tax rates for those profits coming onshore) that mean company investment may reflect the regional structure of their profits, for some companies trapping their R&D away from their notional headquarters. This is a secondary effect of the regionalization of production and may have a very significant impact on the growth path of many

countries. If significant shares of R&D spending follow production due to the linkage to the production process and the controls on the movement of capital, one of the key inputs into growth in the West may be weakened.

HAVING LOST INTEREST IN industrial policy, how are Western and other governments around the world now responding? Has the financial crash and subsequent changes in the context for trade led to a refocusing on manufacturing and industrial policy?

Possibly the most important aspect of this discussion, new production technologies has been attracting attention from governments around the world. The major economies have included additive manufacturing (AM) or 3D printing in their strategies, many with explicit research and development programs. For example the Japanese government is targeting additive manufacturing as key to their ambition to transform their industrial base with a particular focus on regional growth.[37] South Korea has included 3D printing in a number of its technology roadmaps, with very specific targets including having five globally leading firms in this space by 2020 and achieving 15 percent market share for 3D-printing related products.[38] Similar plans have been drawn up in the United States with additive manufacturing being a key strand in the National Network for Manufacturing Innovation (NNMI), which was recently renamed Manufacturing U.S.A.[39]

In the new future of global trade, each country will face different circumstances. The U.S. could be even stronger than before, linking the shale gas boom to significantly increased domestic production, leveraging cheaper input costs with its large domestic market. Australia, as a source of raw materials such as iron ore and copper, has a strategic role to play in supporting production across the globe and so could continue to avoid the worst of the financial crash and its aftermath, although there are questions as to how its domestic production capabilities are evolving. China faces a difficult choice, as it will no longer be able to depend on its role as a producer to the world to continue its development, while at the same time its consumer base is growing—more iPhones were sold in China in 2014 than in the U.S.

Germany, having based a significant portion of its economic strength on exports, especially within the EU, will face a difficult balancing act. It

could lose out as other countries increase domestic production or it could forge ahead as the productive center of the European Union. The U.K. will be competing with Germany and the new EU accession countries both to retain the manufacturing base it has and to act as a locus for new production as the regionalization of manufacturing takes place. However, not being in the European Union will cause the U.K. problems, making exports to the mainland more expensive while the extended political conversation within the U.K. over EU membership risks short-term market access. As a heavyweight in information and communications technology (ICT) and with a new ten-year strategy to develop 3D printing, South Korea appears to be already preparing itself for a significant return of manufacturing using new production technologies embedded into the country's dense telecommunications network. The question is whether the chaebols and their legacy can adapt from export-intensive business models to those based primarily on ownership.

The Chinese government faces some unenviable choices as it tries to maintain high growth rates and improve the standards of living for the millions and millions of people within its borders. Its strategy toward manufacturing was initially based on low-skill assembly and many-hands manufacturing. That strategy has by choice and necessity changed for China over the past decade. This is not a country that can just depend on force of numbers anymore; it has to upgrade its industrial commons to meet the severe challenges it faces.

The industrial focus for China moving forward was outlined in their Manufacturing 2025 report, which many believe is a retread of the German Industry 4.0 approach outlined earlier. According to the Chinese Ministry of Science and Technology, the plan aims to transform the industrial base from "big" to "strong," to consolidate the scale of manufacturing that takes place in China but to develop new multinationals who have more and more valuable activities in their control as opposed to just being suppliers or assemblers.[40] They see investment in R&D as a key bottleneck, as there are not enough manufacturers who can innovate either in terms of their products or in terms of the machines that make the products. Remember the drive toward automation? Whether China can service its own need for robots into the future will determine much of the landscape for machine tools and automation in the coming decades. The second element of the

plan is a focus on intelligent manufacturing, which is a catch-all phrase for the introduction of automation and the digitization of manufacturing to as large a degree as possible.

At the same time as implementing the Manufacturing 2025 strategy, China has outlined an ambitious plan to extend and reconnect China's trade routes through what is referred to as the "One Belt, One Road." There are two main elements to the plan—a land route from China to Europe via sixty countries and a sea route, again to Europe, through the South China Sea and the Indian Ocean. The plan was launched by President Xi Jinping in 2013 and comes with a development fund of between $40 billion and $50 billion to support the required infrastructure development to make the routes a reality.[41] There are significant doubts that such a large project, touching so many countries and asking so many questions of politicians, companies and countries, can succeed. However, one interpretation of "One Belt, One Road" is that it is a massive hedge against the changes we are seeing, aiming to drive down the transit time between Asia and Europe so that the temporal component of location decisions is tilted back in the direction of China. This may be a wise move at present, but if the infrastructure development takes decades as opposed to years the changes in production technologies, automation and environmental controls during that period may make it obsolete before it has a chance to have an impact.

GOVERNMENTS CAN HAVE POSITIVE OR NEGATIVE effects on how industries evolve and whether countries prosper or flounder. Many times in the past offshoring has been imposed, dictated by trade barriers that a country has erected in order to force some of the production to be in their country. Brazil has erected such strategic trade barriers, for example in the automotive industry, in order to force at least the final assembly of cars that will be sold in Brazil to be in Brazil. In 2012, as Chinese cars were becoming more prominent on the roads of Brazil, the government of Dilma Rousseff levied greater taxes on cars with less than 65 percent local content in them.[42] The continued high rates of local content regulation has led to challenges at the WTO, for example by the European Union.[43] As is the nature of such disputes, resolving them takes a long time and this challenge has yet to unwind.[44] The current state of the Brazilian economy

leaves much to be desired, going from an average growth rate of 2 percent from 2010 to 2014, to contracting by over 3 percent each year since.[45]

The starting point for this book was that we believe in stories about the economy that have gone well past their use-by date. Another current story may make it difficult to achieve equitable growth even if we can update our thinking on globalization. That is the story of the public sector as a static, bureaucratic set of institutions that do not play a role in moving technology forward. In some people's eyes the public sector is the source of problems rather than the source of innovation. Recently Mariana Mazzucato has taken on the task, as the subtitle of her 2013 book *The Entrepreneurial State* says, of "debunking public vs. private sector myths."[46]

Governments around the world had to a greater or lesser extent retreated to setting "framework conditions"—that is trying to make the market work efficiently through appropriate regulation and taxation. The innovative action was left to the private sector, as that is where all the dynamism resides, or so the story goes. Here the public sector is just a provider of the basics "but too large and heavy to be the dynamic engine."

As she comments, "most of the radical, revolutionary innovations ... from railroads to the Internet ... trace the most courageous, early and capital-intensive 'entrepreneurial' investments back to the State." Again, unless we are willing to update our stories of how the economy works, in this case the relationship between the private and the public sector, we're likely to lose our way.

The actions of governments around the world will determine in large part whether there are positive or negative outcomes from the changes that are happening right now in the global economy. Will countries manage the tensions of foreign ownership and repatriation of profits to ensure growth? Or will economic protectionism take over? We are seeing tax laws becoming tighter and tighter and more and more pressure being put on multinationals to pay their way. The rise of economic nationalism as represented by Trump and other politicians seems to point toward a fractured world. Until the votes are counted and the decisions made we cannot know whether our political systems will push countries and industries further apart. But these are the choices that we face and they are not well recognized in most current political debates.

· · ·

HOW WILL WE KNOW if these changes, physical deglobalization, are actually happening? What may be an early signal for the localization of activity around the world is that the growth of trade, and specifically trade in physical goods, has recently been lower than the rate of growth of world GDP. Having grown since the 1980s, with dips around the recession of 2001, the ratio of global trade to global GDP has flatlined at best since 2011. This is a key indicator for our story as it highlights that there is growth in the world economy, but that trade that traditionally grew faster than GDP has slowed down. Trade may have been a motor of global growth but it appears that linkage is weakening. Into the future the clear signal that we are moving into a deglobalization phase for physical products will be a rise in regional trade without a rise in global trade. That is, that the emphasis of trade will move away from the global level and instead will be even more focused within regions.

Do we need globalization to continue? Many voices, from the director general of the WTO Roberto Azevêdo down, have been warning that without continued globalization, without strong trade, world growth is likely to stall. The WTO forecast for trade growth has been revised and revised throughout 2016. In April the WTO believed that world trade would increase by 2.8 percent during the year. However, just six months later that forecast had been lowered to 1.7 percent, almost a whole percentage point drop.[47] Looking forward to 2017, they are also worried, providing a very wide window for their projection of trade growth, saying it will be somewhere between 1.8 and 3.1 percent. Two things are concerning policymakers—that this would be another year of trade growth lower than global economic growth, and that there is such uncertainty in the projection.

Other commentators are more sanguine about the prospects for the global economy. Dani Rodrik, professor of international political economy at Harvard, contends that "we should not fret too much about a reversal in globalization. We should instead take it as an opportunity to redress the imbalance between global markets and national responsibilities." For Rodrik, this is a chance to strengthen domestic governance, providing a stronger foundation which can in the long run support globalization: "[T]he risk is that mainstream politicians will cling to an unsustainable model of hyper-globalization and fail to seize the moment."[48]

This coming period of physical deglobalization may be just another phase in the long history of world trade, a teenage moment of change in the life of the global economy. But as deglobalization plays out over the coming ten to twenty years it will have an impact on international relations, the power structures of the world and whether we are able to meet ambitious but desperately necessary targets for development. Whether we take the position of Azevêdo or Rodrik depends on which story of the global economy we have more faith in, but both positions reinforce our need to update how we think the world works. Holding on to comfortable or familiar stories about the global economy is not an option, as the political and economic landscape changes rapidly beneath our feet and makes a mockery of any consensus of the past.

Epilogue
The Post World

The week for turning

January 2017 will go down as the month in which many of the political and economic signals reversed, when the leading players in the global economy decided to indulge in some serious cross-dressing. In the space of a week we went from the chilly mountain air of Davos where the leader of the Chinese Communist Party Xi Jinping became the foremost cheerleader for globalization, to an overcast Washington D.C. where the 45th president, Donald J. Trump, was invoking a new age of protectionism. Along the way we had Theresa May simultaneously claiming the U.K. was a global citizen while turning its back on one of the largest markets in the world, the equal or better of the United States in terms of GDP. All change in the carousel of global leadership.

Davos has lost some of its luster. As 2016 turned into 2017, many leaders were staying away including Angela Merkel and François Hollande, possibly not wanting to be represented as the 1 percent and detached from the concerns of ordinary people.[1] The main attraction was the Chinese leader, giving the keynote on the first day of the meeting. His statements were an echo of those we had heard through the late 1990s and into the 2000s, those that said globalization is an irresistible force. It is interesting to see that the Chinese perspective is one of historical inevitability rather than one of constant change as they continue to grow and take on greater power in the world economy. "Whether you like it or not, the global economy is the big ocean that you cannot escape from. Any attempt to cut off the flow of capital, technologies, products, industries and people

between economies, and channel the waters in the ocean back into isolated lakes and creeks is simply not possible."[2] This takes us back to the start of this story, when we had similar statements from leaders of the West and the multilateral institutions they created. Is this history repeating itself or are Chinese leaders preparing the ground for a fundamental change in how China sees itself within the global system?

At almost the same time, on the same day, the Prime Minister of the United Kingdom Theresa May gave her confirmation of Brexit speech. In the gilded hall of Lancaster House, where Thatcher gave her call-to-arms speech for the U.K. to support the completion of the Single Market in 1988, Theresa May said that the U.K. would, in every sense, leave the European project, but would become in her words "Global Britain."[3] Caught between the politics of immigration and the need for economic growth, the Conservative party has chosen to prioritize control of borders. As the Prime Minister acknowledged in her speech this means there can be no way to sustain the U.K. within the Single Market. "I want to be clear. What I am proposing cannot mean membership of the single market. European leaders have said many times that membership means accepting the "four freedoms" of goods, capital, services and people . . . It would to all intents and purposes mean not leaving the EU at all." Now the U.K. is attempting to negotiate a free trade deal, a process that would need to be completed within two years so that the exit would not lead to a default to the higher tariffs of WTO schedules. Two days later Theresa May was also at Davos and again spoke of the need to protect globalization. "The forces of liberalism, free trade and globalization that have had—and continue to have—such an overwhelmingly positive impact on our world . . . are somehow at risk of being undermined." The possibility that the U.K.'s actions are themselves undermining the international order was possibly never entertained.

Meanwhile in the United States as Davos was breaking up and the U.K. was contemplating how to manage its exit from the EU, at the end of the week we had the pomp and circumstance of the inauguration of President Trump. Much has already been written on the change this president signifies and many more columns and tweets will be written before we know what the long-term impact of this choice will be for America and the wider world. However, if there was any doubt that Trump would step

back from international economic engagement that was removed imme-
diately. "We must protect our borders from the ravages of other countries
making our products, stealing our companies and destroying our jobs. Pro-
tection will lead to great prosperity and strength."[4]

Behind all of the speeches and the talking heads interpretations is the
reality of uncertainty. All of these changes make it much harder to predict
where the world is heading, with the probability of greater constraints,
greater frictions being placed on the global trading system. What shape
this will take though is unclear—we don't know how literally we should
take the protectionist rhetoric of Trump or how the U.K. and the EU will
resolve their trading relationship. All is in flux.

Punctuated equilibrium

In 1972 Stephen Jay Gould and Nils Eldredge published a paper which
reinterpreted how evolution works over time.[5] Rather than happening
slowly, with many very small changes aggregating to differentiate species,
they proposed that once a species appears it has very little change for an
extremely long time and then there are rare and brief periods of great
change. This is punctuated equilibrium, long periods of stasis followed by
short periods of rapid change.

It feels like we have just passed through such a moment in the world
of politics into what some claim to be the "post" world—post truth, post
facts, post certainty. A huge jump in a very short period of time, taking
us far away from what were thought to be certainties in the recent past.
Sometimes the world moves faster than you thought possible and in a
direction that was more than unexpected. We don't have facts anymore
we have "alternative facts."[6] There is no truth in the world, there is merely
the echo chamber that we each construct online and in life, surrounding
ourselves with similar voices and compatible positions.

In the heat of the moment are commentators going too far in rushing
to declare catastrophe? The usually calm Martin Wolf recently wrote in
the *Financial Times*, "We are, in short, at the end of both an economic
period—that of western-led globalization—and a geopolitical one—the
post–cold war 'unipolar moment' of a U.S.-led global order."[7] Wolf is not
usually so depressingly definitive in his reading of the political economy
of the moment, but he could be right. This could be an inflection point

in the political and economic order. Whether it has a positive ending is doubtful, although the surge in populist positions in many countries should be a clear signal that what was thought to be a stable consensus was not going to hold. Wolf's reading of where this might lead is pessimistic about the global order. "By succumbing to the lure of false solutions, born of disillusion and rage, the West might even destroy the intellectual and institutional pillars on which the postwar global economic and political order has rested."[8] The end of the world as we know it?

The dangers of another false narrative and overshooting

What does this mean for trade? Specifically, what does it mean for trade in goods and the existence of global value chains? It is obvious now that the landscape for any discussion on making and globalization changed radically through 2016. But these changes were not the "expected" outcome. The polls and pundits were punched on the nose, as things that were laughed off as too strange to be true suddenly became real. At the time of announcing his candidacy Trump's odds were as long as 25/1.[9] But as the year unraveled the odds for Brexit and for Trump were the same as they came to a head, each were 3/1 to pay out, leaving many betting companies with a large bill at the end of the year.[10]

The rise of various flavors of nationalism, and with it varying degrees of protectionism, through 2016 is well documented. From the decision of the U.K. to leave the EU, through the near success of Norbert Hofer in Austria and on to the election of Donald Trump to the presidency of the United States, much ink has been spilt after the fact. Whether 2017 continues this trend depends on how the reality of politician Trump (because he is now undeniably an insider, one of the Beltway creatures) plays out, and what if any aftershock there is from the failed presidential campaign of Marine Le Pen and the shape of the political landscape in Germany following their federal elections. What had been a broad consensus (or so it appeared) fell apart, driven in part by divisive nationalism and rising populism. However, we should be clear, if globalization has aggregate benefits they have not been shared equally and many individuals and communities rightly feel that they have been sacrificed on the altar of economic integration. These sentiments are real and will shape our politics into the immediate future.

The main impact of these changes on our story is the risk of over-shooting. If the rhetoric of economic nationalism is followed through into action it means that the likelihood of greater tariffs appearing is high. With the risk of boundaries of all kinds being imposed post Brexit and the inauguration of President Trump the move to localization will be amplified. If one end of the swinging pendulum was hyper-globalization, then the other end is trade protection, increased constraints on the movement of people and capital, and autarky where economies attempt to be self-sufficient. While hyper-globalization is dead, that doesn't mean that the best position to be in is at the other end of the pendulum's swing. But that is the risk in this political climate, that in correcting to the new conditions the political pressures placed on companies forces them into positions which are sub-optimal for them and for the economy.

Reading the signals in the wrong way

Along the way we are getting an "alternative" account for the global economy, one that is based on "America First," that a country with the clout of the U.S. can effectively dictate to the rest of the world its terms of trade. This is not true but if the process is allowed to take hold it will take time to refute. Who will people believe—the media, experts or the political class—when unilateral tariff imposition damages the economy and there is a search for a scapegoat? The fatigue of the discursive space in modern politics damages our ability to update or share views in a productive way, as the flurry of executive orders, misleading briefings and out-and-out lies makes it difficult to see through to the reality of what is going on.

The early signals from the U.S. are that the new administration will be looking to force the repatriation of supply chains. Peter Navarro was announced by the transition team as the head of a new National Trade Council[11] and as the new administration took office "Mr. Navarro said one of the administration's trade priorities was unwinding and repatriating the international supply chains on which many U.S. multinational companies rely, taking aim at one of the pillars of the modern global economy."[12]

Companies adapting to the changing nature of production, automation and consumer demand by bringing their production into their domestic market should not be misread as support or proof of the need for economic nationalism. The discussion throughout this book does

not support protectionism or forcing companies to place factories in one country or another. It does not mean that countries should try to do everything themselves. It does not mean that local is best in all cases. It does not justify tariffs, sanctions or non-tariff barriers in any way. The context for making has changed due to automation, new production technologies and other concerns such as regulation of emissions. The context breaks any consensus that says global value chains are the default and best option for companies, and managers will have to decide for their products and their markets how best to organize. Given the diversity that manufacturing represents (remember how many different products we can buy) a one-size solution of bringing it all back home just will not work. It is more subtle than that.

Here is the coming conflict—between the political climate of populism and nationalism and the reality that companies see as they attempt to achieve some advantage in the global economy. One system is retreating behind strong borders while the other is attempting to work at the appropriate level whether that is within or between countries. And if the resolution of this tension is to have any stability it has to take on board the mistakes of the past thirty years, most clearly the folly of not attending sufficiently to the losers in the rise of globalization. According to the new cheerleader for globalization President Xi Jinping "[W]e should adapt to and guide economic globalization, cushion its negative impact, and deliver its benefits to all countries and all nations." This remains true for a more regionalized world as well.

Where to from here?

Companies have always had to work within the political context of the day. It is possible that companies became too used to the relative stability of past decades, with a settled position on globalization for many politicians, pundits and economists. The rapid changes in the political context will make the job of structuring companies harder, as managers will have to deal with greater border restrictions and the uncertainty of how these will evolve.

There are some voices trying to put these changes into a more positive light. For example Frank Mattern, the chairman of the McKinsey Global Institute, has written a piece that claims all is not lost as "Trade agreements

may be out of favor, but the digitally-enabled era of commerce that is arriving will defy all protectionists, everywhere."[13] The vision here is the overly optimistic high-technology version though, as ". . . an entrepreneur in Nairobi, Nuremberg, or Nanjing today has the ability to leverage e-commerce platforms such as Amazon or Alibaba and create a 'micromultinational' offering products around the world, printed digitally, and delivered by drone." Even though this is the most positive interpretation possible, there is an element of truth that our digital infrastructure may offset some of the negatives from strong protectionism.

Uncertainty is unfortunately the only certainty in the political space at present. The scale and breadth of trade barriers that will be introduced between various countries cannot be predicted with accuracy. The impacts on trade volumes and economic growth are as yet unclear. However, in terms of the forces pressing on companies to have shorter supply chains and a closer mapping between their markets and their footprint, the political has moved from just a background hum to an insistent beat filling the heads of managers around the world. In some cases, the choices of governments will be more important than the changes in production technologies and the increases in automation.

Having clear and accurate narratives on the world of making is critical now more than ever. We may be shedding the hyper-globalization position but we risk replacing it with an extreme form of nationalism, forcing companies into shapes they would not naturally take. We must accurately represent the reality of the choices that companies face. They have to live within the political context but we should not allow the production of alternative facts on the global economy to dominate our political and economic choices.

Finbarr Livesey
February 2017

Notes

Chapter 1: Go East, Young Man?

1. Fukuyama, F., The end of history? *The National Interest,* Summer 1989.
2. Stanley, T. and A. Lee, It's still not the end of history, *The Atlantic,* 1 September 2014.
3. UN, Role of the United Nations in promoting development in the context of globalization and interdependence, United Nations fifty-fourth session of the General Assembly, Agenda Item 104, September 1999.
4. Quotes taken from Tony Blair's statement as part of the 1998 WTO Ministerial Conference in Geneva, www.wto.org/english/thewto_e/minist_e/min98_e/anniv_e /blair_e.htm.
5. Stiglitz, J., *Globalization and Its Discontents,* Penguin Books, 2002.
6. IMF, Globalization: A brief overview, *IMF Issues Brief,* Issue 02/08, May 2008.
7. Epstein, R. and McCain Nelson, C., Donald Trump lays out protectionist views in trade speech, *Wall Street Journal,* updated 28 June 2016, www.wsj.com/articles/donald -trump-lays-out-protectionist-views-in-trade-speech-1467145538.
8. See, for example, Mason, R., How did the U.K. end up voting to leave the European Union? *Guardian,* 24 June 2016, www.theguardian.com/politics/2016/jun/24 /how-did-uk-end-up-voting-leave-european-union.
9. The statement was used in Theresa May's first speech as the prime minister and leader of the Conservative party, see Withnall, A. and Mortimer, C., Theresa May says "Brexit means Brexit and we will make a success of it" in first speech as leader, *Independent,* 11 July 2016, www.independent.co.uk/news/uk/politics /andrea-leadsom-theresa-may-conservative-leadership-election-live-tory-latest -updates-next-prime-a7130671.html.
10. Global Trade Alert 2014 report, www.globaltradealert.org/16th_GTA_report.
11. Azevêdo, R., How an activist approach on trade could stimulate global demand, *Financial Times,* 15 April 2016.
12. Fisher, W., The narrative paradigm: In the beginning, *Journal of Communication,* Autumn 1985.
13. Kuhn, T., *The Structure of Scientific Revolutions,* University of Chicago Press, 1962.
14. Text of Blair's foreword available at www.theguardian.com/world/2002/sep/24/iraq .speeches.

15. From transcript of Powell's remarks at www.theguardian.com/world/2003/feb/05/iraq.usa.

16. Quote from www.economist.com/node/1942341.

17. See the Irish CSO press release www.cso.ie/en/newsandevents/pressreleases/2012pressreleases/pressreleasecensus2011profile7religionethnicityandirishtravelers/.

18. Visit Tyler Vigen's site and you can play with the data to see if you can find some new spurious correlations: http://tylervigen.com/spurious-correlations.

19. Huwert, J.-Y. and Verdier, L., *Economic Globalisation: Origins and Consequences,* OECD Insights, OECD Publishing, 2013.

20. A troubling trajectory, *The Economist,* 13 December 2014.

21. Das, D., Globalization in the world of finance: An analytical history, *Global Economy Journal,* 6(1), 2006, article 2.

22. Data from Crafts, N., Globalisation and economic growth: A historical perspective, *The World Economy,* 27(1), 2004, pp. 45–58.

23. Anon., Is financial globalization beginning a process of reversal? *The International Economy,* Summer 2011.

24. Manyika, J. et al., *Digital Globalization: The New Era of Global Flows,* McKinsey Global Institute, 2016.

25. See https://about.twitter.com/company for what the numbers look like now.

26. Again this will have been updated on the company information page at http://newsroom.fb.com/company-info/.

27. Maddison, A., The West and the rest in the world economy: 1000–2030, World Economy 9(4), 2008, pp. 75–100, quoted in the WTO, *World Trade Report 2013,* p. 46.

28. Office for National Statistics, 2011 Census analysis: 170 years of industry, ONS, 2013.

29. The World Intellectual Property Organization (WIPO), for example, has a comparative index of national innovation strength based on eighty-two indicators: www.wipo.int/publications/en/details.jsp?id=4064.

30. The measurement of R&D spending and at a broader level the innovation capacity of companies and countries has attracted a lot of attention over the past thirty years and more. There are large manuals on what counts as R&D, the Frascati Manual being the touchstone, and many rankings and lists have been created, such as the Global Innovation Index.

31. National Science Foundation, *Science and Engineering Indicators 2015,* NSF, 2016.

32. Shih, W. and Pisano, G., Restoring American competitiveness, *Harvard Business Review,* July–August 2009.

33. Smith, A., *An Inquiry into the Nature and Causes of the Wealth of Nations,* Strahan and Cadell, 1776, Book IV, Section ii, 12.

34. Krugman, P., Increasing returns and economic geography, *Journal of Political Economy,* 99(3), 1991, pp. 483–499.

35. Charles Wilson in his 1953 confirmation testimony, when pressed to sell his shares in GM, was asked if he could make a decision as Secretary of Defense that would be adverse to the interests of GM. He said he would struggle to see such a situation arising as "for years I thought what was good for our country was good for General Motors, and vice versa."

36. Krugman, P., A country is not a company, *Harvard Business Review,* July–August 1996.

37. Bernard, A. et al., Firms in international trade, CEP Discussion Paper no. 795, Center for Economic Performance, London School of Economics, 2007.

38. The terms also can be used together as companies can make both decisions—to outsource abroad. As a rough guide there are four categories for each activity of a company that has a clear nationality: within the company in their home country, within the company outside of the home country, outside of the company in their home country and outside of the company outside of the home country. No one has clarified and disambiguated these terms well.

39. Milberg, W. and Winkler, D., *Outsourcing Economics: Global Value Chains in Capitalist Development,* Cambridge University Press, 2013.

40. Sirkin, H. L. et al., Made in America, again: Why manufacturing will return to the U.S., Boston Consulting Group, 2011: www.bcg.com/documents/file84471.pdf.

41. Figures taken from Pierce, J. and Schott, P., *The Surprisingly Swift Decline of U.S. Manufacturing Employment,* Federal Reserve Board, Washington D.C., 2014.

42. Knight, W., China is building a robot army of model workers, *Technology Review,* 26 April 2016: www.technologyreview.com/s/601215/china-is-building-a-robot-army-of-model-workers/.

43. Office of National Statistics, Balance of payments: Oct. to Dec. and annual 2015, ONS Statistical Bulletin, 2016.

Chapter 2: From Putting Out to Getting Out

1. The figures for global and country level manufacturing output are taken from Bairoch, P., International industrialization levels from 1750 to 1980, *Journal of European Economic History,* **11**(2), 1982, pp. 269–333.

2. Latest figures taken from Rhodes, C., Manufacturing: International comparisons, House of Commons Library Briefing Paper 05809, June 2015.

3. See the Federal Reserve Bank of St. Louis, https://fredblog.stlouisfed.org/2014/04/the-decline-of-manufacturing/.

4. In 2015 they were China, the U.S., India, Commonwealth of Independent States (CIS) and Japan: www.economywatch.com/economic-statistics/economic-indicators/GDP_Share_of_World_Total_PPP/.

5. Bythell, D., Cottage industry and the factory system, *History Today,* **33**(4), 1983, pp. 17–23.

6. Fening, P. A., The state of cottage industries in Ghana: A case of cast aluminum pot fabrication industry, *Asian Journal of Humanities and Social Sciences,* **3**(2), 2015, pp. 100–108.

7. See their website at www.grupofenix.org/our-groups#mujeres.

8. Figures taken from Tugend, A., It's unclearly defined, but telecommuting is fast on the rise, *New York Times,* 7 March 2014: www.nytimes.com/2014/03/08/your-money/when-working-in-your-pajamas-is-more-productive.html.

9. Mokyr, J., The rise and fall of the factory system: Technology, firms, and households since the Industrial Revolution, paper prepared for the Carnegie-Rochester Conference on macroeconomics, Pittsburgh, 17–19 November 2000.

10. Ibid.

11. Weber, M., *Economy and Society,* University of California Press, 1922.

12. Carlsson, B., New knowledge: The driving force of innovation, entrepreneurship and economic development, paper presented at DRUID summer conference, 2009.

13. You can download the full text of the act online at the Library of Congress website, www.loc.gov/law/help/statutes-at-large/3rd-congress/c3.pdf.

14. Quotation from Hounsell, D., *From the American System to Mass Production, 1800–1932: The Development of Manufacturing Technology in the United States,* Johns Hopkins University Press, 1984.

15. Adler, K., Innovation and amnesia: Engineering rationality and the fate of interchangeable parts manufacturing in France, *Technology and Culture,* 38(2), 1997, pp. 273–311.

16. See, for example, Bresnahan, T. and Trajtenberg, M., General purpose technologies: Engines of growth? NBER Working Paper 4148, August 1992.

17. Helpman, E., ed., *General Purpose Technologies and Growth,* MIT Press, 2003.

18. Crafts, N., Steam as a general purpose technology: A growth accounting perspective, London School of Economics Working Paper 75/03, 2003.

19. http://corporate.ford.com/innovation/100-years-moving-assembly-line.html.

20. De Backer, K. and Miroudout, S., Mapping global value chains, European Central Bank Working Paper 1677, May 2014.

21. Linden, G. et al., Who captures value in a global innovation system? The case of Apple's iPod, Study Paper, Personal Computing Industry Center, 2007: pcic.merage .uci.edu/papers/2008/whocapturesvalue.pdf.

22. Grimes, S. and Sun, Y., China's evolving role in Apple's global value chain, *Area Development and Policy,* 1(1), 2016, pp. 94–112.

23. Who's smiling now? OECD Observer 296, Q3 2013, www.oecdobserver.org/news /fullstory.php/aid/4227/Who_92s_smiling_now_.html.

24. In 2011 Kraft decided to split in two, creating Mondelēz International to take forward its confectionery and food brands. It is based in Chicago.

25. Sturgeon, T. et al., Globalization of the automotive industry: Main features and trends, *International Journal of Technological Learning, Innovation and Development,* 2(1/2), 2009, pp. 7–24.

26. Prahalad, C. K. and Hamel, G., The core competence of the corporation, *Harvard Business Review,* May–June 1990: globex.coe.pku.edu.cn/file/upload/201606/27 /1756365219.pdf.

Chapter 3: "Tea, Earl Grey, Hot," or How We Will Make

1. These figures from http://asklib.hcl.harvard.edu/a.php?qid=137327. In the combined collection across the Harvard library system there are apparently over 17 million books accessible to students and staff.

2. Have a look at the machine in action on the Harvard Bookstore webpage www .harvard.com/clubs_services/books_on_demand/.

3. More details of the technology and the company's history can be found on the On Demand Books website at www.ondemandbooks.com/.

4. OPTN/SRTR Annual Data Report 2012, *American Journal of Transplantation,* 14(S1), pp. 5–192. The Organ Procurement and Transplantation Network (OPTN) came into existence through the National Organ Transplant Act (NOTA) in 1984.

5. Figures from the American Transplant Foundation website www.americantransplant foundation.org/about-transplant/facts-and-myths/.

6. If you're interested in registering to be a donor in the United States visit www.organ donor.org and in the U.K. www.organdonation.nhs.uk/how_to_become_a_donor/.

7. O'Brien, F. J., Biomaterials & scaffolds for tissue engineering, *Materials Today,* 14(3), March 2011, pp. 88–95: www.sciencedirect.com/science/article/pii/ S136970211170058X; Wilshaw, S.-P. et al., Development and characterization of acellular allogeneic arterial matrices, *Tissue Engineering Part A,* 18(5–6), February 2012, pp. 471–483: http://online.liebertpub.com/doi/abs/10.1089/ten .TEA.2011.0287.

8. The full video of his presentation is available on the TED website www.ted.com /talks/anthony_atala_printing_a_human_kidney#t-323052 and the bladder makes an appearance from the back of the stage about eleven minutes in.

9. Yandell, K., Organs on demand, *The Scientist,* 1 September 2013: www.the-scientist .com/?articles.view/articleNo/37270/title/Organs-on-Demand/.

10. For further details on the 3D human tissue models Organovo is developing see their website at www.organovo.com/.

11. www.bbc.co.uk/news/technology-16907104.

12. Bioengineers, physicians 3-D print ears that look, act real, *Cornell Chronicle,* 20 February 2013: www.news.cornell.edu/stories/2013/02/bioengineers-physicians-3-d -print-ears-look-act-real.

13. Wainwright, O., Faces to order: How 3D-printing is revolutionising prosthetics, *Guardian,* 8 November 2013: www.theguardian.com/artanddesign/architecture -design-blog/2013/nov/08/faces-3D-printing-prosthetics.

14. Griffith, H., Pioneering 3D printing reshapes patient's face in Wales, BBC News, 12 March 2014: www.bbc.co.uk/news/uk-wales-26534408.

15. For a review of bioprinting techniques and advances see Tasoglu, S. and Demirci, U., Bioprinting for stem cell research, *Cell,* 31(1), 2013, pp. 10–19.

16. Need different types of tissue? Just print them! Fraunhofer press release, 1 October 2013: www.fraunhofer.de/en/press/research-news/2013/oktober/need-different-types -of-tissue-just-print-them-2.html.

17. See http://will.i.am/about/ for more detail of will.i.am's awards and activities.

18. Howarth, D., Will.i.am calls for ethical stance on 3D-printing human bodies, *Dezeen,* 6 March 2015: www.dezeen.com/2015/03/06/will-i-am-interview-future-3D-printing -people/.

19. D'Aveni, R., 3-D Printing will change the world, *Harvard Business Review,* March 2013: http://hbr.org/2013/03/3-d-printing-will-change-the-world/ar/1: www.architectural-review.com/home/products/3D-printing-will-destroy-the -world/8658346.article.

20. For a review of methods and materials used in additive manufacturing see Guo, N. and Leu, C., Additive manufacturing: Technology, applications and research needs, *Frontiers of Mechanical Engineering,* 8(3), 2013, pp. 215–243.

21. For more detail and a video of Ford's use of 3D printing see www.computerworld .com/article/2490192/emerging-technology-inside-ford-s-3D-printing-lab-where -thousands-of-parts-are-made.html.

22. If you want to get into this, here is CNET's guide to printing an iPhone case: www .cnet.com/uk/how-to/diy-3D-printing-a-custom-iphone-case/.

23. *Forbes* reported an American jeweler making $250,000 custom pieces using 3D printing: www.forbes.com/sites/clareoconnor/2014/02/28/how-a-jewelry-company -is-making-250000-pieces-using-3D-printing-and-google-earth/.

24. *The Economist* reported how GE had purchased a small 3D maker in Cincinnati to make parts for their engines: www.economist.com/blogs/schumpeter/2012/11 /additive-manufacturing.

25. The full details for the Printrbot are available at http://printrbot.com/shop /assembled-simple-metal/.

26. Numbers from the Wohlers Report quoted in *Technology Review*: www .technologyreview.com/s/601268/airplanes-are-getting-lighter-thanks-to-3-d-printed -parts/.

27. Kellner, T., The FAA cleared the first 3D printed part to fly in a commercial jet engine from GE, GE Reports, 14 April 2015: www.gereports.com/post/116402870270/the -faa-cleared-the-first-3D-printed-part-to-fly/.

28. http://makerfaire.com/makerfairehistory/.

29. The full text of the speech is online at www.whitehouse.gov/the-press-office/2013/02 /12/remarks-president-state-union-address.

30. Joon-bae, K., Ministry of Science, ICT & Future Planning promotes intelligent 3D printing infrastructure integrated with internet of things (IoT), etnews, 25 September 2014: http://english.etnews.com/news/article.html?id=20140925200004.

31. See, for example, the ongoing work at PARC on flexible and printed electronics: www.parc.com/services/focus-area/flexible-and-LAE/.

32. *Wired* recently covered the Sugar Lab which is trying to develop a commercial food printer, see Venkataramanan, M., Print your own psychedelicious sugar cubes, 6 May 2014: www.wired.co.uk/magazine/archive/2014/05/play/print-your-own-sugar -cubes. For Hershey's, see http://mms.businesswire.com/media/20141217005885 /en/445806/19/2117268_3-D_Chocolate_Printing.mp4&.mp4.

33. Kayser's Solar Sinter was nominated as a Design of the Year by the London Design Museum in 2012. See the video of the printer working in the desert online at www .markuskayser.com/work/solarsinter/.

34. See www.adidas.co.uk/customise and start playing with the trainer designer.

35. www.rolls-roycemotorcars-manchester.co.uk/bespoke.

36. Singh, A., Inside Rolls-Royce: Where bespoke meets bling, *Telegraph*, 14 March 2014: www.telegraph.co.uk/motoring/news/10702547/Inside-Rolls-Royce-where-bespoke -meets-bling.html.

37. Levy, S., *Hackers: Heroes of the Computer Revolution—25th Anniversary Edition*, O'Reilly Media, 2010.

38. Hatch, M., *The Maker Movement Manifesto: Rules for Innovation in the New World of Crafters, Hackers and Tinkerers*, McGraw-Hill Professional, 2013.

39. You can see Alice's work in action at https://vimeo.com/73705160. Unfortunately the Levi's Makers part of their website doesn't appear to have any other makers listed as of mid-2016.

40. It is worth exploring the website for FirstBuild, https://firstbuild.com/ to see how professionalised the maker movement can become.

41. See the description in this Fast Company article from 1999: www.fastcompany.com/36433/digital-companies.

42. Have a go at customizing your bike at www.trekbikes.com/gb/en_GB/project-one/.

43. www.brooksbrothers.com/mtm-about/mtm-about,en_GB,pg.html.

44. Sherman, E., Mass customization: Let your customers have it their way, Inc., 18 November 2013: www.inc.com/erik-sherman/mass-customization-let-your-customers-have-it-their-way.html.

45. This section based on a number of sources including Ferdows, K., et al., Rapid-fire fulfillment, *Harvard Business Review,* November 2004: https://hbr.org/2004/11/rapid-fire-fulfillment, and Ruddick, G., How Zara became the world's biggest fashion retailer, *Telegraph,* 20 October 2014: www.telegraph.co.uk/finance/newsbysector/retailandconsumer/11172562/How-Inditex-became-the-worlds-biggest-fashion-retailer.html.

46. Results from Inditex for 2014: www.inditex.com/documents/10279/144955/INDITEX_Resultados14_Eng.pdf/a83094ff-ca26-496d-be1c-c4e4d461a4d6.

47. According to the 2016 *Forbes* billionaires list at www.forbes.com/profile/amancio-ortega/?list=billionaires.

48. www.theguardian.com/business/2016/may/13/hands-behind-the-heritage-inside-the-burberry-factory.

49. Hessman, T., The dawn of the smart factory, *Industry Week,* 14 February 2013: www.industryweek.com/technology/dawn-smart-factory.

50. Schwab, K., The fourth industrial revolution, *Foreign Affairs,* 12 December 2015: www.foreignaffairs.com/articles/2015-12-12/fourth-industrial-revolution.

51. See www.forschungsunion.de/pdf/industrie_4_0_final_report.pdf for further details.

Chapter 4: All Hail Our Robot Overlords

1. There is a brilliant almost silent video of these robots at work online at www.youtube.com/watch?v=quWFjS3Ci7A.

2. See the basics of BigDog at www.bostondynamics.com/robot_bigdog.html including links to videos of the beast in action.

3. History of ASIMO from Honda available at http://asimo.honda.com/asimo-history/.

4. The Tesla Origin story in Tech Insider: www.techinsider.io/tesla-the-origin-story-2014-10.

5. MacKenzie, A., Shocking winner: Proof positive that America can still make (great) things, *MotorTrend,* n.d., www.motortrend.com/news/2013-motor-trend-car-of-the-year-tesla-model-s/.

6. You can look up Baxter's specification here www.rethinkrobotics.com/baxter/tech
-specs/.

7. Zheng, C., Robots go it alone at factory with no assembly workers, *China Daily*, 5
May 2015: www.chinadaily.com.cn/china/2015–05/05/content_20620184.htm.

8. Qiu, Q., A brave, new world of robots on the rise in China, *Telegraph*, 3 July 2015:
www.telegraph.co.uk/news/world/china-watch/technology/industrial-robots
-china/.

9. Knight, W., China is building a robot army of model workers, *Technology Review*, 26
April 2016: www.technologyreview.com/s/601215/china-is-building-a-robot-army-of
-model-workers/.

10. Ibid.

11. Chu, K. and David, B., As China's workforce dwindles, the world scrambles for
alternatives, *Wall Street Journal*, 23 November 2015: www.wsj.com/articles/as-chinas
-workforce-dwindles-the-world-scrambles-for-alternatives-1448293942.

12. World Record Academy www.worldrecordacademy.com/technology/strongest_and
_largest_robot_world_record-set_by_KUKA_70226.htm.

13. Here are the rules for the 2016 version of the challenge http://amazonpicking
challenge.org/APC_2016_Official_Rules.pdf.

14. Figures taken from a survey of the APC 2015 contestants, published as Correll, N.
et al., Lessons from the Amazon Picking Challenge, *Journal of LaTeX class files*, 6(1),
January 2007: http://arxiv.org/pdf/1601.05484v1.pdf.

15. Quote from Greg Selke, CEO of ONExia in PWC 2014 report The new hire: How
a new generation of robots is transforming manufacturing: www.pwc.com/us/en
/industrial-products/assets/industrial-robot-trends-in-manufacturing-report.pdf.

16. Brinkman, W. F. et al., A history of the invention of the transistor and where it will
lead us, *IEEE Journal of Solid State Circuits*, 32(12), 1997, pp. 1858–1865.

17. Moore, G., Cramming more components onto integrated circuits, *Electronics*, 38(8),
1965, pp. 114–117.

18. Statistic from Knight, W., This robot could transform manufacturing, *Technology
Review*, September 2012: www.technologyreview.com/s/429248/this-robot-could
-transform-manufacturing/.

19. See their website at www.ifr.org/home/ for more detail.

20. Baker, N., A fourth state of matter: Inside South Korea's LCD revolution, *The New
Yorker*, 8 July 2013: www.newyorker.com/magazine/2013/07/08/a-fourth-state-of
-matter.

21. Frey, C. B. and Osborne, M., The future of employment: How susceptible are jobs to
computerization? Paper for the Oxford University Engineering Sciences Department
and the Oxford Martin School program on the impacts of future technology
workshop on Machines and Employment, September 2013: www.oxfordmartin.ox.ac
.uk/downloads/academic/The_Future_of_Employment.pdf.

22. Citigroup, Technology at Work v2.0, Oxford Martin Program on Technology and
Employment, 2016: www.oxfordmartin.ox.ac.uk/downloads/reports/Citi_GPS
_Technology_Work_2.pdf.

23. Pilat, D. et al., The changing nature of manufacturing in OECD economies, OECD
Science, Technology and Industry Working Papers, 2006.

24. Keynes, J. M., Economic possibilities for our grandchildren (1930), reprinted in Keynes, *Essays in Persuasion*, W. W. Norton & Co., 1963.

25. Rodrik, D., Premature deindustrialization, *Journal of Economic Growth*, **21**, 2016, pp. 1–33.

26. Ibid.

27. Brynjolfsson, E. and McAfee, A., *The Second Machine Age: Work, Progress, and Prosperity in a Time of Brilliant Technologies*, W. W. Norton & Co., 2014.

28. Data on manufacturing employment from the Bureau for Labor Statistics (BLS) online at http://data.bls.gov/timeseries/CES3000000001.

Chapter 5: Getting from A to NA in a Hilly World

1. Friedman, T., *The World Is Flat*, Farrar, Straus and Giroux, 2005.

2. Stiglitz, J., Global playing field: More level but it still has bumps, *New York Times*, 30 April 2005, www.nytimes.com/2005/04/30/books/global-playing-field-more-level-but-it-still-has-bumps.html, 2005.

3. This section is based on Levinson, M., *The Box: How the Shipping Container Made the World Smaller and the World Economy Bigger*, Princeton University Press, 2006, which provides a wonderful history of the shipping container, which up to that point had received very little attention.

4. Estimates taken from www.worldshipping.org/about-the-industry/containers/global-container-fleet.

5. Hummels, D., Transportation costs and international trade in the second era of globalization, *Journal of Economic Perspectives*, **21**(3), 2007, pp. 131–154.

6. https://kontainers.com/.

7. Manthorpe, R., Shipping cargo? Kontainers wants to do the heavy lifting, *Wired*, 27 April 2016: www.wired.co.uk/article/kontainers-cargo-shipping.

8. See Lingenheld, M., The Baltic Dry enigma, *Forbes*, 23 July 2015: www.forbes.com/sites/michaellingenheld/2015/07/23/the-baltic-dry-enigma/#47841ec05dec.

9. UNCTAD, Oil Prices and Maritime Freight Rates: An Empirical Investigation, Technical Report UNCTAD/DTL/TLB/2009/2, United Nations Conference on Trade and Investment, 2010.

10. See for example the special issue of *Philosophical Transactions of the Royal Society A*, published in January 2014 on the future of oil. http://rsta.royalsocietypublishing.org/content/372/2006/20130179.short.

11. See the *New York Times* interactive www.nytimes.com/interactive/2016/business/energy-environment/oil-prices.html.

12. Brown, C., *Self Enforcing Trade: Developing Countries and WTO Dispute Settlement*, Brookings Institution Press, 2009.

13. http://history.house.gov/People/Detail/14749.

14. The battle of Smoot–Hawley, *The Economist*, 18 December 2008: www.economist.com/node/12798595.

15. WTO, *World Trade Report 2013*.

16. Irwin, D., The Smoot–Hawley Tariff: A quantitative assessment, *Review of Economics and Statistics*, 80(2), 1998, pp. 326–334.

17. FT View, The Doha Round finally dies a merciful death, *Financial Times*, 21 December 2015.

18. This section uses data from Hummels, D., Transportation costs and international trade in the second era of globalization, *Journal of Economic Perspectives*, 21(3), 2007, pp. 131–154.

19. Bartlett, B., Donald Trump's protectionism has a good pedigree, *Financial Times*, 5 April 2016.

20. Lakshmi, A., CMA CGM's Benjamin Franklin Ends U.S.-Asia Route, *Maritime Professional*, 11 May 2016: www.maritimeprofessional.com/news/cgms-benjamin -franklin-ends-usasia-289434.

21. www.icontainers.com/what-fits-20-foot-container/.

22. Florida, R., *Who's Your City? How the Creative Economy Is Making Where You Live the Most Important Decision of Your Life,* Basic Books, 2008.

23. UNHCR, Mid-Year Trends 2015: www.unhcr.org/uk/statistics/unhcrstats /56701b969/mid-year-trends-june-2015.html.

24. UN, World Urbanization Prospects 2014 Revision: www.un.org/en/development /desa/publications/2014-revision-world-urbanization-prospects.html.

25. National Science Foundation, *Science and Engineering Indicators 2015*, 4.36: www.nsf .gov/statistics/2016/nsb20161/uploads/1/nsb20161.pdf.

26. Levinson, *The Box.*

Chapter 6: Manufacturing the Environment

1. London, B., *Ending the Depression Through Planned Obsolescence,* n.p., 1932.

2. See www.idsa.org/content/brooks-stevens-fidsa for a brief overview of his life and work.

3. Packard, V., *The Waste Makers,* David McKay, 1960.

4. See, for example, Campbell, M., Lawsuit seeks more than $5M from Apple for slowing older iPhones with iOS 9 upgrade, AppleInsider, 29 December 2015: http:// appleinsider.com/articles/15/12/29/lawsuit-seeks-more-than-5m-from-apple-for -allegedly-slowing-older-iphones-with-ios-9-upgrade.

5. Thielman, S., Neate, R. and Hern, A., Decline in iPhone sales leads to first revenue decline in 13 years for Apple, *Guardian*, 27 April 2016: www.theguardian.com /technology/2016/apr/26/apple-iphone-first-revenue-decline-13-years.

6. Echegaray, F., Consumers' reactions to product obsolescence in emerging markets: The case of Brazil, *Journal of Cleaner Production*, 134, October 2015, pp. 1–13.

7. Cox, J. et al., Consumer understanding of product lifetimes, *Resources, Conservation and Recycling*, 79, 2013, pp. 21–29.

8. Friends of the Earth, *Overconsumption: Our Use of the World's Natural Resources,* Friends of the Earth Europe, 2009.

9. Allwood, J. et al., Options for achieving a 50 percent cut in industrial carbon emissions by 2050, *Environmental Science and Technology*, 44(6), 2010, pp. 1888–1894.

10. Figures from U.K. Consumer Council for Water www.ccwater.org.uk/savewaterand money/averagewateruse/.

11. Figures from U.S. Geological Survey: http://water.usgs.gov/edu/qa-home-percapita .html.

12. UN, World Population Prospects: 2015 Revision: www.un.org/en/development/desa /publications/2014-revision-world-urbanization-prospects.html.

13. Barton, D., Chen Y. and Jin, A., Mapping China's middle class, *McKinsey Quarterly*, June 2013: www.mckinsey.com/industries/retail/our-insights/mapping-chinas-middle -class.

14. National Research Council, *Minerals, Critical Minerals, and the U.S. Economy*, National Academies Press, 2008.

15. Graedel, T. et al., On the materials basis of society, *Proceedings of the National Academies of Science*, **112**(20) , 2015, pp. 6295–6300.

16. MacArthur sails into record books, BBC News, 8 February 2005: http://news.bbc.co .uk/sport1/hi/other_sports/sailing/4229079.stm.

17. From *Guardian* excerpts from her logbook: www.theguardian.com/uk/2005/feb/08 /sailing.sport3.

18. For the latest date and for details of how the overshoot is calculated see www .overshootday.org/.

19. See the original 2007 video at www.youtube.com/watch?v=9GorqroigqM watched close to four million times since it was released.

20. Leonard, A., *The Story of Stuff*, Free Press, 2010.

21. Ellen MacArthur Foundation, *Toward the Circular Economy*, vol. 1, Ellen MacArthur Foundation, 2012.

22. See IKEA's entry in the Ellen MacArthur Foundation database at www.ellen macarthurfoundation.org/ce100/directory/ikea.

23. Farell, S., We've hit peak home furnishings, says IKEA boss, *Guardian*, 18 January 2016: www.theguardian.com/business/2016/jan/18/weve-hit-peak-home-furnishings -says-ikea-boss-consumerism.

24. Nguyen, H., Stuchley, M. and Zils, M., Remaking the industrial economy, *McKinsey Quarterly*, February 2014: www.mckinsey.com/business-functions/sustainability -and-resource-productivity/our-insights/remaking-the-industrial-economy. Ellen MacArthur Foundation directory entry for H&M available online at www .ellenmacarthurfoundation.org/ce100/directory/h-m, 2014.

25. Hass, W. et al., How circular is the global economy? An assessment of material flows, waste production, and recycling in the European Union and the world in 2005, *Journal of Industrial Ecology*, 19(5), 2015, pp. 765–777.

26. Ellen MacArthur Foundation, *Growth Within: A Circular Economy Vision for a Competitive Europe*, Ellen MacArthur Foundation, 2015.

27. Wiens, K., The New MacBook Pro: Unfixable, Unhackable, Untenable, *Wired*, 14 June 2012:www.wired.com/2012/06/opinion-apple-retina-displa/.

28. World Economic Forum, Toward the circular economy: Accelerating the scale-up across global supply chains, WEF, 2014: www3.weforum.org/docs/WEF_ENV _TowardCircularEconomy_Report_2014.pdf.

29. Ellen MacArthur Foundation, *Growth Within*.

30. Taylor, A., 5 years since the 2011 Great East Japan Earthquake, *The Atlantic*, 20 March 2016: www.theatlantic.com/photo/2016/03/5-years-since-the-2011-great-east-japan-earthquake/473211/.

31. Japan says quake rebuilding to cost as much as 25tn yen, BBC News, 23 March 2011: www.bbc.co.uk/news/business-12828181.

32. Reed, J. and Simon, B., Car components hit by Japan aftershock, *Financial Times*, 28 March 2011: www.ft.com/content/9ac4d7e2-595f-11e0-bc39-00144feab49a.

33. Cai, W. et al., Increasing frequency of extreme El Nino events due to greenhouse warming, *Nature Climate Change*, 4, 2014, pp. 111–116. Dominey-Howes, D., Explainer: are natural disasters on the rise? *The Conversation*, 24 March 2015.

34. Kewalramani, D. and Sobelsohn, R. J., "Greenwashing": Deceptive business claims of "eco-friendliness," *Forbes*, 20 March 2012: www.forbes.com/sites/realspin/2012/03/20/greenwashing-deceptive-business-claims-of-eco-friendliness/#34d1fd9758b1.

35. These details taken from Nike's FY 14–15 Sustainable Business Report, available online at http://about.nike.com/pages/sustainable-innovation.

36. COP21 climate change summit reaches deal in Paris, BBC News, 13 December 2015: www.bbc.co.uk/news/science-environment-35084374.

37. Quoted in Briggs, H., Global climate deal: In summary, BBC News, 12 December 2015: BBC news article www.bbc.co.uk/news/science-environment-35073297.

38. UN News Center, 22 April 2016: www.un.org/apps/news/story.asp?NewsID=53756#.Vypt9dKDGko.

39. Key findings from the Third IMO GHG study 2014: www.imo.org/en/OurWork/Environment/PollutionPrevention/AirPollution/Pages/Greenhouse-Gas-Studies-2014.aspx.

40. EU paper http://ec.europa.eu/clima/policies/transport/shipping_en/.

41. Ibid.

42. Maddox Consulting, Analysis of market barriers to cost effective GHG emission reductions in the maritime transport sector, final report to the European Commission, 2012.

43. The overview of the strategy is available online at http://ec.europa.eu/environment/circular-economy/index_en.htm. For the plan itself see European Commission, Closing the loop—An EU action plan for the Circular Economy, Communication from the Commission to the European Parliament, the Council, the European Economic and Social Committee and the Committee of the Regions, 614 final, COM, 2015: http://eur-lex.europa.eu/legal-content/EN/TXT/?uri=CELEX:52015DC0614.

44. Matthews, J. and Tan, H., Lessons from China, *Nature*, 531(7595), 2016, pp. 440–442.

45. World Economic Forum, *Toward the Circular Economy: Accelerating the Scale-Up Across Global Supply Chains*, WEF, 2014.

Chapter 7: Looking Through the Other End of the Telescope

1. Quote from Bell's speech which was reproduced in the *Annals of the New York Academy of Science*, 302, December 1977, pp. 685–689.

2. See the UN's Global Forum on International Statistics and Economic Globalization online at http://unstats.un.org/unsd/trade/globalforum/about.asp.

3. This example and data from Martinez-Mora, C. and Merino, F., Offshoring in the Spanish footwear industry: A return journey? *Journal of Purchasing and Supply Chain Management,* 20, 2014, pp. 225–237.

4. Ibid.

5. Adidas press release: www.adidas-group.com/en/media/news-archive/press-releases /2015/adidas-first-speedfactory-lands-germany/.

6. Meyer, D., Why Adidas is turning to robots in Germany and the U.S., *Fortune,* 25 May 2016, http://fortune.com/2016/05/25/adidas-robot-speedfactories/.

7. Figures from the TSMC website: www.tsmc.com/english/aboutTSMC/index.htm.

8. For a great and geeky history of the Raspberry Pi from the founder himself see the Center for Computing History's video at www.computinghistory.org.uk/det/41927 /Eben-Upton-The-Story-of-Raspberry-Pi/. Be prepared for many acronyms and chip names and programming languages to be thrown at you, but it gives a wonderful sense of the development. For a slightly easier introduction Eben Upton's TEDxGranta talk in 2012 is a good place to start https://youtube/6xFzVuxldqs.

9. Cellan-Jones, R., Raspberry Pi—a rapturous reception, BBC News, 29 February 2012: www.bbc.co.uk/news/technology-17196115.

10. Paul, I., 10 insanely innovative, incredibly cool Raspberry Pi projects, PC World, 13 March 2015: www.pcworld.com/article/2895874/10-insanely-innovative-incredibly -cool-raspberry-pi-projects.html.

11. Raspberry Pi blog post: www.raspberrypi.org/blog/made-in-the-uk/.

12. Rundle, M., The $5 Raspberry Pi Zero could be as revolutionary as the original, *Wired,* 26 November 2015: www.wired.co.uk/article/raspberry-pi-zero-launch.

13. Raspberry Pi blog post: www.raspberrypi.org/blog/ten-millionth-raspberry-pi-new -kit/.

14. Beautyman, M., Jopo, Finland's most popular city bike is a chopper with serious style, treehugger, 25 June 2012: www.treehugger.com/bikes/test-drive-jopo-finland-most -popular-city-bike-review.html.

15. See the company's website: www.helkamavelox.fi/en/helkama-2/.

16. Boston Consulting Group, Made in America again, December 2015: www.slideshare .net/TheBostonConsultingGroup/made-in-america-again-55937000.

17. Heikkila, J. et al., Is production returning to Finland? Policy Brief, No. 2/2016, Tampere University of Technology, 2016.

18. Engineering Employers Federation, Backing Britain: A manufacturing base for the future, 7 September 2014: www.eef.org.uk/resources-and-knowledge/research -and-intelligence/industry-reports/backing-britain-a-manufacturing-base-for-the -future.

19. Reshoring Initiative website: www.reshorenow.org/companies-reshoring/.

20. Shih, W., What it takes to reshore manufacturing successfully, *MIT Sloan Management Review,* Fall 2014: http://sloanreview.mit.edu/article/what-it-takes-to -reshore-manufacturing-successfully/.

21. The figures for this section are from Hanemann, T. and Rosen, D., New neighbors 2016: Chinese investment in the U.S. by congressional district, a report by the

National Committee on U.S.–China Relations and the Rhodium Group, 12 April 2016: http://rhg.com/reports/new-neighbors-2016.

22. Based on Paulson Institute case study California Dreaming: How a Chinese battery firm began making electric buses in America, 22 June 2015: www.paulsoninstitute .org/think-tank/2015/06/22/california-dreaming-how-a-chinese-battery-firm-began -making-electric-buses-in-america/.

23. UNCTAD, *World Investment Report 2016: Investor Nationality, Policy Challenges,* United Nations, 2016.

24. Expenditures by foreign direct investors for new investment in the United States, Bureau of Economic Analysis News Release, BEA 15–57, 30 November 2015: http:// www.bea.gov/newsreleases/international/fdi/fdinewsrelease.htm.

25. Ibid.

26. UNCTAD, *World Investment Prospects Survey 2014–2016,* United Nations, 2014.

27. Data taken from http://unctad.org/en/Pages/Statistics.aspx; all values used in the calculations in current U.S. dollars.

28. Hansard text: www.publications.parliament.uk/pa/cm201011/cmhansrd/cm110323 /debtext/110323-0001.htm#11032368000001.

Chapter 8: Mapping the Fracture Between the Physical and the Digital

1. The website for the Atlas of Economic Complexity has the most up-to-date data presented in a great format to visualize the complexity of the world economy and trade, available at http://atlas.cid.harvard.edu/. See also the interview with Hidalgo, Why information grows, *The Economist,* 15 June 2015: www.economist.com/blogs /freeexchange/2015/06/cesar-hidalgo-economic-complexity.

2. As Beinhocker points out in his notes to his book, Beinhocker, E., *The Origins of Wealth: Evolution, Complexity, and the Radical Remaking of Economics,* Random House Business, 2007: "Although I have not found any reliable estimates of the number of unique products and services on offer in a modern economy, under these assumptions, we would have about 12 billion SKUs [stock keeping unit], or in the range of 10^{10} [products]."

3. For those still confused on the financial crash of 2008 a good overview is provided by the Council on Foreign Relations (CFR) in their interactive presentation Crisis guide: The world economy which won a Business and Financial Reporting Emmy Award in 2009, available online at www.cfr.org/world/crisis-guide-global-economy /p19710.

4. It is important not to get distracted in replaying the crisis and the response but it is instructive in terms of narrative blindness to see the firsthand accounts from around the world, for example Lewis, M., *The Big Short,* W. W. Norton & Co., 2010; Sorkin, A. Ross, *Too Big To Fail,* Viking Press, 2009; or Darling, A., *Back from the Brink: 1000 days at Number 11,* Atlantic Books, 2011.

5. Data from the World Bank Databank: http://data.worldbank.org/indicator/NE .TRD.GNFS.ZS.

6. See the World Trade Organization International Trade Statistics 2013, section IV "Trade in Global Value Chains": www.wto.org/english/res_e/statis_e/its2013_e/its13_highlights4_e.pdf.

7. Carrere, C. and Schiff, M., On the geography of trade: Distance is alive and well, *Revue Economique,* 56(6), 2005, pp. 1249–1274.

8. Disdier, A. and Head, K., The puzzling persistence of the distance effect on bilateral trade, *Review of Economics and Statistics,* 90(1), 2008, pp. 37–48.

9. Mangalindan, J. P., Amazon's Prime and Punishment, *Fortune,* 21 February 2012: http://fortune.com/2012/02/21/amazons-prime-and-punishment/.

10. BI Intelligence, UPS will start testing Saturday delivery in the U.S., *Business Insider,* 19 July 2016: www.businessinsider.com/ups-will-start-testing-saturday-delivery-in-the-us-2016-7?IR=T.

11. Marshall, A., *Principles of Economics,* Macmillan, 1920.

12. Bond, B., The geographic concentration of manufacturing across the United States, ESA Issue Brief #01–13, Economics and Statistics Administration, Department of Commerce, 2013.

13. The data for Nike's contract factory structure can be found at http://manufacturingmap.nikeinc.com/.

14. Frey, C. B. and Osborne, M. A., The future of employment: How susceptible are jobs to computerization? Paper for the Oxford University Engineering Sciences Department and the Oxford Martin School program on the impacts of future technology workshop on Machines and Employment, September 2013: www.oxfordmartin.ox.ac.uk/downloads/academic/The_Future_of_Employment.pdf.

15. See the Conference Board for international comparisons as they took on this time series after the U.S. Bureau of Labor Statistics discontinued official collection of the data: www.conference-board.org/ilcprogram/.

16. Calculations from Boston Consulting Group report on the future of robotics, a summary of which is available at www.slideshare.net/TheBostonConsultingGroup/robotics-in-manufacturing.

17. Figures from the World Bank Statistics database: http://data.worldbank.org/.

18. The regions that the WTO uses to group the statistics are North America, South/Central America, Europe, the Commonwealth of Independent States (CIS), Africa, the Middle East and Asia.

19. Inter and intra regional trade data from the WTO international statistics database: www.wto.org/english/res_e/statis_e/its_e.htm.

20. The world's shifting center of gravity, *The Economist,* 28 June 2012: www.economist.com/blogs/graphicdetail/2012/06/daily-chart-19.

21. See Baden, B., What America exports to China, *China Business Review,* 15 May 2013: www.chinabusinessreview.com/what-america-exports-to-china/; Office of the U.S. Trade Representative, U.S.–China Trade Facts: https://ustr.gov/countries-regions/china-mongolia-taiwan/peoples-republic-china and www.wto.org/english/res_e/statis_e/statis_e.htm.

22. Figures taken from United States Census Bureau at www.census.gov/foreign-trade/balance/c5700.html.

23. See Sirkin, H. L. et al., Made in America, again: Why manufacturing will return to the U.S., Boston Consulting Group, 2011: www.bcg.com/documents/file84471.pdf, and U.S. manufacturing nears the tipping point: Which industries, why, and how much? Boston Consulting Group, 2011: www.bcgperspectives.com/content/articles /manufacturing_supply_chain_management_us_manufacturing_nears_the_tipping _point/.

24. Kakaes, K., The All-American iPhone, *Technology Review,* 9 June 2016: www .technologyreview.com/s/601491/the-all-american-iphone/. For a country to country comparison of iPhone costs in 2015 see Titcomb, J., How much does an iPhone 6s cost in each country around the world? *Telegraph,* 25 September 2015, www.telegraph .co.uk/technology/2015/12/11/how-much-does-the-iphone-6s-cost-in-each-country -around-the-world/.

25. Walker, D., Local Motors wants to print your next car out of plastic, *Wired,* 24 March 2016: www.wired.co.uk/article/3D-printed-cars-local-motors-lm3D.

26. Figures from Siemens, Background Information: Local Motors, 2016: www .siemens.com/press/pool/de/events/2016/digitalfactory/2016–04-hannovermesse /background-local-motors-e.pdf.

27. Lever, R., Olli, A 3D printed, self-driving minibus, to hit the road in U.S., Phys.org, 16 June 2016: http://phys.org/news/2016–06-olli-3D-self-driving-minibus-road.html.

28. See the Yogasmoga website at http://yogasmoga.com/. See also Segran, E., Why clothing start-ups are returning to American factories, *Fast Company,* 16 March 2016: https://medium.com/@FastCompany/why-clothing-startups-are-returning-to -american-factories-94331015004f.

29. Bensinger, G., When drones aren't enough, Amazon envisions trucks with 3D printers, *Wall Street Journal,* 26 February 2015: http://blogs.wsj.com/digits/2015/02/26/when -drones-arent-enough-amazon-envisions-trucks-with-3D-printers/.

30. Murray, A., GE's Immelt signals end to 7 decades of globalization, *Fortune,* 20 May 2016: http://fortune.com/2016/05/20/ge-immelt-globalization/.

31. GDP figures from World Bank: http://data.worldbank.org/indicator/NV.IND .MANF.ZS.

32. Germany Trade and Invest, Industrie 4.0: Smart manufacturing for the future, 2014: www.gtai.de/GTAI/Content/EN/Invest/_SharedDocs/Downloads/GTAI /Brochures/Industries/industrie4.0-smart-manufacturing-for-the-future-en.pdf.

33. Ibid.

34. The reporting of her speech and the lack of broad German industrial engagement in this agenda was reported in Karnitschnig, M., Why Europe's largest economy resists new industrial revolution, *Politico,* 6 July 2016: www.politico.eu/article/why-europes -largest-economy-resists-new-industrial-revolution-factories-of-the-future-special -report/.

35. See the BBC microsite for the full results and commentary on the referendum at www.bbc.co.uk/news/politics/eu_referendum.

36. Andrew Liveris's remarks reported by the All Party Parliamentary Manufacturing Group (APPMG) via Twitter: https://twitter.com/TheAPMG /status/783290370490793984.

37. See www.netherlandscircularhotspot.nl/nlch-campaign.html for details of the campaign.

38. Netherlands Trade and Investment, The Netherlands switches to the circular economy, 15 September 2016: www.hollandtradeandinvest.com/latest/news/2016 /september/15/the-netherlands-switches-to-circular-economy.

Chapter 9: The Changing Politics of Manufacturing

1. The text of the speech is available online at www.britishpoliticalspeech.org/speech -archive.htm?speech=139.

2. See the full text of the speech at www.britishpoliticalspeech.org/speech-archive .htm?speech=202.

3. Owen, G., Industrial policy in Europe since the Second World War: What has been learned? ECIPE Occasional paper, 1. The European Center for International Political Economy, Brussels, 2012.

4. See the full text of the speech at http://webarchive.nationalarchives.gov.uk /20130109092234/http:/number10.gov.uk/news/transforming-the-british-economy -coalition-strategy-for-economic-growth/.

5. Her government bio is online at www.gov.uk/government/people/theresa-may.

6. May, T., Machinery of government changes: Written statement to the House of Commons, HCWS94, 18 July 2016, available online plus links to further details at www.parliament.uk/business/publications/written-questions-answers-statements /written-statement/Commons/2016-07-18/HCWS94/.

7. Full text of the speech available online at www.presidency.ucsb.edu/ws/?pid=63752.

8. Cox News Service, Top candidate to become Bush's manufacturing czar withdraws, *Baltimore Sun,* 12 March 2004: http://articles.baltimoresun.com/2004-03-12 /business/0403120205_1_manufacturing-china-job-losses.

9. Applebaum, B., Why are politicians so obsessed with manufacturing? *New York Times Magazine,* 4 October 2016: www.nytimes.com/2016/10/09/magazine/why-are -politicians-so-obsessed-with-manufacturing.html.

10. Haberman, M., Donald Trump says he favors big tariffs on Chinese exports, First Draft, *New York Times,* 7 January 2016: www.nytimes.com/politics/first -draft/2016/01/07/donald-trump-says-he-favors-big-tariffs-on-chinese-exports/.

11. Farnsworth, C., U.S. raises tariff for motorcycles, *New York Times,* 2 April 1983: www .nytimes.com/1983/04/02/business/us-raises-tariff-for-motorcycles.html.

12. Reagan, R., Proclamation 5050—Temporary Duty Increase and Tariff-Rate Quota on the Importation Into the United States of Certain Heavyweight Motorcycles, 15 April 1983.

13. See the detail of the act from the Office of the Legislative Counsel, U.S. House of Representatives, available online at http://legcounsel.house.gov/Comps/93–618 .pdf.

14. Zarroli, J., Clinton promises to help create manufacturing jobs of the future, *All Things Considered, NPR,* 5 September 2016: www.npr.org/2016/09/05/492727584 /clinton-promises-to-help-create-manufacturing-jobs-of-the-future.

15. Elliott, L., Did Margaret Thatcher transform Britain's economy for better or worse? *Guardian,* 8 April 2013: www.theguardian.com/business/2013/apr/08/margaret -thatcher-transform-britain-economy.

16. Philips, K., U.S. industrial policy: Inevitable and ineffective, *Harvard Business Review,* July–August 1992: https://hbr.org/1992/07/us-industrial-policy-inevitable-and -ineffective.

17. Data sourced from the Conference Board available online at www.conference-board .org/ilcprogram/.

18. Ibid.

19. Data taken from the OECD.stat database available online at http://stats.oecd.org/.

20. Applebaum, Why are politicians so obsessed with manufacturing?

21. See for example Worstall, T., Slow U.S. manufacturing growth doesn't actually matter very much, *Forbes,* 5 January 2015: www.forbes.com/sites/timworstall/2015/01/03 /slow-us-manufacturing-growth-doesnt-actually-matter-very-much/.

22. Data from the Office for National Statistics released in December 2014, available online at http://tinyurl.com/jbwledd.

23. See for example Sullivan, R., A rare look at design genius Jony Ive: The man behind the Apple watch, *Vogue,* 1 October 2014: www.vogue.com/1415025/apple -design-genius-jonathan-ive/; or Parker, I., The shape of things to come: How an industrial designer became Apple's greatest product, *The New Yorker,* 23 February and 2 March 2015: www.newyorker.com/magazine/2015/02/23/shape-things -come.

24. Smith, A., *An inquiry into the Nature and Causes of the Wealth of Nations,* Strahan and Cadell, 1776, Book I, Chapter 1.

25. Pisano, G. and Shih, W., Restoring American competitiveness, *Harvard Business Review,* July–August 2009: https://hbr.org/2009/07/restoring-american -competitiveness.

26. Ibid.

27. Rodrik, D., Premature deindustrialization, *Journal of Economic Growth,* **21,** pp. 1–33, 2016.

28. Amsden, A., *The Rise of "the Rest": Challenges to the West from Late-Industrialising Economies,* Oxford University Press, 2003.

29. The text of the Ministerial Statement from the meeting is online at www.wto.org /english/thewto_e/minist_e/min05_e/final_text_e.htm. See also OECD and WTO, Aid for trade at a glance 2013: Connecting to value chains: www.wto.org/english /res_e/booksp_e/aid4trade13_e.pdf.

30. All figures here taken from the U.S. Census Bureau: www.census.gov/foreign-trade /balance/c5700.html.

31. Grimes, S. and Sun, Y., China's evolving role in Apple's global value chain, *Area Development and Policy,* **1**(1), 2016, pp. 94–112, citing Sturgeon, T. J. and Kawakami, M., "Global value chains in the electronics industry: Was the crisis a window of opportunity for developing countries?," in O. Cattaneo, G. Gereffi and C. Staritz (eds.), *Global Value Chains in a Postcrisis World: A Development Perspective* (Washington, D.C.: The World Bank, 2010), pp. 245–302.

32. Ibid.

33. Rubin, R., U.S. Companies are stashing $2.1 trillion overseas to avoid taxes, Bloomberg, 4 March 2015: www.bloomberg.com/news/articles/2015–03–04 /u-s-companies-are-stashing-2-1-trillion-overseas-to-avoid-taxes.

34. Kick off article for this: Dolfsma, W., China buys into corporate mergers, and proves better at it than the West, The Conversation, 3 May 2016: https://theconversation .com/china-buys-into-corporate-mergers-and-proves-better-at-it-than-the-west-58437.

35. Steinberg, J. et al., China is on an overseas buying spree, *Wall Street Journal*, 15 March 2016: www.wsj.com/articles/china-is-on-an-overseas-buying-spree -1458042732#:cqcd3gZqx5oIuA.

36. China Science and Technology Newsletter No. 9, Department of International Cooperation, Chinese Ministry of Science and Technology, 15 August 2015: http:// www.cistc.gov.cn/upfile/769.pdf.

37. Full text of their approach available online at www.meti.go.jp/english/aboutmeti /policy/fy2014/pdf/0906_001a.pdf.

38. You can see the roadmap for 3D printing at http://english.motie.go.kr/?p=5363.

39. See www.manufacturingusa.com/pages/program-details for more details.

40. China Science and Technology Newsletter, No. 9, 15 August 2015.

41. Source from Chinese government website, quoted in Economist Intelligence Unit, Prospects and challenges on China's "one belt, one road": A risk assessment report: www.eiu.com/public/topical_report.aspx?campaignid=OneBeltOneRoad.

42. Seeking protection, *The Economist,* 14 January 2012: www.economist.com /node/21542780.

43. See the WTO's news article on this in their dispute settlement news archive: www .wto.org/english/news_e/news13_e/ds472rfc_19dec13_e.htm.

44. See the current status of the challenge on the WTO's website www.wto.org/english /tratop_e/dispu_e/cases_e/ds472_e.htm.

45. Brazilian waxing and waning, *The Economist,* 18 April 2016.

46. Mazzucato, M., *The Entrepreneurial State: Debunking Public vs. Private Sector Myths,* Anthem Press, 2014.

47. Miles, T., WTO cuts 2016 world trade growth forecast to 1.7 percent, cites wake-up call, *Reuters,* 27 September 2016.

48. Rodrik, D., There is no need to fret about deglobalisation, *Financial Times,* 4 October 2016.

Epilogue: The Post World

1. McDonald, D. Ten things you need to know about Davos, (2017) *Irish Independent,* 21 January 2017.

2. The full video of the speech is available online at https://www.weforum.org/events /world-economic-forum-annual-meeting-2017/sessions/opening-plenary-davos-2017 and the text of the speech is available at https://www.weforum.org/agenda/2017/01 /full-text-of-xi-jinping-keynote-at-the-world-economic-forum.

3. Her speech is available online at the Prime Minister's Office https://www.gov.uk /government/speeches/the-governments-negotiating-objectives-for-exiting-the-eu -pm-speech.

4. The full text and video of President Trump's inaugural address is available online at https://www.whitehouse.gov/inaugural-address.

5. Gould, S. J. and Eldredge, N., Punctuated equilibrium comes of age, *Nature,* 366, pp. 223–227, 18 November 1993.

6. Swaine, J. Donald Trump's team defends "alternative facts" after widespread protests, *Guardian,* 23 January 2017.

7. Wolf, M., The long and painful journey to world disorder, *Financial Times,* 5 January 2017 https://www.ft.com/content/ef13e61a-ccec-11e6-b8ce-b9c03770f8b1.

8. Ibid.

9. Shen, L., Here's how much you could have won betting on Trump's Presidency, *Fortune,* 9 November 2016.

10. Griffin, A., Odds for Donald Trump to win U.S. election exact same as they were for Brexit, *Independent,* 8 November 2016.

11. The announcement text is available on the Trump transition team website https://greatagain.gov/navarro-national-trade-council-c2d9oc10eacb#.wmtwo5dz3.

12. Donnan, S., Trump's top trade adviser accuses Germany of currency exploitation, *Financial Times,* 31 January 2017.

13. Mattern, F., As trade agreements fall out of favor, all is not lost for companies that thrive on commerce, McKinsey Global Institute, 31 January 2017.

Select Bibliography and Further Reading

Amsden, A., *The Rise of "the Rest": Challenges to the West from Late-Industrializing Economies,* Oxford University Press, 2003.

Beinhocker, E., *The Origins of Wealth: Evolution, Complexity, and the Radical Remaking of Economics,* Random House Business, 2007.

Brown, C., *Self Enforcing Trade: Developing Countries and WTO Dispute Settlement,* Brookings Institution Press, 2009.

Brynjolfsson, E. and McAfee, A., *The Second Machine Age: Work, Progress, and Prosperity in a Time of Brilliant Technologies,* W. W. Norton & Co., 2014.

Darling, A., *Back from the Brink: 1000 days at Number 11,* Atlantic Books, 2011.

Ellen MacArthur Foundation, *Growth Within: A Circular Economy Vision for a Competitive Europe,* Ellen MacArthur Foundation, 2015.

Florida, R., *Who's Your City? How the Creative Economy Is Making Where You Live the Most Important Decision of Your Life,* Basic Books, 2008.

Friedman, T., *The World Is Flat,* Farrar, Straus and Giroux, 2005.

Hatch, M., *The Maker Movement Manifesto: Rules for Innovation in the New World of Crafters, Hackers and Tinkerers,* McGraw-Hill Professional, 2013.

Helpman, E., ed., *General Purpose Technologies and Growth,* MIT Press, 2003.

Hounsell, D., *From the American System to Mass Production, 1800–1932: The Development of Manufacturing Technology in the United States,* Johns Hopkins University Press, 1984.

Huwert, J.-Y. and Verdier, L., *Economic Globalisation: Origins and Consequences,* OECD Insights, OECD Publishing, 2013.

Keynes, J. M., Economic possibilities for our grandchildren (1930), reprinted in Keynes, *Essays in Persuasion,* W. W. Norton & Co., 1963.

Kuhn, T., *The Structure of Scientific Revolutions,* University of Chicago Press, 1962.

Landes, D., *The Unbound Prometheus,* Cambridge University Press, 1969.

———., *The Wealth and Poverty of Nations,* Abacus, 1998.

Leonard, A., *The Story of Stuff,* Free Press, 2010.

Levinson, M., *The Box: How the Shipping Container Made the World Smaller and the World Economy Bigger,* Princeton University Press, 2006.

Levy, S., *Hackers: Heroes of the Computer Revolution—25th Anniversary Edition,* O'Reilly Media, 2010.

Lewis, M., *The Big Short,* W. W. Norton & Co., 2010.

London, B., *Ending the Depression Through Planned Obsolescence,* n.p., 1932.

Manyika, J. et al., *Digital Globalization: The New Era of Global Flows,* McKinsey Global Institute, 2016.

Marshall, A., *Principles of Economics,* Macmillan, 1920.

Mazzucato, M., *The Entrepreneurial State: Debunking Public vs. Private Sector Myths,* Anthem Press, 2014.

Milberg, W. and Winkler D., *Outsourcing Economics: Global Value Chains in Capitalist Development,* Cambridge University Press, 2013.

Morris, I., *Why the West Rules for Now: The Patterns of History and What They Reveal About the Future,* Profile Books, 2010.

National Research Council, *Minerals, Critical Minerals, and the U.S. Economy,* National Academies Press, 2008.

National Science Foundation, *Science and Engineering Indicators 2015,* NSF, 2016.

Packard, V., *The Waste Makers,* David McKay, 1960.

Pierce, J. and Schott, P., *The Surprisingly Swift Decline of U.S. Manufacturing Employment,* Federal Reserve Board, 2014.

Schlefer, J., *The Assumptions Economists Make,* The Belknap Press of Harvard University Press, 2012.

Schumpeter, J. A., *Capitalism, Socialism and Democracy,* Harper and Brothers, 1942.

Smith, A., *An Inquiry into the Nature and Causes of the Wealth of Nations,* Strahan and Cadell, 1776.

Sorkin, A. R., *Too Big to Fail,* Viking Press, 2009.

Stiglitz, J., *Globalization and Its Discontents,* Penguin Books, 2002.

Studwell, J., *How Asia Works: Success and Failure in the World's Most Dynamic Region,* Profile Books, 2013.

UNCTAD, *World Investment Prospects Survey 2014–2016,* United Nations, 2014.

UNCTAD, *World Investment Report 2016: Investor Nationality, Policy Challenges,* United Nations, 2016.

Weber, M., *Economy and Society,* University of California Press, 1922.

World Economic Forum, *Toward the Circular Economy: Accelerating the Scale-Up Across Global Supply Chains,* WEF, 2014.

Index

Note: the letter n following a page number indicates an endnote.

ABOUT THE AUTHOR

Finbarr Livesey is a senior lecturer in the Department of Politics and International Studies at Cambridge University. He has consulted for a number of national governments and presented to multinational corporations on new models of industrial policy. Livesey studied public policy at the Kennedy School at Harvard University and was a director of GeoPartners, a consultancy based in London. He also assisted in setting up the Harvard Open Access Project at the Berkman Klein Center for Internet & Society at Harvard.